½ litre _____

450ml ___

400ml ___

350ml ___

300ml ___

¼ litre _____

200ml ___

150ml ___

100ml ___

50ml ___

Rory O'Connell is a teacher at, and co-founder of, the Ballymaloe Cookery School in East Cork. He has cooked in some of the world's best kitchens, with some of the biggest names in food, and has taught many of the rising stars of the next generation of chefs. With over thirty years' experience cooking and teaching, he is uniquely equipped to share his expertise and knowledge.

Master it
How to cook today

Rory O'Connell

FOURTH ESTATE · London

First published in Great Britain by Fourth Estate
a division of HarperCollins*Publishers*
77–85 Fulham Palace Road
London W6 8JB
www.4thestate.co.uk

1 3 5 7 9 10 8 6 4 2

A catalogue record for this book is available from
the British Library

ISBN 978-0-00-744728-2

Printed by South China Printing Co. Ltd.

This book is dedicated to the memory of my mother Elizabeth O'Connell, and to my sisters Darina, Blanaid and Elizabeth, and my brothers William, David, Aidan, Tom and Richard

Freshly Packed

IRISH
POTATOES

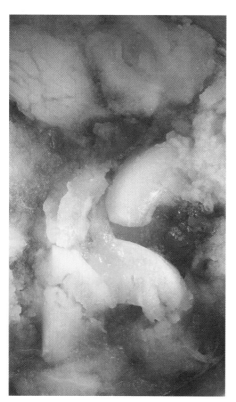

Contents

Introduction

I love cooking and I love teaching people how to cook – that is why I have written this book.

To cook well, it helps if you love and value food, as this is where it all starts. I cannot separate the cooking from what I am cooking. I feel bound to do well by the ingredients, and learning how to recognise good ones is crucial to becoming a good cook.

By cooking them well I honour the soil, the waters, the air, the planet, the efforts of the farmers, fishermen, producers and purveyors – everyone who got the ingredients to my kitchen.

This repertoire of recipes that I have chosen, though by no means exhaustive, should be a good starting point for the modern cook. The recipes are based on important techniques that all cooks will benefit from. When you master a technique, such as making a shortcrust pastry and lining a flan ring, a year-round soup formula to follow the changing ingredients of the seasons, using gelatine, making mayonnaise and so on, you open up a huge range of possibilities. That is the aim of this book – to demystify; to arm you with skills; to help you avoid the mistakes that my cooks, students and indeed I myself have made; to cook lovely food.

I have chosen my words carefully, highlighting the crucial ones to describe the particular details of a technique or the distinguishing features of a good ingredient.

This is not a 'chuck it in and see how it goes' book. I find that approach irksome and unfair, as unless the cook is utterly instinctive and much practised, this approach is fraught with pit falls. Food is too precious and expensive for that sort of game of chance.

So many times, I have witnessed the wide-eyed amazement and delight of a cook who, when finally cajoled into reading, weighing, heating and timing a set of ingredients, has produced a dish that has previously eluded them.

My approach to cooking is simple and not new. Use the best ingredients you can find, get organised and follow the recipe.

A potter will have his own recipe for success and will measure his carefully chosen clay, set his kiln at the correct temperature, shape his pots and bake them for the correct length of time. If he doesn't follow all of the steps, he will most likely have an oven full of pieces of pot rather than the desired perfectly formed vessel. So it is with cooking.

On a deeply personal level, I am charmed by what the earth produces to nourish and pleasure us. I am thrilled by the unconventional beauty of a cabbage leaf, the cross-section of a kiwi fruit closely observed, the heady smell and ticklish feel of a peach, the razor-like edges and sharp fizzing flavour of a verbena leaf, the sound of an egg shell being cracked and an egg spluttering in hot butter, the intensely modern shape and markings of a mackerel. I love it all.

Cooking is my beautiful game, my centre court, my George Best moment. Few things make as much sense to me as cooking the ingredients that fuel and pleasure us. Nothing else grounds me as cooking does – it makes me happy.

A note on cream

In Ireland, the cream I generally use, and the one that is most widely available, is called 'fresh cream' with a fat content of 35–40%, I refer to it in the recipes as 'regular cream'. It is a good all-rounder, rich enough for whipping and for use in sweet and savoury sauces and in ice cream. It is similar to the British 'whipping cream' but you can also use double cream in its place.

Spoon measurements

All spoon measurements in this book are rounded unless stated otherwise. 'Rounded' means the same volume of ingredient on top of the spoon as below. For example, a rounded spoon measurement is the same as two level spoon measurements.

Oven temperatures

All oven temperatures in this book are for conventional ovens. If you have an exclusively fan oven, refer to your oven manual for instruction. The general rule is that you subtract 20°C (about 36°F) from the recommended temperature when using a fan oven.

Shop well – eat well

If you don't shop well, you won't eat well – it's as simple as that. So this requires a bit of effort. If you rely on the corner store for all your food, much as we love them, need them and use them for their convenience, the chances are, except in most unusual circumstances, that you will not get the variety and quality of ingredients you need in order to have a varied basket of food that is full of the nutritional value we require.

Make a plan and make a list
Be aware of what seasonal ingredients are available and use that information to help you plan your meals. Seasonal ingredients taste better, are easier to cook and are the best value for money. Some weekend newspapers have lists in their food sections of what is in season at any time of the year. Use these lists to help you plan your meals.

If your house is a place where meals need to be cooked every day, it's worth sitting down for half an hour at the weekend to make a simple list. This will save you time and money when you go shopping, help prevent waste and give you a chance to cast your eye over the variety of foods that you and those you care for will be eating in the days ahead. This list will help you to buy the five oranges you really need rather that the ten you might not use, and so on.

When shopping, be 90% focused and 10% open-minded – that 10% gap gives you the freedom to snap up the ingredient not planned for, but clearly at the time in great condition and a good addition to your basket.

With your list in hand, use specialist shops such as the butcher, fishmonger and greengrocer. Build up a relationship with the person whom you rely on for the food to sustain you through life, because that person has an important role to play in your wellbeing. Ask them what they consider to be the best value at that time of the year. Let them know when an ingredient was a success, and also if it did not meet your expectations.

Try to allow time to get to a farmers' market. In some cases that will require a bigger effort. When you get there, have a walk around. Take your time to have a look at everything that's available. Look for the ingredients that are practically jumping off the table with freshness. Those are most likely local, and due to their short journey may be the best value going.

Some of the specialist ingredients such as smoked fish or cheese, meat and poultry, may seem expensive – they are a treat, but you can balance the cost of those hand-crafted artisan products with the less expensive but no less worthwhile seasonal vegetables and fruit.

Buy just what you need. Balance your budget in this way.

Shopping can be pleasant, even enjoyable. It can be sociable and educational and it's a crucial part of the process that ends up with good food on the table.

Accurate measuring spoons:

teaspoon, dessertspoon and tablespoon

Getting started – get organised

Being organised is a great help in the kitchen. Once you have decided what you are going to cook and have completed your shopping, you are ready to start cooking.

Sit down for a moment before you start and write out a work list, '**an order of work**'. Read through the recipes and decide how you will divide up your time, what needs to happen first and so on. This will mean you are organising your cooking in the correct order. The dishes that take longest to cook or that need to rest and chill, such as pastry, need to go on first and so on. When you do this, nothing is forgotten and it helps you to make the best use of your time. You then have the added pleasure of ticking things off your list as you go, a simple pleasure that I enjoy greatly.

Having written out your order of work, I suggest that you **measure out all your ingredients before you start to do any cooking.** Keep plastic containers and the like for this purpose. Keep the measured ingredients for each recipe on a separate tray, or, if you want to be pedantic like me, line them up in a row in the order they go into the dish. I find this time-saving and satisfying, and I can then focus on the dish rather than juggling with cooking and measuring at the same time.

Multiple ingredients that go into a dish at the same time can be combined in one bowl or on a plate, thereby leaving less clutter on your work surface. I get a considerable amount more done when I measure ahead like this. The clearer my workspace is, the clearer my brain seems to be and the more I enjoy the cooking process.

Try to **wash up as you go**. You don't want a mountain of washing-up facing you when you have finished cooking.

I keep my salt and sugar in little open-faced bowls beside the hob, along with the pepper mill, so that they are immediately available when I need them.

I like to keep a little butter at room temperature in a butter dish, so that if I am grilling or pan-frying it is soft and easily spreadable – this means I can smear the ingredient with the minimum amount of fat, but still enough to add flavour and prevent the ingredient from sticking.

Store cupboard

Have a small store cupboard of essential and regularly used ingredients to make the shopping for a particular meal less onerous, and to have the key ingredients for the making of a meal at short notice. See the suggested list below, and tailor it to suit your likes and needs. Shop for quality rather than quantity for the store cupboard. This is not a war chest to see you through a crisis, but a regularly used source of flavoursome ingredients that will add the oomph to the more easily found staples.

Maldon sea salt
Olive oil
Sunflower oil
White and red wine vinegar
French mustard
Anchovies, salted or in oil
Capers
Dried chillies
Lentils
Chickpeas
Local honey
Chocolate, best quality, 62% and 70% cocoa solids
Dried fruit: prunes, raisins, sultanas and cherries

A pot of raspberry jam
Flour: plain, self-raising, strong white
Small quantities of regularly used whole spices, such as cumin, coriander, cardamom, nutmeg
Ground turmeric
Basmati rice
Risotto rice
Couscous
Olives
Chicken stock (in freezer)
Fish sauce (nam pla)
Parmesan and Cheddar cheese (in the fridge)
Chorizo

The freezer

I find the freezer very useful for preserving certain foods, cutting down on waste and generally as an organisational aid. However, the bigger your freezer is, the more likely you are to have it packed with food that you may not get to use quickly enough. The most important thing to remember when freezing foods is that the sooner you use the food, the better it will taste.

Only freeze food that is in perfect condition.

Freeze foods in suitable containers such as freezer bags. Recycled food containers such as those used for yoghurt or milk can be perfect, providing you have remembered to save the lids.

Freeze foods in small quantities, so that you will not have to defrost more than you need.

Put a clear label listing the food and the date of freezing on each item.

Be careful when defrosting certain raw foods such as chicken and pork to ensure that the food is completely defrosted before cooking. I usually remove chicken and pork from the freezer the evening before use, sit them in the fridge overnight and finish defrosting them at room temperature the next day.

I buy **fruit** during the local growing season to ensure best quality and value, and freeze it in tightly sealed bags or punnets. Raspberries, loganberries, tayberries and blackberries, black, white and redcurrants freeze well. Cranberries and blueberries are also worth the effort. Bitter Seville oranges for marmalade freeze surprisingly well and after defrosting the rind softens easily during the cooking. This means you don't have to make all your marmalade for the year during the oranges' short winter season.

Basil is the only **herb** I freeze. I freeze a little basil in August to use straight from the freezer later in the year, but only in sauces. The trick with basil is not to remove the container it has been frozen in from the freezer when you are retrieving some for a sauce. If the container is removed from the freezer, the basil defrosts and oxidizes instantly and when refrozen will be bitter, disappointing and a pointless exercise. When carefully handled as suggested, this frozen basil is surprisingly good and is perfect for perking up a winter tomato sauce of tinned, bottled or frozen tomatoes. The basil needs no preparation before freezing. Just make sure the leaves are fresh and unblemished.

Tomatoes are the only **vegetable** I freeze. Like basil, tomatoes need no preparation before freezing. They should be as ripe as possible, and will when defrosted be suitable only for cooked sauces, soups and purées. Freeze them when at their best and in season. If you have frozen the basil as well as the tomatoes, it is possible to make an excellent preserved tomato sauce during the winter months. This is a prime example of how to use your freezer to maximum effect. You have trapped the summer's flavours for releasing during the winter. If you achieve this, bravo you.

Firm-textured **fish** such as salmon, turbot, brill and monkfish freeze well, but only when impeccably fresh. Before freezing, wash the fish well and make sure no trace of blood remains on the flesh or near the bones.

All **poultry** freezes well, either on the bone or jointed. I occasionally freeze cooked chicken bones to use for stock. That is the only case in which I freeze cooked meat. Poultry should be perfectly fresh and lightly dried with kitchen paper before freezing.

I rarely freeze **meat**, but if I have to save an ingredient, such as a steak or a few lamb chops, I will wrap it carefully and try to use it as soon as possible after freezing. Minced meat is really not worth freezing and will be dull and watery when defrosted.

Most **soups** freeze well. I don't freeze green soups, though, as they lose their colour and delicate flavour. Freeze soups in small tightly sealed containers.

When **puff or shortcrust pastry** is frozen on the day it is made, it is quite successful. These are the only pastries that I feel are worth freezing. Freeze the pastry, well wrapped, in blocks close to the weight you use for your specific recipes.

I freeze white sourdough **bread** while still fresh to save it being wasted and then use the defrosted bread for breadcrumbs and pangrattata. The bread can of course be crumbed before freezing. Soda breads do not freeze successfully.

Clearly, freezing is an essential part of the process of making and serving **ice creams, sorbets and granitas**. Sorbets and granitas need to be used as soon as possible after freezing, ideally within a couple of days, as they become more icy over time and lose flavour quite quickly. Ice creams are more robust, but they too will be better the sooner they are eaten.

All **meat, poultry and fish stocks** freeze well, as do meat juices left from a roast.

I occasionally freeze **nuts** if I have overbought. They lose some of their texture as a result of freezing, but the flavour is preserved and they will not go rancid, which is what will happen to them if you store them for too long at room temperature. They are perfectly acceptable for using in pesto, pralines and cakes. Pine nuts, hazelnuts and Brazil nuts are the ones I freeze. I generally buy walnuts in the shell, so the necessity to freeze them does not arise; however, shelled walnuts can be frozen.

Egg whites freeze perfectly and will be wonderful for meringues and soufflés when defrosted. They defrost in an hour. Organised cooks will freeze the whites in ice-cube trays and pop them out individually as needed. Otherwise, drop the defrosted whites on to a scale, allowing 25g per individual white.

Kit

You must have equipment that will work. A knife that is not sharp will blunt your enthusiasm. A saucepan that is so light that it would burn water will spoil your food and drive you mad. None of us would go out for a game of football and kick a burst ball around, and so it is in the kitchen – you need the proper bits of kit to make it work properly. Have a look at my suggested list.

Knives
    Chopping knife
    Flexible filleting knife
    Vegetable or fruit knife
    Carving knife and fork
    Steel, for keeping your knives sharp

Chopping boards
    2 heavy wooden chopping boards (use the different sides for specific tasks, i.e. raw meat, cooked foods, fruit and vegetables, and fish)
    Small board, for garlic

Measuring
    Scales (I find the battery-operated or electric modern scales to be the most accurate)
    Measuring jugs (I use heavy Pyrex jugs)
    Measuring spoons: teaspoon, dessertspoon and tablespoon

Tools
    Wooden spoons, a selection with round and flat bottoms (make sure the handles are not too thin, otherwise they will just swivel in your hand when you are stirring a heavy mixture)
    2 flexible heatproof rubber spatulas, 1 small and 1 large
    2 fish slices, 1 metal and 1 heavy plastic

Flexible palette knife
Balloon whisk
Sharp vegetable peeler
Microplane grater and protective covering
Stainless steel box grater
Japanese mandoline and safety guard
Set of thin meat skewers
2 stainless steel sieves, 1 large and 1 medium
Large straining colander
Potato masher with a medium fine mesh, or mouli-légumes with
3 different-sized grating discs
Ladles, 1 large and 1 small
2 large stainless steel serving spoons, 1 perforated
Rolling pin
2 pastry brushes

Pots and pans
Heavy-based stainless steel saucepans: at least 1 large, medium and
small, with lids (I have some glass saucepan lids that I find really
useful)
Small low-sided heavy-based stainless steel saucepan, with lid –
this is like a cross between a saucepan and a sauté pan
Medium low-sided heavy-based stainless steel saucepan, with lid
Large and wide low-sided heavy-based stainless steel saucepan,
with lid
Casseroles: ideally 1 large, medium and small, with lids
Cast-iron grill pan
Cast-iron frying pan
Heavy-based non-stick frying pan

Bowls
Selection of stainless steel and Pyrex bowls
Selection of plastic bowls
Extra large light stainless steel or plastic bowl for mixing bread and
dressing salad leaves

Tins
    Heavy-quality, rustproof tins to suit the sizes as specified in your
    recipes
    Heavy-quality baking trays or sheets of various sizes

Machines
    Food processor
    Food mixer
    Hand-held blender

Other essentials
    Pestle and mortar
    Pepper mill
    Baking parchment

Using a Microplane is a really good way to crush garlic
to a paste

Essentials

This is a selection of techniques and recipes that I find are essential in today's kitchen. Though the béchamel sauce may sound rather old fashioned, it is still vital. Others, like the salsa verde, seem more contemporary. Roasting and grinding spices, though a new experience for some, has been an essential technique in the kitchen for millennia.

Crushing garlic

The reasons for crushing garlic are twofold. Garlic when raw and crushed to a paste is at its strongest and fieriest, and as a smooth paste it will generally disappear into the dish it is being added to. I take the old-fashioned approach of a knife and timber chopping board or a more contemporary approach, with a Microplane. What I don't use is a garlic press. I find them awkward, inefficient and wasteful.

Place the unpeeled cloves of garlic on a heavy chopping board. With a chopping knife, press heavily on each clove. I use the part of the knife closest to the tip of the blade. The knife will crush the garlic. Peel off the skin, and if there is a hard bit at the bottom remove that as well. Sprinkle a tiny pinch of salt on to the garlic – this helps the knife to grip. Again using the tip end of the knife, press heavily on the garlic in rhythmic movements to render it a smooth paste.

If using a Microplane to crush the garlic, there is no need to peel the individual cloves. Grip the clove of garlic by the end closest to the root and rub it up and down the blade of the Microplane. The papery skin will remain on the sharp side of the implement where it helps to protect your fingers from the bladed surface, while the crushed garlic is pushed through to the blunt rear. Discard the skin and scrape the paste off the Microplane.

Peeling tomatoes

Peeling tomatoes will either be easy and enjoyable, or a penance that you may swear never to repeat. The crucial requirements here are really ripe tomatoes and boiling water. Underripe tomatoes are not worth eating and are torturous to peel, hence not worth considering. Water that has once boiled is no good to you. It must be still boiling when poured over the tomatoes. When the tomatoes are ripe and the water is boiling, this task is actually quite pleasurable.

Remove the stalks from the tomatoes and with a small knife make a shallow cross-shaped cut where the stalk was. This cut encourages the skin to lift off. Bring enough water to cover the tomatoes to the boil and pour the **still boiling** water over, to submerge the tomatoes completely. Count out **ten seconds** and immediately pour off all the water. Refresh the tomatoes in cold water for a few seconds. Pour off the cold water, then simply peel off the skins. I discard the skins, adding them to the hens' bucket. You can save the strained water for the washing up.

Drying your own tomatoes

At the end of the summer, when there is a glut of really ripe and inexpensive tomatoes, I cut them in half, put them on a wire rack, season them with a little salt and pepper, pop them into a very low oven and forget about them for about 12 hours. They dry out and become wizened and intense. Then, when cooled, I put them into jars with basil or marjoram leaves, cover them completely with olive oil, label and date them, and put them in a cold place, to be used right the way through the months when good tomatoes are scarce. The basil or marjoram, while flavouring the tomatoes, is beautifully preserved in the oil, and is also fished out for use when otherwise getting those herbs would involve an aeroplane.

Slowly drying tomatoes in a low oven

Roast peppers

I find this simple technique for roasting peppers very successful. The secret is to allow the peppers to get blistered, almost burnt and collapsing before removing them from the oven. The peeled peppers can be stored in the fridge for weeks. I usually cover them with olive oil and add a few basil leaves if I have them. Annual marjoram is also an excellent herb here.

Serves 4–6 6 best-quality (preferably organic) peppers
A drizzle of olive oil for roasting, and more olive oil
to cover the roasted and peeled peppers
Maldon sea salt and freshly ground black pepper

Preheat the oven to 190°C/375°F/gas 5.

Place the peppers in a bowl and drizzle lightly with olive oil. There is no need for pools of oil, it will just go to waste. Season with salt and pepper. Transfer to a roasting tray and roast for about 40 minutes, or until the skin is dark and blistered, the flesh is soft and the peppers are starting to collapse.

When ready, remove from the oven and tip the contents of the roasting tray into a bowl. Cover the bowl tightly with cling film and allow to cool completely.

Gently pull the cooled peppers apart and remove the skin and seeds. Put the peppers into a jar. If you like, at this stage you can add leaves or sprigs of the herb of your choice. They will keep for longer, several months in fact, if you cover them completely with olive oil. The leftover oil can be used for cooking when the peppers are finished.

Cover and chill until needed. Always allow the peppers to come back to room temperature before serving.

Roasting and grinding spices

If you like to use spices in your cooking, grinding your own as you need them will give you the very best results. It is an easy and essential kitchen technique. Most of the pre-ground spices you buy are a pale imitation of the freshly ground results you can achieve with ease in your own kitchen. Whole spices are sometimes lightly dry-roasted before being used or ground. The roasting lifts the flavour and aroma of the spices, giving them a nutty tone. I generally roast the different spices for a recipe in separate batches, as because of the variation in size and shape, they colour unevenly when they are roasted together. For example, if you roast cumin and coriander together, the cumin will have reached the required toasted colour before the coriander; hence if you allow the coriander to toast properly, the cumin will burn and become unpleasantly bitter. If you burn spices when dry-roasting, it is better to cut your losses and start again. Do not be put off by the last sentence, though, as this is so easy and rewarding. The roasted spices can be ground in a spice grinder or in the more manual pestle and mortar, which is my preferred spice-grinding apparatus. An electric coffee grinder makes a perfect spice grinder, though if your first cup of coffee of the day is as important to you as it is to me, I suggest that perhaps you have a separate grinder, clearly marked for the purpose of grinding spices only.

Spices are best bought in small quantities and stored in tightly sealed containers. If you grind too much spice for a recipe, store any left over, again in tightly sealed containers, and use it up as soon as possible. I use jars with tightly fitting screw-on lids.

To dry roast spices, heat a heavy cast-iron or heavy-based non-stick frying pan over a medium heat and add the spice. Stir gently or shake the pan to keep the spices moving.

Watch as the colour changes. If you are not sure of the colour change, **refer to the colour of the unroasted spice** to indicate what is happening in the pan. The roasting spice should be lightly browned. Do not leave the pan at any stage, as a small quantity of spice can roast in as short a time as 1 minute.

Spices, roasted to a golden-brown colour, and ready to grind

As soon as the spice is lightly browned, remove it from the pan immediately and place in the grinder or mortar. Grind the spice right away, generally to a fine powder, unless a recipe specifies a coarser finish.

Do not forget to catch the aroma of the spices as the little plume of warm and fragrant smoke arises from the grinder or mortar. Only the cook/grinder gets to enjoy this brief moment, and every time I inhale that exotic offering I give silent thanks to the spice god. It is at that point you will know it is worth the small effort of grinding your own. Magic.

Checking if the bird is cooked

Fowl must be fully cooked. There is no grey area here and no question of personal preference. There should be no sign of blood or pink flesh. It is crucial to be able to recognise this stage, and there are a couple of ways to determine this. The first thing to do is to look at the bird and see if it looks cooked. That's the starting point. If it appears to be cooked, take preferably a thin metal skewer, otherwise a small thin-bladed knife, and insert it into the flesh between the leg and the breast, that is, at the bone, right down where the leg is attached to the carcass. Leave it there for exactly 10 seconds and remove. Now immediately test the temperature of the tip of the skewer or knife on your hand. It should be red hot and make you pull away the skewer with a start. If that is the case, you know the heat has properly penetrated into the place where it takes longest to cook. If the knife tip is not red hot, replace the bird in the casserole or oven, cook for a further 10 minutes and test again. I find this is the best way to check if the bird is cooked. The other way is to pierce the leg of the bird at the base or get a spoon into the spot where the skewer went in and try to release some of the cooking juices on to it. These juices should be clear, with no trace of pink or blood. This method also works, but is in my opinion somewhat more cumbersome than the first.

Find the spot between the leg and the breast, count to ten and then test the heat of the skewer

Carving

To carve the cooked bird, place it on a timber carving board. A carving board will have a little well cut into it to collect any juices that flow out of the poultry or meat being carved. Failing one of these boards, place a board inside a shallow tray; that way any juices will flow into the tray and not all over your counter. If you struggle with carving a bird, there are several reasons why that might be. Remember that when carving, your knife will generally be travelling south.

A sharp knife helps greatly, and I prefer to use a flexible filleting knife rather than the usually recommended long carving knife. I find you can be defter with the medium-sized knife.

The next crucial bit of information is to know what a 'ball and socket joint' is and also to know where these are, because they are at the joints where the wings and legs are attached to the carcass and also where the thigh is attached to the drumstick. These joints are most important in this particular adventure, and they feature strongly in the next piece of text, so please bear with me. The ball and socket joint occurs where one bone with a ball end fits snugly into another bone with a socket end. To separate these bones, you need to cut precisely between the ball and socket. They are held together by a small piece of membrane, and when you cut through that, they are miraculously separated. When you are doing this, you need to be a little bit patient, at least to start off with. Put your knife in the appropriate spot and cut. If you hit a bone, stop. Abandon the brute force and ignorance approach. All that will do is blunt your knife and have you in a sweat. Just move the tip of the knife a little to the right or left and cut again. When you are in the right place, as in exactly between the ball and socket, your knife will slip through as if it is soft butter. This is an important moment because when you can find this spot confidently, you have removed at least three-quarters of the difficulty from carving any bird.

So to start, turn the bird so that the cavity end is facing you. Begin by removing one of the legs, that is, the whole leg consisting of the drumstick and thigh, in one piece. Do this by cutting through the skin between the breast and leg. Push the leg out a little with the side of the knife blade. This makes it easier to see where you are going, and, as you can imagine, being able to see what is going on is a considerable advantage here. You are looking for the ball and socket joint at the base of the carcass. Cut through the middle of this joint and, as I explained above, don't rush it, just concentrate on finding the spot where the knife will slide through easily. Place the removed leg, skin side down, on the board, and separate the drumstick from the thigh by cutting again through the ball and socket joint where they are attached at the top of the drumstick. Place separately on a hot serving plate.

To remove the flesh from the breast, turn the bird around with the cavity now facing away from you and the wishbone towards you. The first piece to be removed here is the wing, and in the case of chicken, duck and guinea fowl, with about 3cm of the breast attached to the wing bone. Carve into the breast and push your knife down towards the wing bone, where it is attached to the carcass. The search for the ball and socket goes on here again, and when found and cut through, the wing and piece of breast meat will come away easily in one piece. Continue carving the breast in neat slices. I like to carve these slices about 7.5mm thick. Serve some of the white breast meat with some of the brown leg meat, arranging the neatest slices of white meat on top of the brown.

When carving a very small bird like quail, the legs and breasts are generally served whole. In the case of a larger bird like turkey, the legs once removed from the carcass will be carved off the bone and sliced, the wings for those who like them can be served whole and the breast meat carved into neat 7.5mm slices.

Serve the carved and neatly arranged fowl on hot serving plates.

Parsley pesto

This is brilliant stuff. Given that fresh basil is only available for a couple of months during the summer, parsley is an obvious year-round and delicious substitute. I strongly believe that most people's experience of the classic basil pesto is an unpleasant one, as basil deteriorates so quickly if not carefully handled. As a result it is generally bitter and rancid.

This parsley pesto made to the classic recipe has a special flavour all of its own. It is very good in soups and broths, on bruschetta, with grilled or roast fish, poultry and meats, and on pasta. It keeps well in the fridge for up to 2 weeks.

Serves 6–8   25g flat-leaf parsley, weighed after removing tough stalks
25g pine nuts
1 fat clove of garlic, peeled and crushed to a paste
75–150ml extra virgin olive oil
40g finely grated Parmesan
Pinch of Maldon sea salt

Place the parsley, pine nuts and garlic in a food processor and pulse-chop to a fine crumb. Add the olive oil in a stream to achieve a soft consistency. Fold in the grated Parmesan.

Taste and correct the seasoning with a pinch of sea salt.

Spring wild garlic pesto
Replace the parsley in the master recipe with wild garlic leaves. Finely chop the wild garlic before processing, as otherwise it may end up being a little stringy. Proceed as in the above recipe.

Rocket leaf pesto
Remove the tough stalks from the rocket leaves before weighing and continue as in the master recipe.

Basil pesto
You can make this sauce at any time of the year if you are happy to

use imported basil, though the notion of eating basil pesto in January leaves me feeling rather cold. I only make it during the summer months, when fresh local basil is available, and then I use a pestle and mortar, which imparts a particular consistency that I enjoy. However, you can achieve a good result using a food processor.

Remove the tough stalks from the basil leaves before weighing and continue as in the master recipe, adding the oil immediately so as to protect the torn leaves from the air. As basil oxidises and becomes bitter after the leaves are chopped or broken, it is essential to get the oil in straight away, so cover the pesto with a layer of olive oil and chill it as soon as possible.

Béchamel sauce

Every cook needs to know how to make a béchamel or white sauce. Even though it seems a bit old-fashioned, and won't be featuring at your local molecular gastronomy restaurant, it is still an essential part of the cook's repertoire. Properly made, this sauce is well flavoured, smooth and shiny, and has a silky consistency. The plain or master version becomes a vehicle for other flavourings such as herbs, mustard, anchovies, capers, spices, vegetables, cheese and so on. You can't really consider a cauliflower or macaroni cheese or a fish pie without it. It can be delicious to serve with a poached chicken, in which case a little of the chicken poaching liquid can be added to the sauce to achieve a thinner consistency than you normally expect from this sauce.

So if your memory of white sauce is a miserable one, of a lumpy, thick, stodgy, floury and bland non-event, perhaps this recipe, carefully followed, will change your mind and remind you why this classic remains important.

Serves 6–8   300ml full-fat milk
1 small carrot, peeled and thickly sliced
¼ of an onion, peeled
1 bay leaf
4 parsley stalks
1 thyme branch
25g butter
25g plain flour
Maldon sea salt and freshly ground black pepper

Place the cold milk, carrot, onion and herbs in a small saucepan and bring to a simmer. Do not allow the milk to boil over, as you will lose some of the milk and the proportions of the sauce will be wrong, yielding a sauce that is too thick – exactly what we are trying to avoid. Turn off the heat and allow to sit for 10 minutes. The vegetables and herbs will add a subtle flavour to the milk.

While the milk is infusing, melt the butter in another small

The sauce should be thick enough to heavily coat the back of a spoon

saucepan and add the flour. Stir with a wooden spoon to combine, and cook on a low heat for 3 minutes, all the time stirring regularly and making sure the mixture does not overheat and burn. It is crucial that you allow it to cook for the 3 minutes as suggested, to remove any raw trace of flour from the sauce. This slightly odd-looking mixture of cooked flour and butter is called a roux, and it will both thicken and enrich the sauce. (You can make exactly the same mixture to whisk into a gravy to thicken it.)

Strain the milk and whisk it into the roux. Place on a low heat and, whisking all the time, bring the sauce to a simmer. The sauce will not start to thicken until the liquid reaches a simmer. At this point, maintain the sauce at a gentle simmer for 2 minutes, still whisking to ensure that there are no lumps of roux left floating in the sauce. You will notice the sauce becoming smooth and shiny.

Remove from the heat and season to taste with salt and pepper. The consistency should be thick enough to heavily coat the back of a spoon. The sauce is now ready to serve. You can prepare a béchamel in advance and reheat when needed.

Parsley sauce
Just before serving, add 3 tablespoons of chopped parsley to the finished sauce and bring back to a simmer. Serve immediately for the freshest taste.

Cheese sauce
Add 2 tablespoons each of grated Parmesan and Gruyère and 1 teaspoon of French mustard to the finished sauce. Whisk in well and simmer for 1 minute before serving.

Pancakes, sweet or savoury

It's a funny name really, pancakes, as they are as far removed from a cake as you could imagine. Mind you, they can be great, and when thin and light and sweetened with a citrusy butter or a warm fruit compote, or stuffed with a carefully chosen vegetable wrapped in a light yet rich sauce, they will bring a smile to most faces.

I use the same recipe whether making the sweet or the savoury version, just adding a small pinch of sugar to the dessert option. The addition of melted butter is a tremendous asset to the texture and flavour.

Keys to success
Whisk all the ingredients thoroughly to ensure there are no lumps of flour in the batter.

The addition of the cooled melted butter is vital for the flavour and texture of the pancakes and makes them less likely to stick when being cooked.

Cook the pancakes on quite a high heat using the correct quantity of batter to ensure you achieve a pancake that is neither too thick nor too thin.

Makes 12   170g plain white flour
Pinch of salt
2 teaspoons caster sugar (omit for savoury pancakes)
2 eggs and 1 yolk
425ml full-fat milk
2 tablespoons cooled melted butter

Sieve the flour, salt and sugar (if you are making sweet pancakes) into a bowl. Make a well in the centre and drop in the eggs and extra yolk. Start whisking the eggs and adding the milk in a steady stream, gradually drawing in the flour from the edges of the bowl. When all the milk has been whisked in, the batter should look smooth and will have a layer of fine bubbles on the surface. I usually pass it through a fine sieve to be absolutely sure all the flour has been properly incorporated.

Stir in the melted butter, which may become a little lumpy-looking. That is fine and to be expected, as when the melted butter hits the cold liquid it tends to solidify into little lumps. These buttery lumps disappear completely in the cooking. Chill the batter if possible for 1 hour before cooking.

To cook the pancakes, I use a 20.5cm heavy-based non-stick or cast-iron pan. Place the pan over a medium heat and allow it to become quite hot. Grease the pan sparingly yet thoroughly with a little butter, making sure to go up 1cm along the sides of the pan. I do this with a bit of baking parchment or greaseproof paper, or a butter wrapper lightly greased with soft butter. Dribble ½ teaspoon of the batter on to the pan to check that it is hot enough. The batter should start to colour and cook immediately. If it doesn't, let the pan get hotter.

Add about 2 tablespoons of the batter per pancake and quickly lift, tilt and swirl the pan to coat the bottom evenly with a fine layer. If you miss a spot and there is a hole in the pancake, just dribble in a tiny bit more batter to fill the hole. Allow to cook until the edges of the pancake start to curl and loosen. Turn the pancake carefully and continue to cook for another minute, until it is a golden colour. Lift out of the pan and place on a plate while you cook the rest. The cooked pancakes can be stacked one on top of the other and, blissfully, they will not stick together.

The cooked pancakes can be eaten there and then in the old-fashioned way with a little butter, lemon juice and caster sugar, or may be reheated later according to your taste.

Sweet pancakes
Serve with: chocolate sauce, roasted hazelnuts and a blob of softly whipped cream; caramel sauce and thickly sliced bananas and a blob of softly whipped cream or crème fraîche; a warm compote of raspberries and geranium and softly whipped cream; a collapsing roast peach and its cooking juices, a sprinkling of almond praline and thick pouring cream.

Savoury pancakes
Stuff savoury pancakes, using the method below, with: broccoli with lemon and Parmesan and a drizzle of hollandaise sauce; chard and Gruyère, as in the gratin recipe on page 272; leeks with olive oil, Parmesan, toasted pine nuts and pangrattata page 295.

First preheat the oven to 180°C/350°F/gas 4.

Lay a pancake one at a time on your work surface. Spoon 1½ tablespoons of the chosen filling on to the centre of the pancake and fold in the edges to make a neatly sealed parcel. Place them, folded side down, on a baking tray lined with baking parchment. Sprinkle a very few drops of water with your fingertips over the pancakes to create a gently steamy atmosphere in the oven. Cover with a sheet of baking parchment and reheat in the oven for about 15 minutes, or until bubbling hot.

Serve as soon as possible, with a leaf salad.

Tomato sauce

This is a general-purpose sauce which is versatile and can be served in a variety of ways, ranging from a simple pasta dish or with grilled meat or fish. It's good with meatballs, and I sometimes use it as a cooking medium for mussels and mackerel, finishing off the dish with a blob of garlicky mayonnaise.

As with any tomato dish, the quality and ripeness of the tomatoes is crucial. If you try making this sauce with watery winter tomatoes, the result will be dull and disappointing. Summer is without doubt the best time of the year for making it, when deep red vine-ripened tomatoes are at their best. You could make a large batch at that time of year, when the tomatoes are also good value, and freeze it in small containers to defrost on cold wintry days and remind you of summer's sweet flavours. Failing that, a very good result can be achieved in winter using best-quality tinned or bottled tomatoes.

The ingredients

Tomatoes for this dish need to be brilliantly ripe, almost to the point of bursting. In fact if they are slightly softening due to their readiness, that is fine, as they will melt into the sauce.

Basil is an obvious choice for this sauce, but other herbs such as marjoram and tarragon are also excellent.

Serves 6–8 2 tablespoons extra virgin olive oil
225g red onions, peeled and finely chopped
2 cloves of garlic, peeled and finely chopped
2 sticks of celery, cut into 5mm dice
1 medium carrot, peeled and cut into 5mm dice
Maldon sea salt and freshly ground black pepper
1.8kg tomatoes, peeled and coarsely chopped (or the
   equivalent quantity in canned or bottled tomatoes)
2 tablespoons basil leaves
Pinch of sugar

Heat the olive oil in a medium-sized heavy-based saucepan. Add the onions, garlic, celery and carrot, and coat them in the oil. Season with salt and pepper and cook uncovered on a moderate heat. Stir the vegetables regularly with a wooden spoon and control the heat to prevent them from both stewing and scorching. After 10 minutes the vegetables will be beginning to soften but in no way collapsing.

Add the prepared tomatoes, season with salt and pepper and stir. Cover the saucepan with a tight-fitting lid, reduce the temperature and allow the tomatoes to cook at a gentle simmer and melt into a sauce. This will take about 20 minutes. Stir the tomatoes a couple of times as they cook. If the sauce seems a bit thin and watery, remove the lid and cook uncovered to thicken the sauce slightly. On the other hand, the sauce should not be too thick and strong. You are looking for a consistency that will just hold its shape on the plate, but still be full of flavour.

Add the basil leaves, torn into smaller pieces if large, and stir in. Taste and correct the seasoning. If the sauce seems a little dull, add a small pinch of sugar to lift it.

With cinnamon to serve with grilled lamb
Add a broken cinnamon stick to the vegetables and do not retrieve it until the sauce is cooked.

With dried chilli to add some heat
Break a small deseeded dried chilli into coarse pieces or use a pinch of dried chilli flakes and add to the vegetables at the beginning of cooking. Use rosemary as the herb in this case.

With rosemary in winter
For a robust and warming winter sauce, add 2 large sprigs of rosemary to the vegetables at the beginning of cooking. The herb stalks can be removed at the end of cooking. Some of the leaves will have fallen off the sprigs – that's fine.

Salsa verde

Salsa verde – or call it Green Sauce if you like, though it doesn't sound quite so good like that – is a delicious and most useful sauce. Full of herbs and piquant from the addition of the anchovies and capers, it packs a punch and will stand up to and sit happily alongside robustly flavoured meats such as beef and lamb or grilled oily fish like bass, mullet and salmon. Though it will keep for a day or two, it is without doubt best eaten within a few hours of being made. This way the flavour of the herbs is fresh and green. When allowed to sit for longer than that, the herbs become muddy in flavour, as the piquant ingredients seem to 'cook' the charm out of the greens.

If using salted anchovies and capers, they will need to be well rinsed under cold water to remove excess salt.

Serve with grilled meats and fish.

Serves 6–8
- 1 large handful of rocket leaves, about 100g
- 1 bunch of flat-leaf parsley leaves, about 100g
- 8 large sprigs of mint, leaves only
- 6 large sprigs of tarragon, leaves only
- 1 tablespoon capers, coarsely chopped
- 2 cloves of garlic, peeled and crushed to a smooth paste
- 6–8 anchovies, very finely chopped
- 1 tablespoon Dijon mustard
- 225ml extra virgin olive oil
- Zest of 1 lemon
- Maldon sea salt and freshly ground black pepper

Chop the rocket and herbs quite finely, but not to a dust, and mix with the other ingredients. Taste and correct the seasoning, if necessary adding a few drops of lemon juice to freshen the taste. Store in a covered container in the fridge.

Mayonnaise

Mayonnaise is an immensely important sauce and if I had to choose a single savoury 'Desert Island' sauce, this would be it.

It pairs perfectly with many different ingredients. Poached salmon or trout are sublime with it. A blob of mayonnaise on top of a halved hard-boiled egg, still a little warm from the pot, is one of my favourite foods. I love it with a simple hamburger when it melts into the beefy juices. With a slice of warm roast chicken, it makes the best sandwich. Lobster, prawns, shrimps, mussels, cockles and clams lap it up. It accepts lots of different flavours happily. Herbs such as tarragon, chives, dill, parsley, watercress and wild garlic, and stronger flavours like gherkin, anchovy, spices, chillies, garlic crushed raw or roasted, tomatoes and roast peppers all work well when stirred into it. More exotic flavours such as tamarind and quince are also good, and sometimes I add the juices from a foil- or parchment-baked fish, to thin, warm and flavour all at the same time. The roast garlic version can be thinned with a little gravy from the roasting pan of lamb, beef or chicken, to make a delicious sauce, again served warm. As you can see, it is versatile.

Some books will terrify you with words of warning before you start making mayonnaise. Others are perhaps a little casual in their approach, but all I will say is be a bit careful, take your time, and just remember the important rules, as stated below. Once you have made it once or twice, it won't cause you a second thought and by then you will realise that there is simply no substitute for the real thing.

The sauce can be made by hand, in a food processor or in a food mixer. The handmade sauce will be softer, the machine-made one firmer.

The ingredients
Use free-range or if possible organic egg yolks for mayonnaise. The egg whites, which are not used in the making of the sauce, can be stored covered in the fridge for 2 weeks, or alternatively they freeze perfectly. Some very organised cooks like to freeze the individual egg whites in ice-cube trays. This makes life easier when using them later. Otherwise you can weigh the whites, which take about 2

hours to defrost at room temperature, allowing 25g for each white. Defrosted egg whites make perfect meringues and whip up perfectly for mousses and soufflés.

Try to find good-quality French mustard and white wine vinegar. A lot of vinegar is poisonously sharp, and if that is the case with yours, use, as I often do, lemon juice to sharpen the sauce.

Good-quality oil is crucial for a good mayonnaise. The combination of oils is also important. If you use all olive oil, you might find the taste too strong, so many people find that a combination of a 'bland' oil such as sunflower or peanut oil, mixed with a smaller proportion of the stronger-tasting olive oil, gives them a balance that they enjoy. However, mayonnaise made solely with grassy green new season's olive oil is truly fabulous, and something I look forward to and am willing to splash out on at least once a year.

Mayonnaise is a cold emulsion sauce. The 'emulsion' refers to the joining together of two liquids. The liquids in this case are egg yolk and oil. There is only a certain speed at which the emulsion can be formed, so if you add the oil too quickly to the egg yolks, the yolks cannot absorb the oil and the two liquids will separate and curdle. This is the most important thing to remember when making mayonnaise, so take your time.

Serves 6–10 2 free-range egg yolks
¼ teaspoon French mustard
1 dessertspoon white wine vinegar or lemon juice
Pinch of fine sea salt and freshly ground black or white pepper
250ml oil (e.g. 50ml olive oil and 200ml sunflower or peanut oil)

Place the egg yolks, mustard, vinegar or lemon juice and a pinch of salt and pepper in a medium-sized Pyrex or glazed ceramic bowl.

Adding the oil, in a thin, steady stream

Place the oil in a jug. I use a Pyrex measuring jug so that I can control the flow of the oil to a slow dribble.

Drop the oil very slowly on to the egg mix while continuously whisking. Adding the oil slowly is the key to success, and other than using good ingredients it is the only rule you need to remember. If your arm gets tired from the whisking, it is fine to stop and leave it for a minute or two before starting again.

After about 3 minutes of whisking in the oil, the mixture will start to thicken slightly. You can start to add the oil a little bit more quickly now, but do not get carried away by your success – continue to add it quite cautiously. Keep adding the oil until it is all incorporated into the sauce, which by now will have the consistency of softly whipped cream.

Taste and correct the seasoning, perhaps adding another drop of vinegar or lemon juice.

Occasionally the mayonnaise may be a little too thick for your liking. This might be caused by an extra large egg yolk. If this is the case, whisk in a teaspoon or two of water to bring it to the required consistency. The small amount of water will have virtually no effect on the flavour of the sauce.

Store the mayonnaise in a covered jar in the fridge, where it will keep happily for a week or more.

*If the mayonnaise curdles, due to the oil being added too quickly, it will start to look grainy and when left to rest for a few minutes will become quite thin and oily on top. If this happens, it is not a disaster. Put another egg yolk into a clean bowl and slowly whisk in the curdled mayonnaise, a teaspoon at a time, until it emulsifies again. Continue and finish the sauce as above.

Puff pastry book

There are certain dishes and techniques that can elevate your food and cooking to a higher level. Puff pastry is one of these techniques. This light, flaky and buttery pastry, with its 729 feathery layers, is peerless and opens up a lot of different avenues that have previously been closed in the sweet or savoury kitchen. Once the technique is mastered, you will find that even though the pastry will need two hours to complete, the actual handling time is quite short. I reckon 10–15 minutes. The rest of the time the pastry sits in the fridge, chilling and relaxing between the all-important rolls and folds.

With this pastry to hand a whole new range of dishes is possible: vol-au-vents and bouches, millefeuilles, palmiers, sacristains, tartes fines, all sorts of delights en croûte and so on.

Puff pastry freezes really well. Get it into the freezer as soon as possible, to trap the flavour of the butter. So bite the bullet and get rolling and folding and you will be richly rewarded with a fine pastry that bears no resemblance to the commercial equivalent.

I've included the recipe for savoury shortcrust pastry in the relevant chapter, see page 99.

Keys to success

The initial dough made with flour and water is called the **détrempe**. It should be neither too wet as in soft and sticky, nor too dry as in firm and cracking.

The butter should be **chilled** and is then beaten and formed into the appropriate shape.

Use flour on the worktop and on the pastry when rolling, but brush off excess flour before folding and chilling.

Line up edges carefully and always fold the pastry **exactly in three** as if it was an important business letter.

Wrap the pastry and chill for at least **30 minutes** between each double roll.

Each time you start to roll the pastry it should be placed on your worktop like **a book ready to be opened**.

If butter squirts out of the pastry when you are rolling, add a sprinkle of flour and keep going. It is better if it doesn't happen, but it sometimes does, and even though you might not end up with the desired 729 layers of pastry, it will still be excellent.

The ingredients
Strong white flour or baker's white flour, a white flour high in protein, is essential for puff pastry.

The butter used is generally unsalted, though I often use salted butter and find the result delicious.

Makes 1kg   450g baker's or strong flour
Pinch of salt
250ml ice-cold water
450g butter, cold from the fridge

Sieve the flour and salt into a large bowl. Add almost all the water, and with your hand, mix to form a dough, adding the remaining drops of water if it refuses to come together. The dough will not look particularly attractive or smooth at this stage. A soft dough will make a flabby pastry that will not rise with straight sides when being cooked later. If your détrempe is too dry the pastry is more likely to crack when you are rolling and folding it.

Cover the détrempe by wrapping it in greaseproof or parchment paper or plastic film, or slip it into a large plastic bag, and chill for 30 minutes.

When the détrempe is chilled, dust the worktop with flour and roll the dough out about 30cm square.

Place the cold butter, wrapper removed, in a strong plastic bag and bash it with your rolling pin to achieve a rectangular slab that is pliable but still chilled. The slab should be about 13cm wide and 17cm long. You will probably have to shape the butter a bit with your hands – that's fine, but do not allow the butter to warm up or start to melt. Place the butter in the middle of the square of dough and fold in the edges of the dough as if making a neat parcel. The butter should be completely enveloped – no butter should be visible.

Now roll the dough and butter 'parcel' into a rectangle about 22cm wide and 45cm long. Don't get too worked up about these measurements. They are approximate, so something close to this size will be fine. What is really important, though, is that the sides and ends of the pastry are straight, so that when you fold the pastry, all of the edges meet in flush lines. If your pastry looks misshapen, apply pressure with your rolling pin wherever necessary to achieve a regular shape.

Brush the excess flour off the surface of the pastry with a pastry brush, and neatly and precisely fold the dough into three – as if folding a business letter! This is crucial, and lining up the edges of the dough neatly is also crucial. With folds and edges carefully aligned, the pastry will rise up straight later. If not carefully aligned, the rising pastry has a tendency to tumble off to one side or the other. You now have three layers in your pastry.

Give the dough a 90° clockwise turn. It should now look like a book ready to be opened on your worktop. Roll out into a rectangle as before, fold in three again, and seal at the edges by pressing gently with your rolling pin. Brush off the excess flour. Place in a plastic bag and chill for at least 30 minutes. Your pastry now has nine layers.

Now the pastry has had two single rolls or one double roll. It needs two more of these double rolls, allowing a 30-minute rest and chill between each. Chill the pastry after the final roll for at least 30 minutes.

The pastry is now ready to be rolled again for cutting, shaping and cooking.

Harissa

I keep a jar of this hot and spiced North African-inspired paste in the fridge most of the time. I find it a really useful condiment for seasoning and marinating and on some occasions for adding a little heat to certain dishes. I use it with grilled lamb, pork and chicken, with oily fish such as salmon and mackerel, on hard-boiled eggs and in an omelette, stirred through mayonnaise as a sauce or through olive oil to make a slightly hot vinaigrette for crisp and cool salad leaves.

I use medium hot chillies such as cayenne, jalapeño or serrano, for a level of heat that is obvious but not too scorching.

Serves 6–8
- 6 medium hot red chillies
- 1½ tablespoons tomato paste or thick purée
- 8 cloves of garlic, peeled and crushed to a paste
- 3 teaspoons cumin seeds, roasted and ground
- 3 teaspoons coriander seeds, roasted and ground
- 6 tablespoons extra virgin olive oil
- 1 teaspoon red wine vinegar or lemon juice
- 3 tablespoons chopped coriander leaves
- Maldon sea salt, freshly ground black pepper and a pinch of sugar

Preheat the oven to 200°C/400°F/gas 6. Place the chillies on a small roasting tray and roast for about 20 minutes. The skins will be blackening and blistering and coming away from the flesh. Place the roasted chillies in a bowl, seal tightly with cling film and allow to cool. When cool, peel off the skins and slit the chillies to remove the seeds. You just want the roasted flesh of the chilli for the harissa.

Place the chillies in a food processor. Add the tomato paste, garlic and ground spices and process to a smoothish purée. Gradually add the oil and vinegar or lemon juice. Add the chopped coriander leaves and season to taste, adding a tiny pinch of sugar if you feel the flavour needs a lift. The taste should be strong, hot and pungent. Store in a covered container such as a jam jar in the fridge. The harissa will keep perfectly like this for several months.

Curry powder

If you would like to make your own spice mix, here is a combination I like to use for a general-purpose mix. Buy the spices whole, and roast and grind them yourself, and the flavour will be fresh and exciting. In this blend, it is the particular flavour and aroma of the fenugreek mixed with the other spices that gives the blend its distinctive 'curry powder' feel.

Makes 35g

1 teaspoon fenugreek seeds

1 teaspoon ground turmeric

2 tablespoons coriander seeds, roasted

1 tablespoon cumin seeds, roasted

2 teaspoons black peppercorns, roasted

1 teaspoon black mustard seeds, roasted

4 cloves, roasted

1 dessertspoon chilli flakes (add more if you want a hotter mix)

Place a heavy-based frying pan over a medium heat and roast the fenugreek and turmeric for 10 seconds. Remove from the heat and add the remaining ingredients before grinding everything to a fine powder in a clean coffee or spice grinder or a pestle and mortar.

Store the spices in a clean sealed container such as a jam jar and keep in a cool dark place. Use within a couple of weeks.

Vegetable stock

Vegetable stock can be a well flavoured, delicious and subtle broth or it can be as dull as dishwater. The key to a good vegetable stock is vegetables. A few bits of randomly chosen vegetables floating around in a saucepan of simmering water will not give you the result you wish for. Neither is this process a vehicle for using up stale vegetables that would find a more productive role on the compost heap or a way to absolve your guilt at the sight of those unused ingredients.

The cooking time of the stock is short. As soon as the vegetables are cooked, so is the stock. You know how horrible overcooked vegetables taste, the same applies here as the overcooked taste will be obvious in the strained liquid.

You may not have all of the vegetables as suggested here, but there is a bit of leeway as long as you do not overpower the stock by using too much of one particular ingredient.

Makes 1.5 litres

4 carrots
2 onions
1 leek
4 sticks of celery (outside greener stalks are fine)
6 button mushrooms
1 small fennel bulb
1 small potato
2 cloves of garlic, unpeeled
4 parsley stalks
½ bay leaf
1 sprig of thyme and tarragon
4 black peppercorns

Peel and coarsely chop the vegetables into 2cm pieces. Leave the garlic cloves unpeeled. Place all of the ingredients into a saucepan they fit into quite snugly and just cover with cold water. Bring to a simmer and cook for 30 minutes. Allow to sit for 10 minutes before straining through a fine sieve. The stock will keep for 2 days in the fridge or may be frozen.

I love how a simple broth can, with the addition of carefully chosen ingredients, be transformed into an elegant dish that combines both humbleness and sophistication. This is comfort food certainly, but that does not mean it can't be smart and acceptable at any table.

Chicken and other broths

I am totally hooked on chicken broth. It is so wonderfully nourishing and with carefully chosen ingredients can be as smart as anything you will serve. I eat it throughout the year, varying the ingredients depending on what is in season. For the success of this recipe, a really good well-flavoured and preferably clear chicken stock is vital. This can be a bit confusing, as in some parts of the world stock and broth mean the same thing. That is not the case here.

On the subject of broth versus stock, Alan Davidson, author of the indispensable *Oxford Companion to Food*, wrote: 'It could be said that broth occupies an intermediate position between stock and soup. A broth (e.g. chicken broth) can be eaten as it is, whereas a stock (e.g. chicken stock) would normally be consumed only as an ingredient in something more complex.' That is exactly the case here.

Chicken broth has not been given the title 'Jewish penicillin' in some cultures without good reason. You can almost feel its goodness coursing through your veins as you eat it. My mother would make it for us when we were young and feeling a bit under the weather. We actually liked it regardless of whether we were unwell or in robust health. Sometimes she would add extra chicken necks and gizzards to the broth when cooking and we loved these delicious extras. We would pick up the necks with our small and nimble fingers, perfect for the task, and nibble the tiny little sweet morsels of flesh off them. The gizzards were chopped into small pieces and consumed with equal pleasure with her brown soda bread, thinly sliced and lightly buttered, the hot gizzards melting the butter, making for greasy chins and much giggling.

I love how a simple broth can, with the addition of carefully chosen ingredients, be transformed into an elegant dish that combines both humbleness and sophistication. This is comfort food certainly, but that does not mean it can't be smart and acceptable at any table.

Keep this broth firmly in season and you will get splendid results and each changing season will give you many options to choose from. In spring use wild garlic leaves and flowers when the countryside is covered with them. Either of the two different types of wild garlic will do. The long skinny-leaved one, sometimes called three-cornered garlic, with its bell-like flowers, or the wider-leaved ramsons, with its allium-shaped flower heads, are both perfect. Watercress is vibrant, peppery and fresh-tasting. Sorrel, wild or cultivated, is tart and slimy.

If you are a forager and interested in wild foods, this recipe will give you lots of opportunities to use the many wild greens you collect. Wood sorrel, dandelion leaves and ground elder are just the tip of the iceberg in terms of what is available to eat from the wild. Arm yourself with Roger Phillips's marvellous book *Wild Food*, and get out there collecting.

Cavolo nero, from the winter garden, is deep-flavoured and slightly brooding. Pea and broad bean leaves are fresh and summery. Spinach is salty and lovely and chard leaves are silky and sophisticated. Beetroot leaves and stalks when combined with dill give a lovely result. The list of possible additions goes on and on, and though I generally urge caution with experimentation, this is as good an opportunity as any to put your own stamp on a dish.

I generally use chicken bones when making stock for a broth; however, there are several other options. A turkey carcass makes a rich and wonderful stock, a perfect base for a broth or, on another day, to be used in a risotto. Guinea fowl and quail are also excellent, though it has to be said that having enough guinea fowl or quail bones to make a stock is generally the reserve of restaurant kitchens.

A duck carcass also produces a good stock for a broth, but you have to be a bit more focused on removing as much of the fat as possible from these greasy little creatures and I tend to add lots of robust and earthy flavours like root vegetables and lentils to the stock extracted from the duck bones.

Chicken stock and roast chicken stock

Keys to success

Start with good-quality ingredients consisting of chicken bones, **raw or cooked, or a combination of both.**

Frozen chicken bones work perfectly and in this instance, due to the long cooking time, can be used directly from frozen.

I also freeze leftover carcasses from a cooked chicken, wings raw or cooked, in other words any bits of chicken raw or cooked with the exception of the liver and wing tips. **The liver and wing tips should never go into the stockpot**, as over long cooking they will make the stock bitter. This is a form of stockpiling of the bones and bits until you have enough to make a pot of stock. You can of course make stock with just one chicken carcass and still get a worthwhile quantity.

Chicken necks are also wonderful in a stock, as is the **gizzard**, though these can be hard to get nowadays.

I sometimes use a **combination of frozen bones and fresh bones**. There is nothing to worry about here, due to the long cooking time of the stock.

Place the bones in a saucepan they fit into snugly. Leave 4cm free at the top of the saucepan so that the stock does not spill out of the pot.

If your saucepan is too big, you may have too much water, ending up with a stock that is too thin in flavour.

Even if you use a saucepan that is too big and are careful to just cover the bones with water, the fact that the level of the liquid is low in the pot can cause the steam to recirculate rather than evaporate and this may cause the stock to be cloudy.

Chicken and stock ingredients ready for cooking

Cold water is always used to draw the flavour out of the solid ingredients and into the liquid.

I **rarely add salt** to stock when it is cooking.

All stocks are brought to simmering point **and cooked uncovered at a bare simmer** to obtain a clear well-flavoured stock. If you have difficulty controlling the heat under your pot, use a heat diffuser mat to achieve the gentle breaking of bubbles on the surface of the liquid.

The stock should never boil. When it boils, a couple of things happen. It reduces, and as this happens it becomes stronger and loses its subtle charm. Also the boiling loosens tiny particles of flesh from the bones and vegetables, resulting in a stock that may be cloudy and with these tiny particles floating in it.

A cloudy stock is not the end of the world and is fine to use, but if you are careful with the gentle simmering you can end up with a deliciously flavoured liquid that is almost as sparklingly clear as a consommé.

Taste the stock on a spoon, blowing on it in the old-fashioned way, as it will be very hot. Underwhelmed? Taste another spoonful while adding a few grains of salt to the spoon... a revelation I hope.

The resulting stock **is gently strained** through a fine sieve and allowed to settle. Any fat will rise to the surface, to be **skimmed** off using a large spoon. You can also use a mais-gras, one of those French ceramic degreasing jugs. If you can lay your hands on an old-fashioned 'skimming bowl', the type used in dairies to separate the cream from the milk, that would be fantastic.

The other effective way to skim the fat off stock is to place the cold stock in the fridge overnight and next day to **skim off the solid or semi-solid fat**.

Stock at a gentle simmer

The cooled stock will keep in the fridge for up to 3 days.

Stock also freezes very well. I use plastic containers such as spotlessly clean yoghurt tubs or milk containers for this purpose. Make sure the stock is cold before decanting it into plastic containers.

The frozen stock will still be fine and safe to use after 6 months, but as always with the freezer, the sooner something comes out, the better it will be.

A richer and darker-flavoured stock is obtained by roasting the raw or cooked chicken bones to a rich golden colour before making the stock. Therefore in the case of the cooked bones from a roast, they will be twice-roasted. Lovely. I call this **Roast chicken stock**. This stock is used for darker sauces and to accompany the more robustly flavoured meats such as beef and venison.

The degreased stock can be reduced by as much as three-quarters, or more if you wish, to achieve a deeply flavoured 'chicken glaze'. The more you reduce or boil it down, the more concentrated the flavour will be. This liquid when chilled will set to a rubber jelly, and in this case you have just made your own stock cube. Bravo. This can then be stored in a covered container in the fridge, where it will keep for up to 3 months, and can also be frozen. You can cut it or tear it into manageable pieces, and these little lozenges of concentrated chicken flavour can be used as they are to perk up a dull gravy or soup, or diluted to taste with boiling water to reconstitute a stock.

Chicken stock

Makes 3 litres 2–3 raw or cooked chicken carcasses, or a mixture of both
3.4 litres cold water (approx.)
2 onions, peeled and sliced
1 leek, split in two
1 outside stick of celery or 1 lovage leaf
2 carrots, scrubbed and sliced
A few parsley stalks
1 large sprig of thyme
1 small bay leaf
6 black peppercorns

Chop or break up the carcasses as much as possible. Put all the ingredients into a saucepan that they fit into snugly. The water should just cover them. Bring slowly up to the boil and skim the fat off the top with a tablespoon. Simmer uncovered and very gently for 2–3 hours.

Allow the stock to sit for 20 minutes before straining to allow any loose particles of meat or vegetables to fall to the bottom of the saucepan. Strain and remove any remaining fat. If you need a stronger flavour, boil down the strained and degreased liquid in an open pan to reduce by one-third or one-half the volume. Do not add salt.

Roast chicken stock

Roast the raw or cooked bones or carcasses in a moderate oven, 180°C/350°F/gas 4, for approximately 30 minutes, or until they have attained a rich golden colour, then proceed with the recipe as above.

Broth with spinach or chard leaves and herbs

The object of the exercise here is a light yet flavoursome broth, spiked with the best greens each season has to offer. The secret of success is in the late addition of the green or defining ingredients to the broth. There is a bit to do, though, before that stage is reached. Dice the onion and potatoes neatly, remembering that they will be clearly visible in the finished broth, and cook them very gently so that they do not collapse before the stock is added. The broth should never boil rapidly, just stay at a gentle simmer, and crucially the saucepan lid stays off once the greens go in.

The ingredients
Spinach or chard leaves are the principal green ingredient here. The fresher they are, the more vibrant and delicious the broth will be. The stalks from the greens are finely diced and sweated with the potatoes and onions. If you choose baby spinach leaves, there is no need to destalk. Just add the whole lot at the end of cooking as directed and they will melt to a silky comforting consistency.

The butter can be replaced with 2–3 tablespoons of olive oil.

The herbs will taste better and fresher if they are chopped just before you add them to the broth.

As always, the addition of salt and pepper are crucial here, so taste carefully and season accordingly.

Serves 4–6 50g butter
175g potatoes, peeled and cut into neat 1cm dice
175g onions, peeled and finely chopped into 5mm dice
400g spinach or chard leaves, or 600ml when pressed into
    a measuring jug, stalks cut into 1cm dice, leaves gently
    torn into bite-sized pieces
2 cloves of garlic, peeled and crushed to a paste
Maldon sea salt and freshly ground black pepper
1.2 litres chicken stock
100ml chopped herbs: a mixture of parsley,
    chives and marjoram

Melt the butter in a heavy-based saucepan and allow to foam. Add the potatoes, onions, diced spinach or chard stalks and garlic. Use a wooden spoon to coat the vegetables in the butter and season with salt and pepper. Cover with a butter wrapper or greaseproof paper and a tight-fitting lid. Cook on a very low heat to allow the vegetables to sweat gently until barely tender. This will take about 10 minutes. Don't overcook and allow the diced potato to collapse.

Add the stock, stir gently and bring to a simmer, and cook for a further 10 minutes. The broth should be barely bubbling. If it cooks too fast at this stage, the delicacy of flavour of the chicken stock will be lost. By now the potato and onion should be completely tender but still holding their shape. Taste and correct the seasoning. This is the base and can be put aside until later.

To finish the broth, bring the base back to a simmer. Add the greens and cook uncovered, allowing the greens to wilt and take on a melted consistency. Spinach leaves can take as little as 3 minutes, 7–8 minutes if tough. Chard leaves will take about 10 minutes. Add the herbs and again watch the cooking time very carefully – 2 minutes will be enough to release the flavour from the herbs. Taste one last time to ensure the seasoning is spot on. Serve immediately.

Wild garlic leaf and flower broth

There are two types of wild garlic that grow in profusion in Ireland. They are both part of the allium family. Around where I live in East Cork, the first variety generally starts to appear as early as March, though it is not unknown to see it in January or February. This is the long, skinny-leaved garlic, sometimes called three-cornered garlic or snow bell. It produces at the end of the stalk a little bunch of white bell-shaped flowers, hence the name snow bell. This variety seems to thrive on the sunny side of the road but will also succeed in the shade. The other variety, called ramsons, arrives later and is happiest growing in the shade. It has long, wide, elegant and shiny leaves and the flowers on this variety are in a little typical allium pom-pom. Either of the two types of wild garlic will do for this recipe. Don't forget that they can be used in other soups, with grilled or braised fish, meat and poultry, in salads, flavoured butters, sauces and so on. It is well worth trying to get a little patch of either type of garlic established in your garden. However, beware, as both varieties will spread in all directions if given the chance, so you may have to limit their progress.

The key to the success of this recipe is the addition of the wild garlic to the broth just a few minutes before you are going to eat it. This way the garlic will still be bright green in colour and vibrant in taste when it arrives at the table. Sometimes the little flowers, which I urge you to use, will float to the surface of the hot broth and sit there like little water lilies or lotus flowers. Now that's a bonus.

The ingredients

The wild garlic, when in season, is readily available for those who live in the countryside and for urban dwellers is increasingly found in vegetable shops and farmers' markets. Every part can be used, bulbs below the ground and leaves and flowers above.

An optional addition of grated Parmesan is delicious here. Allow your guests to sprinkle a light dusting on each bowl of poured soup rather than you adding it to the cooking pot. It will taste sweeter and fresher this way. One generous teaspoon of Parmesan is plenty on each serving.

Serves 6 50g butter
175g potatoes, peeled and cut into neat 1cm dice
175g onions, peeled and finely chopped into 5mm dice
2 cloves of garlic, peeled and crushed to a paste
Maldon sea salt and freshly ground black pepper
1.2 litres chicken stock
600ml finely chopped garlic leaves, tightly packed
      into the measure
50ml garlic flowers, if available

Melt the butter in a heavy-based saucepan and allow to foam. Add the potatoes, onions and crushed garlic. Stir to coat in the butter and season with salt and pepper. Cover with a butter wrapper or grease-proof paper and a tight-fitting lid. Cook on a very low heat to allow the vegetables to sweat gently until barely tender. This will take about 10 minutes. Don't overcook and allow the diced potato to collapse.

Add the stock, stir gently and bring to a simmer, then cook gently for a further 10 minutes. The broth should be barely bubbling. If it cooks too fast at this stage, the delicacy of flavour of the chicken stock will be lost. Taste and correct the seasoning. This is the base and can be put aside until later.

To finish, bring the base back to a simmer. Add the garlic leaves, cook uncovered and allow just to wilt. This will only take a couple of minutes. Taste and correct the seasoning again. Finally, sprinkle in the flowers, and watch and marvel as they float on the surface. Serve immediately.

Kale broth with lemon zest and Parmesan

Kale: the mention of the name is enough to wrinkle many a face in disgust. What a shame, because kale is fantastic. Boiled until soft, and puréed with a grating of nutmeg and a splash of cream, it is one of the best winter vegetables. Again cooked until soft, drained and dressed with olive oil and lemon, it is also marvellous, particularly when served on grilled bread that has been lightly rubbed with a little garlic. You can introduce it to chilli, garlic, Indian spices, southeast Asian flavours, Spanish smoked paprika and chorizo and you aren't even beginning to scratch the surface of the flavours it will marry with. Its winter seasonality also seems to add to its charm, as it doesn't have much green competition and it almost stands alone in the coldest months as the bearer of badly needed vitamins and iron.

For the gardener, it is a thing of beauty, as its tiered, plumage-like foliage looks almost like an exotic in the winter garden. Viewed under snow or frost on a clear sunny morning, its handsome bearing rivals anything in the garden at any time of the year.

The trick with kale is to cook it enough. It needs to be soft and comforting. If you want crisp, have a carrot stick. You are not being clever by undercooking kale. It will be tough and more like fodder and your family and friends will not thank you for it.

Subtle seasoning is required here when finishing the broth to get a good balance between the salt, lemon and Parmesan. Too much lemon zest or Parmesan will overpower. Think of the lemon and Parmesan as added seasonings as you sprinkle them on, and go with a light hand and careful tasting.

As always with the addition of any green vegetable to a broth or soup, once the greens go in the saucepan lid stays off.

The ingredients
The kale in this recipe can be one of several varieties. The most easily available variety, which starts to appear in the shops around October, is the dense and compact curly kale. You can also use cavolo nero, with its long slightly sinister-looking plume-like leaves. It is sometimes called Tuscan kale or Nero di Toscana. Watch out for

other varieties, such as Red Russian kale with its serrated leaves. All these kales become sweeter and more tender after the first frosts.

Try to get an unwaxed lemon for this recipe. Failing that, scrub the lemon well before grating the zest.

Parmesan always tastes best when freshly grated off a larger piece. Pre-grated Parmesan in my experience is not great, and if I could only get that I would just leave it out. Don't spoil all your hard work by adding a substandard ingredient.

Serves 4–6 50g butter
175g potatoes, peeled and cut into neat 1cm dice
175g onions, peeled and cut into 5mm dice
2 cloves of garlic, peeled and crushed to a smooth paste
Maldon sea salt and freshly ground black pepper
1.2 litres chicken stock
600ml curly kale leaves, measured after removing the stalks
    and gently torn into small bite-sized pieces
Finely grated zest of 1 lemon (you may not need it all)
4-6 heaped teaspoons grated Parmesan

Melt the butter in a heavy-based saucepan and allow to foam. Add the potatoes, onions and crushed garlic. Coat in the butter and season with salt and pepper. Cover with a butter wrapper or greaseproof paper and a tight-fitting lid. Cook on a very low heat to allow the vegetables to sweat gently until barely tender. This will take about 10 minutes. Don't overcook and allow the diced potato to collapse.

Add the stock, stir gently, bring to a simmer and cook for a further 10 minutes. The broth should be barely bubbling. If it cooks too fast at this stage, the delicacy of flavour of the chicken stock will be lost. By now the potato and onion should be completely tender but still holding their shape. Taste and correct the seasoning. This is the base and can be put aside until later.

To finish the broth, bring the base back to a simmer. Add the kale and allow to cook very gently and uncovered until quite soft. This can take up to 10 minutes. Taste a little of the kale when you think it is ready, to be certain it is really soft and comforting. Taste and correct the seasoning again and ladle the soup into hot soup bowls. Season each serving with a pinch of the lemon zest and 1 heaped teaspoon of grated Parmesan, and add a drizzle of olive oil. Serve immediately.

Duck, lentil and vegetable broth

Whenever I have a carcass left after roasting a duck, I tend to make a duck stock from it. The stock can be frozen and used for gravy or for a sauce the next time you roast a duck. In this recipe, it is the stock that forms the basis of the dish. Before you make the stock, pick and scrape any little morsels of meat from the cooked carcass. These will be added to the broth at the end of cooking. If a drumstick or a slice or two of breast meat remains, all the better. You don't need a lot of duck meat for this recipe, so don't be worried if the amount is scant. This dish is really about the duck-flavoured broth, the vegetables and the lentils. The stock is made in exactly the same way as a chicken stock, but tends to be fattier. I carefully remove as much fat as I can from the carcass before making the stock. Then I chill the strained, cooked stock overnight. Any surplus fat will rise to the top, solidify and can be easily lifted off, and you end up with a stock that is virtually fat-free.

As you will gather from reading the list of ingredients, this is a hearty dish, and though I normally serve it as a soup course, it can really be served as a meal in itself. You can then congratulate yourself for extracting a second delicious meal from your duck.

The ingredients
I like to use small green lentils such as Puy lentils from France or Castelluccio lentils from Italy.

It may seem like a lot of garlic in the ingredient list, but garlic when cooked gently in its skin like this is mild and delicious. The tender cooked garlic is pressed from its skin and disappears into the broth to give a mild and warming flavour.

The chilli cooked with the lentils adds the merest hint of heat to the broth.

The combination of root vegetables add to the earthy flavour.

The last-minute addition of chopped parsley is refreshing and fresh-tasting.

Serves 6–8
400g lentils
1 carrot, peeled and quartered
1 onion, peeled and studded with 1 clove
6 unpeeled cloves of garlic
1 sprig of sage
1 whole mild red chilli
1 bouquet garni
50g butter or 3 tablespoons olive oil
1 medium onion, peeled and cut into 5mm dice
2 medium carrots, peeled and cut into 5mm dice
4 sticks of celery, cut into 5mm dice
2 cloves of garlic, peeled and crushed to a paste
Maldon sea salt and freshly ground black pepper
1.7–2.3 litres duck or chicken stock
Every scrap of flesh scraped off the roast duck carcass, or 1 roasted duck leg
2 tablespoons chopped flat-leaf parsley

Put the lentils into a saucepan with the quartered carrot, clove-studded onion, unpeeled garlic, sage, chilli and bouquet garni. Cover generously with cold water and bring to a simmer. Simmer the lentils for about 20 minutes, covered with a lid, until they are tender. Keep an eye on the water level in the saucepan and add a little more water as necessary. If the water is just simmering you should not have to add any more liquid. When cooked, the lentils should be tender, but still retaining their shape. Don't allow them to collapse and become muddy. Remove the carrot, onion, sage and bouquet garni. Press the garlic through a sieve back into the lentils. Reserve the cooked lentils in any remaining cooking water.

Heat the butter in a saucepan and allow to foam. If using olive oil, heat it to a shimmer. Add the diced vegetables and crushed garlic, season with salt and pepper and coat in the fat. Cover with a butter wrapper or greaseproof paper and the saucepan lid and sweat on a very gentle heat for about 10 minutes, until the vegetables are starting to become tender. Add the stock and bring to a simmer. Now strain the lentil cooking water from the lentils. Retain the cooking water. Add the lentils to the duck broth and bring to a simmer. Taste and correct the seasoning. At this point a little of the strained lentil water can be added to the broth if it all looks too thick. Remember, this is a broth not a stew.

Add the scraps of roast duck and warm through gently. Taste and correct the seasoning again, add the chopped parsley and serve in hot old-fashioned soup bowls.

Pumpkin, leek, tomato and fennel broth
with parsley pesto

This is a comforting, robust and nourishing broth for autumn and winter. Choose a ripe and firm pumpkin. I like the variety called Uchiki Kuri, also known as Red Kuri. The flesh is close-textured and a deep golden orange colour. The flavour is intense and nutty. It also roasts well and makes an excellent purée. Butternut squash is an excellent replacement for the pumpkin. Even though we are using robustly flavoured ingredients here, the resulting broth is surprisingly delicate. The recipe makes a large quantity, but you can successfully halve these amounts if you wish.

The ingredients

Use a richly coloured pumpkin or squash for this recipe, such as a Red Kuri pumpkin or a butternut squash. Always exercise great care when peeling these tough-skinned curcurbits, and try to always have your knife pointing down and away from you, so that if it slips it hits the chopping board and not you. I usually cut the squash or pumpkin down into a few manageable pieces before removing the seeds and then the tough skin.

The tomatoes should be dark red and ripe. I am happy to use best-quality tinned or bottled tomatoes if the fresh ones are not up to scratch.

The fennel seeds, with their aromatic and aniseed flavour, should be carefully roasted before being coarsely ground.

The chicken stock should be sweetly and delicately flavoured, exactly the result you will get from following the chicken stock recipe on page 60.

Serves 10   450g pumpkin or squash, peeled and deseeded,
            weighed after peeling and deseeding
4 tablespoons olive oil
2 teaspoons fennel seeds, lightly roasted and
            coarsely ground
3 cloves of garlic, peeled and crushed
225g leeks, washed and thinly sliced against the grain
225g potatoes, peeled and cut into 1cm cubes
Maldon sea salt, freshly ground black pepper
            and sugar, to taste
300g very ripe tomatoes, peeled and chopped,
            or tinned tomatoes
1.8 litres chicken stock
2 tablespoons chopped flat-leaf parsley
1 recipe quantity of Parsley Pesto (see page 29)

Cut the pumpkin into 2cm dice. Heat the olive oil in a heavy-based saucepan until it shimmers gently. Add the pumpkin, fennel seeds and garlic. With a wooden spoon, stir to coat in the olive oil and cook on a gentle heat for 2 minutes. Add the leek and potatoes, season with salt and pepper and cover with a butter wrapper or greaseproof paper and the saucepan lid. Sweat on a very gentle heat for 10–15 minutes. Anything more than the gentlest heat at this stage can render the vegetables to a mush, and that would be a disaster. The vegetables should be just beginning to tenderise.

Add the tomatoes, a pinch of sugar and the stock. Cover again and bring to a gentle simmer. Cook until all the vegetables are tender – about 15 minutes should do it. Do not allow the soup to boil furiously, otherwise the stock will reduce and become too strong, the vegetables will break up and the soup will disintegrate into a mush. Taste and correct the seasoning.

Just before serving, add the chopped parsley. Serve with parsley pesto or just a drizzle of olive oil and a dusting of grated Parmesan.

The first stage of the cooking is the 'sweating' of the potato and onion base. This technique starts to soften the potato and removes the harshness from the onion, creating a base that will both flavour and thicken the soup, but still allow the primary ingredient to stand out.

Vegetable soups

I love soups. There are so many options to choose from. You could eat a different soup every day of the year and still not come near exhausting the possible options. Soups can be an ambrosial smooth purée. They can be as thin as water and sparklingly clear, with just a few jewel-like ingredients, or so thick you can almost stand a spoon up in them. They can be a great collection of ingredients, with beans and pulses rubbing shoulders with vegetables which are all in a tangle of noodles or spaghetti, topped off with a blob of some oily, herby relish. The possibilities are endless and perhaps that is where some of the problems start. There is a notion that a soup can be made from the leftover and sometimes tired remains of the vegetable rack. Tired ingredients will yield an exhausted soup.

The most beautiful soups can be made from the minimum amount of ingredients. Potatoes and onions, with the addition of a good stock and some seasoning, can produce a finely flavoured, textured and coloured soup. The other side of the coin are the soups with a long list of ingredients, where layers of flavours and textures are skilfully worked together to give a complex and multi-dimensional result. All the different types of soup have their merits and can be, with care, placed in any balanced menu, or of course can just be eaten on their own with perhaps a little bread to accompany.

The onion and potato base should be tender, but still holding
its shape

Keys to success

Prepare all the vegetables before you start cooking. Cut the onion and potatoes for the base of the soup into **neat 1cm dice**. A neat dice of vegetables will cook evenly and will be less likely to burn.

Prepare the green vegetable as appropriate. Leaf vegetables such as cabbage, spinach and chard should have the stalks removed, and in this case discarded (save them and cook them as a vegetable if the particular stalks are tender), and the leaves cut into neat 2cm dice. Radish or wild garlic leaves should be finely sliced across the grain and then cut into **2cm pieces**. Leeks should be very finely sliced across the grain. The master recipe can also be made with cucumbers and courgettes as the green addition. They are left unpeeled and cut into 2cm dice. **The carefully diced or sliced vegetables will cook quickly and evenly, yielding a fresher-tasting and greener soup.**

The first stage of the cooking is the 'sweating' of the potato and onion base. This technique starts to soften the potato and removes the harshness from the onion, creating a base that will both flavour and thicken the soup, but still allow the primary ingredient, in this case a green vegetable, to stand out. Melt the butter **in a heavy-based saucepan** which is appropriate in size to the quantity of soup being made. The butter should gently foam, and then the potato and onion dice are added. A seasoning of salt and pepper is added and the vegetables are turned and coated in the butter with a wooden spoon.

Cover the vegetables with a disc of greaseproof paper and then the tight-fitting saucepan lid. The paper and saucepan lid are there to trap in any steam that is created as the saucepan heats up. **This base is then cooked over a very low heat**. Use a heat diffuser mat if necessary. Remember, there is no liquid so far, so you are relying on the steam to prevent the vegetables from sticking to the bottom of the saucepan. This steam should keep enough moisture in the saucepan to prevent the vegetables from burning.

The sweating of the onion and potato takes about 10 minutes. Lift the lid and have a look. If a large plume of steam comes out, you know you have successfully trapped in the steam. **The potatoes will be just starting to soften** at the edges but with no colour, and the onions will be softening, also without colour. If you are doubling the recipe and so on it will take longer.

Now add the stock, which if you are in a hurry to get the soup cooked could be already at simmering point. Stir the bottom of the saucepan to be certain that the potato and onion base has not stuck. Replace the saucepan lid and bring to a simmer for a further 10 minutes. **By then the potatoes and onions should be tender.**

This is the base for your soup. **This can be made up early in the day**, put to one side, and you can finish the soup closer to the time of serving. That way you are assured of a brilliant green colour when serving the soup. You can of course continue on and finish it immediately, to eat it there and then or to reheat later.

Regardless of when the green vegetable is added, the base must be simmering and, very importantly, **the lid of the saucepan must be removed.** If you replace the lid when the green vegetable is in the saucepan, it will spoil the colour of the soup.

The type of green vegetable you are using will determine the cooking time. Radish, lettuce or wild garlic leaves will cook in a matter of 3–5 minutes. Spinach or chard leaves will take longer, 6–7 minutes for the summer varieties and 10–12 minutes for the winter ones. Leek greens can take 20 minutes to soften. Peas and courgettes will take around 10 minutes, and courgettes around 15 minutes.

When the green vegetable appears cooked, **taste a little to be certain that it is indeed tender.**

Purée the soup immediately with a hand-held blender or in a liquidizer. This prompt blending sets the colour and gives the soup a silky consistency. When you think it is suitably smooth, keep going for another 30 seconds to ensure an even smoother result.

Taste the soup and correct the seasoning.

The consistency should be like pouring cream, so if it is too thick, add a little more hot chicken stock or a splash of creamy milk (half cream and half milk, mixed). If it is too thin, you are having thin soup.

If I am not serving the soup until later, I like to decant it into a large wide bowl to speed up the cooling time. **Do not cover the soup** until it is completely cold again, to retain the lovely colour. The cold soup can then be covered and refrigerated.

Serve the soup in hot bowls, with an appropriate garnish.

Year-round green vegetable soup

In this master recipe we are aiming to achieve a smooth and silky soup, packed full of flavour and nourishment and bright green in colour. This recipe can be seen as a year-round formula for the various vegetables that come and go as the seasons change. By varying the green ingredient, you need never tire of this recipe. The green vegetables that can be used here are many, but we have to choose one to get us going, so my choice is spinach.

Choose strong, handsome and really fresh-looking leaves and the results will be dazzlingly green.

If the spinach leaves are big, the central rib will need to be removed before measuring the spinach leaves. If you are using baby spinach, the tender stalks can remain.

Nutmeg is one of the traditional flavourings for spinach and a small grating would be good here, but always be cautious with the addition of nutmeg, as you know that too much can spoil the pudding, or the soup in this case.

The ingredients
Potatoes and onions are used in the soup base. The onion adds lots of flavour and the potato thickens the soup.

The green vegetable you use will be the determining flavour of the finished soup. Spinach is my choice here, but any of the following vegetables produce an excellent result. Green cabbage at any time of the year with tough ribs removed from the leaves and finely chopped is excellent. Also nettles, watercress, wild garlic leaves, diced courgettes or cucumbers, Swiss chard leaves, pea and bean leaves, dark green lettuce leaves and so on.

Chicken stock produces the most flavoursome result here.

Serves 6   50g butter
110g onions, peeled and diced
140g potatoes, peeled and diced
Maldon sea salt and freshly ground black pepper
1.2 litres chicken or vegetable stock
350g spinach leaves or your green vegetable of choice,
weighed after removing stalks
Freshly grated nutmeg
Creamy milk, i.e. milk and cream mixed in
equal proportion

Melt the butter in a heavy-based saucepan and allow to foam. Add the onions and potatoes, season with salt and pepper, and toss with a wooden spoon to coat the vegetables in the butter. Cover with a greaseproof paper lid and the lid of the saucepan and cook on a very low heat for 10 minutes or so. This is called 'sweating' the vegetables. The object of the exercise is to soften them slightly, with no colour at all.

Add the stock, bring to a simmer and cover again with the saucepan lid. Simmer until the onion and potato is completely tender and starting to collapse. This will take about 15 minutes. Remove the lid of the saucepan and add the spinach and nutmeg. Do not replace the saucepan lid. Bring to a simmer and cook until the spinach is tender. This can take from 1–2 minutes for baby spinach to 5 minutes for large leaves. If you cannot tell by looking at the vegetable if it is cooked, taste a little – it should be tender and slippery.

Purée immediately with a hand-held blender or in a liquidiser. Add a little more stock or creamy milk if the soup is too thick. Taste and correct the seasoning. If not serving immediately, do not cover, as this will spoil the green colour. Serve in hot soup bowls, garnished with a little blob of cream or a few drops of olive oil.

The soup can be prepared ahead and reheated later, though the green colour will not be as strident as when it was first made.

Potato soup with parsley pesto and black pudding

A single slice of black pudding, sizzling from the pan, is great in each bowl of this comforting and nourishing soup. The parsley pesto, a great and versatile sauce, combines brilliantly with the potato and the pudding. Failing black pudding, a few slices of chorizo warmed in olive oil or a sprinkle of crispy lardons of bacon are excellent.

The ingredients
Black pudding varies in quality, and on the whole puddings made by artisan producers tend to be considerably better than the factory-produced equivalent.

Serves 4–6
50g butter
425g potatoes, peeled and cut into 1cm dice
175g onions, peeled and cut into 1cm dice
Maldon sea salt and freshly ground black pepper
900ml chicken stock
120ml creamy milk
4–6 slices of black pudding
4–6 teaspoons Parsley Pesto (see page 29)

Melt the butter in a saucepan and allow to foam. Add the diced vegetables and stir to coat in the butter. Season with salt and pepper. Cover with a greaseproof paper lid and the saucepan lid and cook on a very low heat for about 10 minutes. The potatoes should be just beginning to break down at this point.

Now add the stock and bring to the boil. Replace the saucepan lid and simmer gently until the vegetables are soft and cooked. This takes about 15 minutes. Purée the soup in a liquidiser or with a hand-held blender until a smooth and silky consistency is achieved. Add creamy milk as necessary if the soup needs thinning out. Taste and adjust the seasoning. Fry the black pudding gently in butter or olive oil on both sides to heat through. Serve the soup in hot bowls, with a teaspoon of parsley pesto and a slice of sizzling black pudding per person.

Carrot, coconut and lemongrass soup

I tasted a soup with these ingredients in Laos a few years ago, and when I came home I set about recreating that delicious flavour. Carrot soup is a funny thing – you imagine it would be easy, but in fact it can be difficult to achieve a really flavoursome result. However, with this lovely combination of flavours I think it works really well.

It is worth noting that lemongrass grows successfully in this country in a glasshouse or conservatory, or even just on a south-facing windowsill. If possible buy carrots with the earth still on them, as generally they have much more flavour than pre-washed ones.

The ingredients

I like to make this soup with big carrots that have been sold with some earth still on them, and preferably after the first frosts, when they seem to become deeper in flavour, so this becomes a late autumn and winter soup.

Lemongrass is easy to source now and is a lovely ingredient with its sweet, scented and astringent flavour. Bright green when fresh, it dulls to a pale straw colour when dried, which is the way it is sold generally in the West. Here it needs to be sliced as finely as you can, so that it will cook down and disappear into the puréed soup. Be careful when running your hands over the grass, as its leaves can be razor sharp. If you have not cooked with it before, give it a go, as it will open up a world of different recipes to you.

Coconut milk, like lemongrass, is an essential ingredient in the cooking of south-east Asia and indeed all of southern India. Like lemongrass, using it is an entry ticket to a repertoire of dishes bigger than you can imagine. The first time you open a can, you may be surprised by the rather grey-white colour of the contents. That's fine, that's the way it looks. Apart from the colour, the general appearance can also vary. Sometimes there will be a thick and solid layer on top, which is the richer cream, with a thinner, watery milk-like liquid underneath. If the can has been shaken, the two different consistencies can appear rather curdled, and again that's all quite all right. Just stir the two liquids together to mix. Some brands of coconut milk have been emulsified to prevent the two liquids from separating and to give the coconut a creamy appearance. I avoid these brands, because apart from the fact that in some recipes the thick and the thin are added separately, I really just want the coconut and water that is used as part of the process and don't want the stabilizers and emulsifiers. The quality of tinned coconut milk varies quite a bit, so search out a good brand such as Chaokoh.

Serves 6–8
40g butter
700g carrots, peeled and thinly sliced
225g onions, peeled and thinly sliced
1 clove of garlic, peeled and chopped
2 stalks of lemongrass
Maldon sea salt, freshly ground black pepper
     and sugar, to taste
850ml chicken stock
500ml coconut milk
Fresh coriander leaves, to garnish

Melt the butter in a heavy-based saucepan and allow it to foam. Add the carrots, onions and garlic and stir to coat in the butter. Remove the coarse outer leaves and the tough ends from the lemongrass. Slice the trimmed stalk finely against the grain and add to the vegetables. Tie the tough outer leaves together with string and add to the pan. Season with salt, pepper and a pinch of sugar. Cover with a greaseproof paper lid and the saucepan lid and cook on a low heat for about 20 minutes, or until the carrots are beginning to soften.

Add the chicken stock, return to a simmer and cook, covered, until the vegetables are completely tender. Remove and discard the tied-up lemongrass stalks. Purée the ingredients to achieve a smooth and silky consistency. Heat the coconut milk to a simmer, add to the carrot purée and mix well. Return the soup to a simmer. The consistency will be slightly thick. Taste and correct the seasoning, bearing in mind that carrots sometimes benefit from a small pinch of sugar to really lift the flavour. Serve hot, garnished with coriander leaves.

Jerusalem artichoke soup
with avocado and roast hazelnut salsa

This is a lovely combination of flavours and textures. The soup is smooth and silky, the avocado almost buttery, and the hazelnuts add a gentle crunch. An excellent alternative to this artichoke soup, which will only be in season during the winter months, is a potato soup – the avocado and hazelnuts are great with that also.

The ingredients
The fresher the artichokes are, the less likely it is that you will have to peel them, though if they look in any way discoloured, peeling is necessary because discoloured skins will yield a discoloured and less fresh-tasting soup. Jerusalem artichokes cook quite unevenly, so test a couple of pieces of the vegetable to ascertain that it is all properly cooked. If the vegetable is not properly cooked, the soup will be slightly grainy in consistency and not the smooth and silky result we are aiming for.

An avocado in perfect condition is a wonderful food, but an underripe one is not worth eating. You have to plan and shop ahead a little with avocados to be sure they will be in the correct condition when you want to serve them. Test them like you would a mango, that is, gently press the heel of your thumb into the flesh of an unblemished avocado and the vegetable should yield to that pressure – a subtle indent will be left by your thumb. Some people like to wrap underripe avocados in newspaper and put them in a warm place such as an airing cupboard to help them ripen, but I find it really only works with certainty for me if I have bought them in plenty of time and allowed them to ripen at room temperature in my kitchen.

Serves 6   60g butter

110g potatoes, peeled and diced

220g onions, peeled and diced

500g Jerusalem artichokes, peeled and diced

Maldon sea salt and freshly ground black pepper

1 litre chicken stock

300ml creamy milk, i.e. cream and milk in
    equal proportions

AVOCADO AND ROAST HAZELNUT SALSA

1 ripe avocado, halved, stone removed, peeled and
    cut into neat 1cm dice

3 tablespoons hazelnuts, roasted, skinned and
    coarsely chopped

3 tablespoons hazelnut or olive oil

1 tablespoon chopped flat-leaf parsley

Maldon sea salt and freshly ground black pepper

Melt the butter in a heavy-based saucepan and allow to foam. Add the potatoes, onions and artichokes and stir to coat in the butter. Season with salt and pepper, then cover with a butter wrapper or greaseproof paper lid and a tight-fitting lid. Sweat on a very gentle heat for about 10 minutes, until the vegetables are just beginning to soften. Add the chicken stock and simmer, covered, until the vegetables are soft and collapsing. Purée the soup to achieve a smooth consistency. Correct the thickness with the creamy milk. Sometimes it may not take all the milk. Taste and correct the seasoning.

Mix together all the ingredients for the avocado and hazelnut salsa. Taste and correct the seasoning. This mixture will sit quite happily in your fridge for an hour, as the oil coating the avocado will prevent it discolouring.

Serve in hot soup bowls, with each serving garnished with a dessert-spoon of the avocado and hazelnut salsa and a drizzle of its oil.

Wild garlic soup

As you will have discovered in the introduction to Wild Garlic Leaf and Flower Broth, I love this wild and free food. Either of the two varieties is suitable here, and regardless of which one you choose it will be the perfect green for this recipe. It is flavoursome and full of goodness and cooks to a smooth and silky consistency. The pretty white flowers from either variety make a delicious and lovely garnish.

Serves 6
55g butter
110g onions, peeled and diced
140g potatoes, peeled and diced
Maldon sea salt and freshly ground black pepper
1.2 litres chicken or vegetable stock
350g wild garlic leaves, finely chopped
Creamy milk, i.e. milk and cream mixed in equal proportion

Melt the butter in a heavy-based saucepan and allow to foam. Add the onions and potatoes, season with salt and pepper, and stir to coat in the butter. Cover with a butter wrapper or greaseproof paper and the lid of the saucepan and cook on a very low heat for 10 minutes or so. This is called 'sweating' the vegetables. The object of the exercise is to soften them slightly, with no colour at all.

Add the stock, bring to the boil and cover again with the saucepan lid. Simmer until the onion and potato are completely tender and starting to collapse. This will take about 15 minutes. Remove the lid of the saucepan and add the garlic leaves. Do not replace the saucepan lid. Bring to the boil and simmer for about 5 minutes, until the garlic leaves are tender. Purée immediately in a liquidiser or with a hand-held blender. Add a little more stock or creamy milk if the soup is too thick. Taste and correct the seasoning.

Serve in hot soup bowls, garnished with a little blob of cream or a few drops of olive oil and some of the pretty garlic flowers.

Lining a flan ring with pastry is one of the techniques that strikes fear into some cooks. But it really is worth persevering with this technique, because once mastered it opens up hundreds of possible recipes of both a sweet and savoury nature.

Savoury tarts

The savoury tart, sometimes called an 'open-faced tart', can be varied depending on the ingredients available, and perfectly illustrates the value of mastering a particular technique that can be used year round to illustrate the glories of the changing seasons.

There are two separate techniques involved here. Making the savoury custard to hold all the ingredients together is simple. Making the pastry and lining the flan ring is more complicated. In fact, lining a flan ring with savoury or sweet pastry is one of the techniques that strikes fear into some cooks, and I have to be honest here and say that in the earlier days of my career I was one of those cooks who avoided the task whenever possible. But to progress as a cook, you sometimes have to bully yourself into performing a task that scares you a bit. It is really worth persevering with this technique, because once mastered it opens up hundreds of possible recipes of both a sweet and savoury nature, and you will have a great sense of achievement when you can approach the task with no fear.

Good eggs and butter are essential for the pastry, and the eggs feature again in the custard, along with cream, to give a rich and rather luscious consistency to the filling.

Read over the pastry section of the recipe a couple of times before starting, so that you have the different stages in your head. Making the pastry takes only a matter of minutes. What is vital to remember with a shortcrust pastry, is not to overhandle it. On the other hand I do sometimes think that some recipes urge too much caution as to the handling. So when you add the egg it should look like smooth pastry dough. If it doesn't, and hasn't come together, knead it a little more until it takes on that smooth and finished appearance.

Keys to success
The pastry is a 'short crust' and needs careful handling.

The 'short' in the pastry name refers to the amount of fat, generally butter, that is used. The more butter used, the shorter the pastry is, and this shortness refers to the pleasantly crumbly but not brittle texture of the cooked pastry. It is important not to confuse the word crumbly with collapsing. The tart must hold its shape both when cooking and being served. The dilemma here is that the more butter you add, the more difficult the pastry is to handle. So I suggest that to start with, you use half the weight of butter to flour. When you can handle that with confidence, you can increase the quantity of butter a little, thereby achieving a finer pastry.

Weigh all the ingredients accurately.

Cold butter is first rubbed into the flour to achieve a texture like **fine breadcrumbs**. This can be done by **hand or in a food processor**. If you are using a food processor, it will happen quickly, but proceed with caution using the pulse button to ensure the butter does not become overworked, as this may lead to a tough pastry.

The beaten egg is then added to the crumb and gently mixed to create a pastry dough that is **neither too dry nor too wet**, but can be rolled and manipulated to line your flan ring.

A pastry that is too wet will not hold its shape and will be tough and flabby when cooked.

A pastry that is too dry is impossible to handle and shape and will be brittle and likely to collapse when cooked.

The pastry is chilled for **at least 30 minutes** before rolling and lining the flan ring. This takes practice to perfect. If it breaks a little the first time you do it, **don't panic – do a bit of patchwork and it will work out**. If it is a complete fiasco, gather up all the bits of pastry, knead them gently together to form a disc, and have another go. It may not win best in show, but you will get a result and be learning as you go, so that the next time you make it you will be better equipped.

The **flan ring is chilled for at least 30 minutes** before being lined with parchment paper and filled to the brim with dry baking beans. The beans help to keep the base of the tart from rising and the sides from caving in.

The **chilling periods are crucial**, to prevent shrinkage of the pastry when it is cooking, resulting in a misshapen flan ring.

The cooking of the pastry is done in two stages. The first stage, which takes 90% of the cooking time, is done with the beans in it, and the second stage is removing the beans and parchment paper, giving the base of the pastry a light brush with beaten egg and returning the pastry to the oven to finish cooking. Brushing with egg helps to create a seal on the base of the tart, resulting in a crisper bottom and avoiding the dreaded 'soggy bottom syndrome'!

Pastry lined with paper and full to the brim with baking beans and rice

Shortcrust pastry

24cm tart   175g plain flour
Pinch of salt
85g butter, cold from the fridge
1 egg

First make the pastry
Sieve the flour into a bowl. Add a pinch of salt. Cut the cold butter into small cubes and add to the flour. Rub the butter into the flour until it looks like very fine crumbs. This part of the process can also be done in a food processor using the pulse button to break up the butter, but I always like to add the beaten egg by hand in a bowl.

Beat the egg thoroughly, then, using a fork or your fingers, stir in just enough of it, 3–4 tablespoons, to bring the pastry together. Retain the remainder of the beaten egg for later. The dough should feel neither too firm nor too soft. Knead the pastry lightly, again for only a few seconds, to form a smooth mass. The pastry should not be sticking to your fingers. If it does, add a little sprinkle of flour and work in gently. Form the pastry into a little round disc, about 1cm thick. Wrap in greaseproof or parchment paper and chill for at least 30 minutes.

Lining the tin with the pastry
You will need a 24cm tart tin or flan ring, with a removable base. To line the flan ring, dust the worktop with flour. Place the flan ring on the dusted surface and with your fingers draw a circle in the flour around the tin, allowing an extra 2cm for the risen edge of the pastry. Remove the tin. This template should help you to roll the pastry as close to your circular requirements as possible.

If the pastry is hard from the fridge, knead or massage it for a few seconds to make it malleable, always remembering that the less you handle the pastry the better. Place on the floured surface and dust the surface of the pastry with a little more flour. Gently roll the pastry with your rolling pin, rolling to the edge of the pastry but not out over the edges, as this causes the edges to be too thin and makes it difficult to handle when placing in the tin. I like to move the pastry on the work surface a few times during the rolling to prevent it from sticking. To do this, place the palm of your hand with fingers outstretched flat on the pastry and gently move it to and fro in a circular movement. If you feel it starting to catch, lift it and sprinkle a little more flour under it on to the work surface. Keep rolling until the pastry is of an even thickness and reaches the edges of the template you have drawn in the flour. Pop the tin on the pastry again just to be sure the disc is the right size.

Brush off the excess flour and roll the pastry around your rolling pin. Drape the pastry over the top of the flan ring. Gently encourage the pastry to drop into the ring and, with your fingers, firm it on to the base, into the corners and up along the sides of the ring. Allow an excess of 5mm of pastry for a raised edge. Pinch off the pastry by pressing your thumb on the top edge of the tin. Clean and neaten the edges to attain a smart finish. Chill the pastry for at least 30 minutes before cooking.

Baking the pastry 'blind'
Preheat the oven to 180°C/350°F/gas 4. Line the chilled pastry with a circle of greaseproof paper to come 2cm up over the edge of the tin. Fill to the top with dried baking beans or old rice.

Place the tart shell in the centre of the preheated oven for 30 minutes. Remove from the oven and remove the beans and paper. These can be saved for another day. Paint the base and sides of the pastry lightly with a little of the leftover beaten egg. Return to the oven for a further 5 minutes. This will help to crisp up the base and make it liquid-proof. Remove from the oven and place the tin on a wire rack to cool.

Spinach and herb tart

The spinach in this recipe can be replaced successfully with Swiss chard. If you choose to use baby spinach, there is no need to remove the stalks. Serve the tart with a salad of leaves or vine-ripened tomatoes and basil during the late summer and early autumn months. The Spring Mimosa Salad on page 126 is wonderful with it and would make an elegant lunch or supper. A drizzle of hollandaise sauce is a quite delicious addition and rather elevates it.

The ingredients
Spinach leaves should look fresh and vibrant, so avoid wilted and tired-looking leaves.

Nutmeg is a strong spice, so use it with caution. It tastes much better when freshly grated from the whole piece as and when you need it, rather than using the pre-ground powder.

Using all the listed herbs in the recipe makes for a very good balanced flavour, but the rosemary on its own will make an excellent tart.

The Parmesan can be replaced with Gruyère or Cheddar, though the suggested Parmesan gives the most refined result.

Serves 6–8   TART FILLING

1 small onion, about 110g, very finely chopped

25g butter

Maldon sea salt and freshly ground black pepper

600g spinach, stalks removed and finely sliced, leaves gently torn into bite-sized pieces

A light grating of nutmeg

2 eggs and 1 egg yolk

300ml regular or double cream

1 clove of garlic, peeled and crushed

1 tablespoon each chopped marjoram, parsley and chives

1 teaspoon chopped rosemary

50g finely grated Parmesan

Prepare the tart case, as instructed on page 99.

Sweat the onion very gently in the butter until soft, then set aside to cool.

Bring 1.8 litres of water to the boil. Add a pinch of salt. Add the sliced spinach stalks and cook for 2 minutes. Add the spinach leaves to the stalks in the pot and cook for a further 3 minutes. Immediately remove and place in a colander or sieve. Press gently to extract as much water as possible. Lay the leaves and stalks out flat, separating them with your fingers, to let them cool as quickly as possible. Grate a little nutmeg over them as they cool.

Beat the eggs and cream and add the cooled onions, crushed garlic, chopped herbs and grated Parmesan. Squeeze the spinach again to extract any more water, then chop coarsely. Add the cooled spinach and season with salt and pepper. Taste and correct the seasoning.

Pour the filling into the tart shell and place in a preheated oven at 180°C/350°F/gas 4 for 30–40 minutes, or until the tart is set. You will know the tart is set when the filling no longer ripples when gently shaken. Remove from the oven and place on a wire rack for at least 5 minutes.

Remove the tin, place the tart on a large flat plate and serve. It tastes best when served warm.

Smoked mackerel and tomato tart

This tart can be served as a starter with salad leaves, or would make a perfect lunch or supper dish. Remember that some smoked mackerel has never seen the inside of a smokehouse, but has been dipped in dye to simulate the smoked effect. So search out best-quality fish that has been naturally smoked in the time-honoured tradition. The tomatoes, as always, need to be really ripe and firm, and you will be peeling them. Peeling tomatoes can be either a pleasure or torture. There is no grey area here, it either works perfectly or is a nightmare. This is a classic example of how important it is to follow all and not just some of the instructions.

For a special treat, serve this tart with a drizzle of hollandaise sauce.

The ingredients

Smoked mackerel, like salmon, has suffered in the last few years from becoming a mass-produced product, and that is exactly how much of it tastes now. Try to find fish smoked by an artisan producer, as it will have superior flavour, colour and texture. As a general rule the colour created on the fish by the traditional wood-smoking process should look natural, as distinct from the orangey and glowing colour of the mass-produced product. The artisan-produced fish will be more expensive, but just buy exactly as much as you need, don't waste a scrap, and the superior flavour and texture will hopefully make you feel that the extra cost was worthwhile.

The sweet and smoky flavour of the tarragon combines beautifully with the tomato and smoked fish.

Serves 6–8 TART FILLING

1 small onion, very finely chopped

25g butter

3 ripe firm tomatoes

Maldon sea salt, freshly ground black pepper and sugar, to taste

2 eggs and 1 egg yolk

300ml regular or double cream

1 tablespoon chopped chives

1 dessertspoon chopped tarragon

2 large whole smoked mackerel or 4 fillets, skinned and bones removed, pulled into 2cm pieces

Prepare the tart case, as instructed on page 99.

Sweat the onions very gently in the butter until soft, then leave to cool.

Peel the tomatoes, as described on page 20. Quarter the peeled tomatoes, remove the seeds and discard. Cut the flesh into 1cm dice. Season with a pinch of salt, pepper and sugar.

Beat the eggs and cream. Add the cooled onions, chopped herbs and seasoning and mix well. Gently fold in the tomatoes and the skinned and shredded mackerel. Taste and correct the seasoning.

Pour the filling into the tart shell and place in a preheated oven at 180°C/350°F/gas 4 for 30–40 minutes, or until the tart is set. Remove from the oven and place on a wire rack for at least 15 minutes.

Remove the tin, place the tart on a large flat plate and serve. It tastes best when served warm. For a special occasion, serve a drizzle of hollandaise sauce with each slice of tart.

Wild mushroom and tarragon tart

Mushrooms and tarragon are a classic combination of flavours and the combination will work for you in lots of other recipes. The Spring Mimosa Salad on page 126 makes an excellent accompaniment.

The ingredients
Clean all mushrooms really well with a little brush or a damp cloth before using, and preferably avoid using any water, though a little rinse may sometimes be necessary. Wild mushrooms such as ceps, chanterelles, hedgehog and even the common field mushroom will be delicious here. Cultivated 'exotic' mushrooms such as oyster, shiitake, namiko are also good. Cook the prepared mushrooms in small batches over a high heat.

Tarragon should never be chopped ahead of time, as it oxidises and loses its wonderful flavour if not protected from the air by a coating of liquid, so chop it just before it goes into the tart filling.

Serves 6

TART FILLING

1 small onion, very finely chopped
50g butter
600g wild mushrooms, cleaned and coarsely chopped
    into 1cm pieces
Maldon sea salt and freshly ground black pepper
2 eggs and 1 egg yolk
300ml regular or double cream
1–2 tablespoons chopped tarragon
50g finely grated Parmesan
1 clove of garlic, peeled and crushed

Prepare the tart case, as instructed on page 99.

Sweat the onions very gently in half the butter until soft, then leave to cool.

Melt the rest of the butter in a large sauté pan and allow to foam. Add the chopped mushrooms and season with salt and pepper. Cook the mushrooms on a high heat, turning them occasionally until they are tender. Remove the mushrooms and allow to cool completely. If your sauté pan is small, cook them in a couple of batches. If there is some liquid from the mushrooms left in the pan, leave it on the heat and allow it to simmer and reduce until it looks thickened and syrupy. Pour this over the cooling mushrooms.

Beat the eggs and cream and add the tarragon, Parmesan, cooled onions, garlic and salt and pepper. Add the mushrooms and mix well. Taste a little of the mixture and correct the seasoning.

Pour the filling into the tart shell and place in a preheated oven 180°C/350°F/gas 4 for 30–40 minutes, or until the tart is set. You will know the tart is set when the filling no longer ripples when gently shaken. Remove from the oven and place on a wire rack for at least 5 minutes.

Remove the tin, place the tart on a large flat plate and serve. It tastes best when served warm.

Soft goat's cheese and thyme leaf tart with tomato oil

Maybe you will think I am crazy or just plain sad, or at least think I have too much time on my hands, when I tell you that I dry my own tomatoes. I am afraid it is true (for more information, see page 20). I accept that that's all a bit too dedicated for the reality of most people's lives, and you will be happy to know that good-quality, shop-bought, semi-dried or sunblush tomatoes work perfectly here.

The goat's cheese is simply pushed into the tart base, sprinkled with thyme leaves and the savoury batter is poured over. The tomatoes are used not in the tart itself but in a little salsa-like oil that accompanies it. The oil is also good on simply grilled mackerel or sardines, with lamb, chicken, pasta, crab meat and shrimp.

The combination is a good one and I like a simple leaf salad to accompany this.

The ingredients
A fresh goat's cheese that is soft enough to spread is required here. In this part of the world I use Ardsallagh goat's cheese.

The quality of shop-bought sun-dried tomatoes varies enormously, so look out for ones that are deep red and preserved in a good-quality olive oil.

Serves 6   TART FILLING

350g soft goat's cheese

1 heaped teaspoon thyme leaves

2 eggs and 1 egg yolk

300ml regular or double cream

Maldon sea salt and freshly ground black pepper

50g finely grated Parmesan

Prepare the tart case, as instructed on page 99.

Press the goat's cheese into the tart shell and sprinkle over the thyme leaves, gently pressing them into the cheese with your fingers.

Beat the eggs and cream with a pinch of salt and pepper and add the grated Parmesan. Taste and correct the seasoning. Pour into the tart shell. This will seem a little strange, with the cheese on the tart base and the batter on top. It's fine, honestly. You end up with a layer of goat's cheese on the base of the tart and a golden layer of custard on top. I think it looks quite beautiful when cooked.

Place in a preheated oven at 180°C/350°F/gas 4 for 30–40 minutes, or until the tart is set. You will know the tart is set when the filling no longer ripples when gently shaken. Remove from the oven and place on a wire rack for at least 5 minutes.

Remove the tin, place the tart on a large flat plate and serve with the tomato oil drizzled over each slice and a bunch of rocket. This tart tastes best when served warm.

Tomato oil

100g sun-dried or sunblush semi-dried tomatoes

50ml olive oil

Maldon sea salt and freshly ground black pepper

Blend the tomatoes and oil to a coarse purée. Correct the seasoning.

Jerusalem artichoke and ewe's milk cheese tart with roast pepper and olive salsa

Jerusalem artichokes are a marvellous winter vegetable. They make the silkiest of soups, a great purée to serve with game or fish, roast beautifully to a caramelised and nutty brown, and combine with a variety of flavours such as avocado, hazelnuts, saffron, scallops and mussels. They are easy to grow and look wonderful in the late summer garden with their stalks towering to a height of three metres. On top of that handsome stalk is the flower, a small and pretty bright yellow blossom, which when you can see it may remind you of a small sunflower and so it should, as the Jerusalem artichoke is part of the sunflower family. In winter the leafless stalks become skeletal, bleak and sculptural and have an eerie and chilly beauty.

The bounty itself sits under the soil, in clusters just like potatoes, and is every bit as exciting to harvest as the better-known and loved spud. People shy away from using this vegetable for various reasons, mainly because of the knobbly surface, which makes peeling them a bit torturous. I do peel them for this recipe; but when they are really fresh I often omit the peeling, particularly when roasting or making them into soup.

There is a variety called Fuseau, which gardeners might like to note as being the least knobbly of the varieties, though perhaps not the most flavoursome variety.

One of the other reasons for their bad reputation is that after being consumed, they make some people a little 'windy'. Personally I have never noticed any unusual rumblings in their aftermath, though certainly some discover that a little turbulence ensues.

Here I pair them with ewe's or sheep's milk cheese to make a sophisticated tart. Search out a really good cheese for this tart, as mass-produced fetas can be a grim and bland bunch, owing much of their flavour to salt rather than sheep's milk. I use Knocklara from Co. Waterford and find it excellent.

You could serve the tart with a salad of lamb's lettuce, roast hazelnuts and avocado tossed in a hazelnut oil vinaigrette if you don't fancy the pepper and olive salsa.

The ingredients

Jerusalem artichokes, looking like knobbly potatoes, are no relation
of the globe artichoke. The flavour is slightly sweet and smoky and
I find them delicious. The artichokes will need to be peeled if they
are not spanking fresh. When really fresh, they just need a good
scrub, like potatoes. They cook quite unevenly, and regardless of
the recipe you are using you need to test several pieces of the vegetable to determine that they are all tender.

Ewe's or sheep's milk cheese varies greatly in quality. Try to find an
artisan cheese rather than a factory-made one. The factory-made
sheep's cheese can be very dull and salty.

The pepper salsa that I suggest serving with the tart will keep in the
fridge for several days.

See page 22 for instructions for how to make your own roast peppers.

Serves 6–8 TART FILLING

400g Jerusalem artichokes, weighed after peeling
or scrubbing

6 tablespoons water

2 tablespoons olive oil

Maldon sea salt and freshly ground black pepper

2 eggs and 1 egg yolk

300ml regular or double cream

50g finely grated Parmesan

200g ewe's milk cheese

Prepare the tart case, as instructed on page 99.

Slice the peeled artichokes into 1cm thick slices. Heat the water and
olive oil to a simmer in a low-sided saucepan. Add the artichokes and
season with salt and pepper. Cover with a butter wrapper or greaseproof paper and the saucepan lid and simmer gently on a low heat
for about 20 minutes, or until the vegetables are tender. Test several
of the slices of artichoke for doneness, as they tend to cook unevenly.

Roast Pepper and Olive Salsa: lovely for serving with grilled oily fish and grilled chicken, beef or lamb

When cooked, remove from the liquid to drain and cool.

Beat the eggs and cream with a pinch of salt and pepper and add the Parmesan.

Slice or crumble the sheep's cheese on to the tart base. Place the drained and cooled artichokes on top. Pour over the eggs and cream and place in a preheated oven at 180°C/350°F/gas 4 for 30–40 minutes, or until the tart is set. You will know it is set if you press the surface of the tart gently with your fingers and it feels just firm. The surface should have a rich golden colour by now.

Remove from the oven and place on a wire rack for at least 15 minutes. Remove the tin, place the tart on a large flat plate and serve warm with the pepper and olive salsa and a salad of organic leaves.

Roast pepper and olive salsa

This salsa is also terrific with grilled fish such as mackerel and salmon, with grilled lamb and chicken, or just smeared over warm grilled sourdough bread.

Serves 6–8   1 red pepper, roasted, peeled, deseeded and cut into
       5mm dice
1 ripe firm tomato, peeled, deseeded and cut into
       5mm dice (omit the tomato if not really ripe)
2 tablespoons coarsely chopped black olives
2 tablespoons olive oil
1 clove of garlic, peeled and crushed to a paste
10 basil leaves, torn or chopped
1 tablespoon balsamic vinegar
Maldon sea salt and freshly ground black pepper

Mix all the ingredients together, then taste and correct the seasoning.

Red onion, roast pepper, rosemary and anchovy pissaladière

Pissaladière is a flat Provençal onion tart with a distinctive lattice of anchovy on top. Here it is given a little twist with the addition of roast peppers and rosemary. The tart is best served while still warm and with a salad of organic leaves.

The ingredients
Onions, thinly sliced and cooked until soft, are a defining ingredient of this flat tart.

Red or yellow peppers, peeled, deseeded and cut into long thin strips, are used along with the anchovies to create a lattice on the surface of the tart.

Anchovies preserved either in oil or salt can be used here. Salted anchovies, if whole, need to be filleted and rinsed really well in cold water to remove excess salt. Anchovies preserved in oil are drained before using.

Serves 6–8

PASTRY
225g plain white flour
110g butter
1 egg

FILLING
4 tablespoons olive oil
700g onions, peeled and thinly sliced
3 cloves of garlic, peeled and thinly sliced
1 large sprig of rosemary
3 roasted red peppers (2 if the peppers are large), peeled, deseeded and cut into long strips, 1cm wide
40g anchovies

Sieve the flour into a bowl and rub in the butter until you have fine crumbs. Beat the egg and add to the flour and butter. Mix it in with

your hand or a fork to bring the pastry together. Knead very lightly to achieve a smooth dough. Wrap with greaseproof paper and chill for at least 30 minutes.

Heat the olive oil in a heavy-based saucepan and add the sliced onions, garlic and rosemary. Cover with a butter wrapper or grease-proof paper and the saucepan lid and sweat on a low heat for 30 minutes. Remove the saucepan and paper lid and allow the onions to cook uncovered for a further 10 minutes to become more golden in colour. Taste and correct the seasoning and spread out the onions on a tray to cool completely.

Meanwhile, roll out the chilled pastry and use to line the base and sides of a Swiss roll-type tin, 23cm x 33cm. Chill for 30 minutes.

Spread the cooled onions over the pastry in an even layer. Arrange the strips of pepper in a lattice pattern over the onions. Cut each of the anchovies lengthways into 2 strips and arrange these thin strips, again in a lattice pattern, over the onions.

Place the tin in a preheated oven at 190°C/375°F/gas 5 for 30–40 minutes, or until the pastry is cooked to a crisp golden finish.

Brush the cooked pissaladière with olive oil and serve with a salad of organic leaves.

Always accurately measure ingredients for a dressing or vinaigrette. The aim is to balance the sharp ingredient such as vinegar or lemon juice with the richer oils or cream.

Salads and dressings

A salad of leaf greens is a keystone of my cooking and eating. On its own, or as an accompaniment to another dish, it is almost always present at the lunch, supper or dinner table.

It is in theory a simple exercise, but in reality there is a great deal of subtlety and refinement involved. In some restaurant kitchens, a new recruit will be presented with a basket of greens to wash and dry as a first task. The way the task is approached and executed will give the watchful chef a good idea as to the recruit's attitude to food and ingredients. Gentle and caring hands are needed so as not to damage or bruise the tender leaves. Drying the leaves, which is essential, also needs a light touch. If the leaves are not perfectly dry, the dressing will not cling to them and the surplus water will dilute it and the whole thing will become a soggy mess.

So there you were thinking what could be easier than a salad, and now I am ranting on about it as if it was an haute technique. I don't mean to scare or irritate you, but in many ways one's approach to a salad sets the standard for any other task in the kitchen. If you can make a really good, simple leaf salad, it means you possess the necessary patience, care and love of food to do almost any other task in the kitchen. Because what making a salad calls for, more than any other thing, is care, and care makes for really good food.

An entire book could be written about leaf salads, and indeed has been, so I won't try to list all the possibilities here. I will give you some of the recipes and a list of the leaves that I like, and suggest some variations.

Freshness of ingredient is key. Leaves vary enormously – crisp or soft, sweet or bitter, tough or tender and so on. Most of them have their place at some point or other. Really good leaves have really good flavour. Poorly produced leaves taste of practically nothing at all and you would probably be better off without them. Where possible, buy leaves in small quantities to ensure freshness and to avoid waste.

Whereas a bowl of mixed and varied leaves, sweet and bitter, green and coloured, soft and crisp, is of course the goal and a joy, it only works if the leaves are of really good quality. Never be afraid to serve a salad bowl that lacks in variety as long as it is strong on quality.

Leaf salads

Making a perfect leaf salad is a technique that some cooks feel eludes them. It requires care and a light hand, but it is a skill everyone can acquire. Be gentle so as not to bruise the leaves.

Keys to success
Choose leaves that are **as fresh and as seasonal as possible**. Tired-looking leaves will yield a tired salad.

Wash the leaves as soon as possible after getting them to your kitchen, even if you are not planning to use them immediately.

Remove damaged leaves and cut whole heads just above the base of the stalk to release the individual leaves. **Do not wrench the leaves off the root** or you will damage them.

Soak the leaves in cold water for 30 minutes before carefully draining and drying them in small quantities in a salad spinner. If you don't dry the leaves, the dressing will just run off, leaving you with a puddle of watery dressing in the bottom of the salad bowl.

Keep leaves wrapped and cold if not using immediately after drying.

Gently lifting and tossing the salad leaves in the dressing so that you don't bruise them

I like to wrap them in a single layer of kitchen paper or a light damp cloth and then slip them into a large plastic bag or bowl before storing them in the fridge. Fresh leaves will keep very well for a few days this way.

Always **accurately measure ingredients for a dressing** or vinaigrette. The aim is to balance the sharp ingredient such as vinegar or lemon juice with the richer oils or cream, to achieve a pleasant flavour that neither under- or overwhelms the leaves.

Place the leaves for tossing in **a bowl that looks too big for the job**. Plenty of space allows for a delicate tossing of the leaves.

Larger leaves should **be delicately torn** into large bite-sized pieces.

Always **shake or whisk a dressing** to ensure an even distribution of ingredients before adding a little less than you think you need to the leaves. I use my hands to dress the leaves, allowing the leaves to fall through my outstretched fingers. You may use salad servers. Add more dressing if necessary. The leaves should be very lightly glazed, not soggy.

Taste the salad before serving to see if a grain of salt is required.

Serve a leaf salad **immediately** after dressing.

Carefully measured dressing ingredients

Winter salad of organic greens

In theory, winter is the most difficult season to have a salad of leaves, and some people cast the idea of a leaf salad right out of their minds during the darker months. There are in fact lots of great things for the salad bowl at this time, and in many ways the salad bowl is even more important and significant, as there really are few other salad vegetables such as tomatoes, courgettes, cucumbers and beetroots around. Certainly a winter salad requires more creativity than the times when the garden is full of green leafy things, but that just adds to the fun. You will need to think outside the box here.

So what are the greens that are growing at this chilly time? Lamb's lettuce survives snow and frost and is great on its own or as part of a mixture of leaves. Bitter and beautiful radicchios and chicories seem to thrive on glacial conditions. Winter cabbage is underrated and can be very finely shredded – a test of your knife skills. Brussels sprouts can have their leaves separated, or finely shredded like the cabbage. A mild snap will yield watercress and land cress. The land cress self-seeds like mad in my garden and I eat it hairy roots and all. Speaking of a mild spell, Brussels sprout plants, given the correct clement conditions, will throw out little shoots of new fresh green growth which are quite fantastic in a salad or cooked as a vegetable. The widely available kales such as curly and red Russian can be destalked and torn into bite-sized pieces, and these too, like the Brussels sprout, will react to a rise in temperature with quite delicious little new shoots. Small cavolo nero leaves, also destalked and torn into small pieces, are dark and terrific. Broccoli tops or greens add another flavour and texture. If some of your parsley and chives have survived the cold, they can be coarsely chopped and added to the bowl. If it is a really chilly day or the leaves are a particularly bitter bunch, I sometimes add a tiny bit of honey to the dressing, but be cautious as you don't want the dressing to taste sweet.

The ingredients
A selection of possible leafy ingredients are listed below, but choose carefully because you don't want the selection to be too wincingly bitter.

Watch out for the new season's olive oil for this salad. Generally available from mid-November on, it can be sensational and its dazzling green colour looks as though it is the juice of green clover rather than an olive.

The vinegar in the dressing can be replaced with the juice from an aromatic lemon.

Try to use a honey local to where you are, bearing in mind that wonderful honey is being produced now in urban areas as well as in the countryside.

Serves 4

4 large handfuls of mixed leaves, carefully washed and dried and consisting of a mixture of some of the following:

Lamb's lettuce, torn into little bunches or individual leaves
Radicchio and chicory leaves, torn into bite-sized pieces
Brussels sprouts, leaves separated or finely shredded
Cabbage leaves, very finely shredded across the grain
Kale leaves, destalked and pulled into small
    bite-sized pieces
Watercress or land cress, in individual sprigs or leaves
Cavolo nero leaves, tiniest ones left whole, larger ones
    destalked and torn into bite-sized pieces
Chives and parsley, coarsely chopped

DRESSING
¼ teaspoon French mustard
¼ teaspoon honey (optional)
Maldon sea salt and freshly ground black pepper
1 tablespoon white or red wine vinegar
4 tablespoons olive oil

Place the mustard, honey if using, and a pinch of salt and pepper in a small bowl. Add the vinegar and whisk in the olive oil in a steady stream. Taste and correct the seasoning.

To assemble the salad, place the leaves in a large bowl. Whisk the dressing again to make sure the oil and vinegar are properly mixed and add just enough dressing to the leaves to lightly coat them. Lift up the leaves with your fingers open wide to encourage the dressing to coat them evenly. Taste to see if a little extra salt is needed. Transfer to a clean bowl or plates and serve immediately.

Spring mimosa salad

I make this salad all year round, varying the salad content according to the seasons and availability, but I like it best of all in spring. Mixed organic leaves are the most obvious option, but the salad works very well with just crisp watercress or chicory leaves. Wild garlic leaves are a great addition in spring, as are the pretty white garlic flowers. As always, choose the best quality oil and vinegar and measure accurately to ensure a correct balance of acidity in the dressing.

Free-range eggs, hard-boiled and yolks sieved, are what create the mimosa effect here, hence the use of the word in the recipe title. Be careful when assembling the salad to get the balance of ingredients correct. Remember, this is a 'salad', so it is a selection of leaves which are lightly garnished with the other ingredients. Too much egg will make the salad seem too heavy, too much olive oil will overpower and equally too much Parmesan will be too rich. The ingredients should tickle one another as you eat them, giving an overall effect of lightness gilded with a few precious extras.

The ingredients
Try to get free-range or organic eggs.

Large fleshy olives like Kalamata are perfect here.

Using a swivel-headed vegetable peeler, shave the Parmesan thinly off
    a larger piece straight on to the salads. Don't worry if the cheese
    breaks up a little, and certainly perfect curls are of no advantage

here; in fact perfect curls of Parmesan can indicate an immature cheese.

Much of what is sold as balsamic vinegar is of poor quality, so search out a quality vinegar. If in doubt about the quality, replace it in the recipe with lemon juice or a good sherry vinegar.

Serves 4

2 eggs
16 fat Kalamata olives
4 handfuls of mixed organic leaves, washed and dried: watercress, wild garlic, butterhead, chicory leaves, chervil sprigs, coarsely chopped spring chives – basically, whatever is at its freshest and best
12 thin Parmesan shavings or pieces

DRESSING
2 tablespoons olive oil
2 tablespoons sunflower oil
1 tablespoon balsamic vinegar
1 small clove of garlic, peeled and finely crushed
Pinch of Maldon sea salt and freshly ground black pepper

Hard-boil the eggs by lowering them gently into a saucepan of boiling, salted water and cooking them at a boil for exactly 10 minutes. If you don't want the yolk completely hard, cook them for 9 minutes. The salt in the water seasons the egg and will help to coagulate any white that might seep out of a crack in the shell, hence less leakage. Remove from the saucepan immediately and cool under a cold running tap. Remove the shell and cut the hard-boiled eggs in half. Chop the white finely. Press the yolk through a sieve, using the back of a soup spoon to achieve a mimosa-type effect. Keep the chopped white and sieved yolk separate.

Stone the olives by gently squashing them on a chopping board with the back of a chopping knife and removing the stones. Chop the olive flesh finely and reserve.

Mix the ingredients for the dressing together, then taste and correct the seasoning.

To assemble the salad, place the leaves in a large bowl and dress with just enough dressing to make them glisten. On four large plates, first place a wide broken circle of chopped olives on each plate. Divide the chopped egg white and spread in the centre of the circles of olive. Place the leaves in a light pile on top of the egg white. Gently, place 3 Parmesan shavings or pieces on each salad. Finally, sprinkle the egg-yolk 'mimosa' on each salad. Serve immediately.

Autumn salad of organic leaves with pomegranate and walnuts

I always look forward to the first of the new season's walnuts. Fresh off the tree, they are still 'wet' and almost milky inside, and that's when I like them best. The other vital ingredient in this salad, pomegranate, has become hugely popular over the last few years and is a terrific fruit. It is as useful in the savoury kitchen as it is in the sweet.

The ingredients
The leaves for this salad should be crisp and ideally a little bitter, so if possible include some radicchio and chicory.

Wet walnuts, which are only available for a few weeks in autumn, are pale in appearance and creamy in consistency and are the nut of choice for this salad. Dry walnuts can also be used at other times of the year. I like to shell the walnuts myself, using either a nutcracker or a pestle and mortar to extract the nuts from the shell. Be vigilant when cracking the nuts, to ensure no shell ends up in the salad. You can buy walnuts that have been shelled, but it is difficult to get ones that are not rancid. Like most oils, walnut oil should be used in the same year it has been pressed. Store it in a cool dark place.

Pomegranates are now available year round, coming from different parts of the globe depending on what season it is there. The skin ranges in colour from pale yellow to dark ruby red. The skin should not be bruised, and in my experience the darker the skin colour the more richly coloured the seeds inside are, though there are exceptions. The seeds inside the skin sit in little clusters surrounded by a papery skin which is high in tannin, and this skin needs to be removed before eating the seeds. I like to extract the seeds by cutting through the leathery skin of the fruit and prising out a wedge at a time. Then I remove the seeds and separate them from the papery skin as I go. Another way to remove the seeds is to cut the fruit in half around the 'equator', then, holding the fruit over a bowl, with your stretched fingers holding the cut surface, beat the skin of the fruit with a wooden spoon to extract the seeds, while leaving the tannic membrane behind, still attached to the skin. If you don't use all of the pomegranate, wrap the rest in plastic film and store it in the fridge – it will need to be used within a couple of days. The unopened fruit will keep for at least a month in the fridge.

Pomegranate molasses is of a syrupy consistency and is made from the juice extracted from the seeds. It gives a rich and tangy deliciousness to the dressing.

Serves 4

12 walnuts, shelled
2 tablespoons pomegranate seeds
Maldon sea salt
4 handfuls of mixed organic leaves, washed and dried

DRESSING
3 tablespoons walnut oil
1 tablespoon pomegranate molasses
Maldon sea salt and freshly ground black pepper

Whisk the oil and pomegranate molasses together with a pinch of salt and pepper. Taste and correct the seasoning.

Place the walnut pieces and pomegranate seeds in a small bowl. Season with a pinch of sea salt and toss in 1 tablespoon of the dressing. Put the leaves into a large bowl and add enough dressing to lightly and delicately coat the leaves. Place the dressed leaves in a serving dish and sprinkle over the walnuts and pomegranate. Serve immediately.

Warm salad of quail with grapes, honey and bacon

Here, we are expanding the salad theme to include a quail roasted with honey and some grapes and bacon. Quail are wonderful little birds and quite simple to cook. Their flavour is sweet and slightly more pronounced than chicken. The quail and bacon are placed hot on to the dressed leaves, so we are really making a warm salad or salade tiède.

With warm salads there are a couple of important points to remember. There are different flavours, textures and temperatures happening. Salads like this should always be served on hot plates, otherwise the juices, in this case from the quail, will become cold and fatty and be much less appealing.

The grapes in this salad can of course be seedless, but buying big juicy grapes and peeling and deseeding them yourself gives a much more delicious result, as the skins of most grapes now are tough and bitter. The bacon for the lardons should be streaky and fatty, to give a sweet, tender and golden result. I save the tiny leftover quail carcasses for stock. People think I am nuts, but how I love that tiny amount of stock and how it cheers up a broth or a chicken stock or the gravy the next time I am roasting a quail.

This dish can be served as a starter or as a main course. If you are serving it as a main course, some hungry eaters will require two quail to satisfy them, so judge your audience and shop and cook accordingly.

The ingredients

Quail are easy enough to find nowadays, and I am in the enviable position of being able to get free-range ones reared by a local producer. Quail roasted in this way can be simply served as roast quail with a little gravy made from the roasting pan juices.

Lardons of bacon are little fat strips cut from a piece of streaky or belly bacon. The unsmoked bacon should be fatty, so that the lardons will be succulent and sweet when crisped up in the frying pan.

Try to find grapes that look fat, sweet and juicy. Watch out especially for the Muscat grapes that appear in September, as their flavour is quite unique and delicious.

Hazelnut oil needs to be carefully stored in the same way that walnut oil does, as if these oils are stored in a warm place, they can become rancid. So a cool place is the ideal situation for a tin of the oil, and if it is in a bottle, darkness helps as well. When buying the oil, check to see what date it was pressed on – you want to be using the oil not more than twelve months after it was pressed. The flavour, though delicious, is quite strong, so I have tempered it slightly in the dressing here by the addition of 1 tablespoon of a 'bland' oil.

Serves 4

4 free-range quail
4 teaspoons honey
2 teaspoons thyme leaves
24 grapes
1 dessertspoon olive oil
2 tablespoons lardons of bacon
4 handfuls of mixed organic salad leaves, washed and dried

HAZELNUT OIL DRESSING
3 tablespoons hazelnut oil
1 tablespoon sunflower or grape seed oil
1 tablespoon white wine vinegar
¼ teaspoon mustard
Maldon sea salt and freshly ground pepper

Preheat the oven to 190°C/375°F/gas 5.

Put the quail into a small roasting tin. They should be snug, not lost in a large tin. An oval Pyrex dish also does nicely. Spoon the honey over and sprinkle on the thyme leaves. Season with salt and pepper. Place in the oven and roast for about 20–30 minutes, or until cooked through. Baste the birds several times during the cooking to achieve a rich golden glaze on the skin. You want the honey to darken and caramelise so that it loses some of its sweetness and becomes much more interesting in flavour. By basting I mean lifting up the juices from the bottom of the roasting dish with a spoon and pouring those juices over the birds. I can't think of any poultry or meat that does not benefit from being basted a few times while they are roasting.

To make sure the birds are cooked through, check in the same way as you would a chicken (see page 25). The cooked birds will sit happily in their roasting dish in a warm oven, 110°C/225°F/gas ½, for up to an hour. In any event rest them for at least 10 minutes before serving.

While the birds are cooking or resting, make the dressing. Whisk the oils, vinegar, mustard and seasoning together. Taste and correct the seasoning. If you can bear it, peel and pip the grapes. They taste so much better, I promise!

To assemble the salad, heat four plates or one large serving dish. Heat the olive oil in a small frying pan and cook the lardons of bacon until crispy and golden. Toss the salad leaves with enough of the hazelnut dressing to glaze lightly and place the leaves on the hot plates. Toss the grapes in the remaining dressing and sprinkle over and around the leaves. Place the quail, either whole or jointed, on top of the leaves. Drizzle any juices from the quail roasting pan over the leaves too. Finally, divide the hot and crispy bacon between the salads and serve immediately.

Warm salad of grilled beef with beetroot, grilled spring onions and aioli

This is a warm beef salad based around a bed of rocket leaves dressed simply with olive oil and lemon juice. The amount of meat is rather small, but with the leaves, beetroot and spring onions this makes a perfectly balanced dish.

Try to find grass-fed beef that has been dry-aged for at least 4 weeks. You will notice that the recipe calls for one thick steak weighing about 450g. This is about twice the thickness of a normal steak and the reason for this is the way it cooks. You can build up a lovely caramelised crust on the steak and still retain a juicy pink interior if that is what you like. You will not find this size of cut on the supermarket shelves, it's one that your butcher will have to cut specially for you. Failing an accommodating butcher, you can use two conventionally sized steaks, but the cooking time will be shorter.

The sauce here, aioli, is a garlicky mayonnaise thinned out with very good chicken stock or meat juices. The ideal is the caramelised juice from a roasting tin or carving dish in which a piece of beef or chicken has been cooked. Always save these meat juices. These essences are scant and precious and have a fabulous undiluted flavour. Store them in small jars in your fridge. Any fat on the juices will rise to the top and set to form a protective coating on the juices, which invariably turn to a rich jelly in the fridge. The jellied juices will keep for at least a month in the fridge. When you are ready to use them, just lift off the fat and you will have a shiny, sometimes solid, sometimes wobbly, mahogany-coloured disc of pure flavour.

The grated beetroot is easy, and worth remembering for a fast and delicious vegetable to serve another day, as are the grilled spring onions, which I have loved ever since the first time I tasted them in Mexico about twenty years ago. The vino cotto used to dress the beetroot may be a new ingredient to you. It is also known as 'agrodolce' and is made from concentrated grape juice and red wine vinegar. I love its richness of flavour and mildly vinegary taste. It can be replaced with balsamic vinegar. It is great sprinkled over chips or rustic roasted potatoes, either of which would be the perfect accompaniment to this dish.

The ingredients

A thick sirloin steak, preferably dry-aged, is what is required here. 'Dry-aged' means that the beef is hung in a cold room to mature and that the enzyme action in the meat breaks down the connective tissue in the muscles, with a resulting tenderising effect on the meat. The texture and flavour of beef aged in this way is superior to the beef that is now wet-aged in plastic vac packs – I find the resulting meat to be dull, soft and lacking in flavour. You will pay more for the dry-aged beef, but I am happy to do that and just eat less of it.

The spring onions should have plenty of colour when cooked, and I never mind if some of the edges get almost charred.

Serves 4
1 thick sirloin steak, weighing about 450g
1 fat clove of garlic, cut in half
12 thick spring onions, about 20cm long
Maldon sea salt and freshly ground black pepper
6–8 tablespoons olive oil
4 medium-sized beetroot, each about the size of a golfball
1 tablespoon vino cotto or balsamic vinegar
4 large handfuls of rocket leaves, washed and dried
1 tablespoon lemon juice

AIOLI
4 tablespoons pure beef or chicken juice, or very
    flavoursome chicken stock (see page 60)
4 tablespoons thick homemade mayonnaise (see page 40)
Maldon sea salt and freshly ground black pepper

Heat a heavy cast-iron grill pan until very hot and lightly smoking. Rub the surfaces of the steak with the cut clove of garlic and glaze it meanly with a little of the olive oil, just a light massage. Reserve the garlic for adding to the aioli. Place the prepared steak on the hot grill and cook carefully, allowing it to colour well on the first side before turning to cook the other side. Once both sides have been well coloured, season well with salt and pepper. Cook for a total of 15 minutes to achieve a medium rare result, controlling the heat so that the steak neither burns nor stews.

Remove the steak from the pan and place on a rack over a plate to catch any juices. Keep warm in a low oven, 110°C/225°F/gas½. The steak will sit quite happily for up to an hour, as long as the warming oven is not too hot.

Heat another grill pan for the spring onions or use the same pan if it is not burnt. Toss the spring onions in 2 tablespoons of olive oil and season with salt and pepper. Put them on the grill pan, turning them regularly to build up plenty of golden brown colour and to cook them through until almost melting. This takes about 15 minutes and could be happening at the same time as the steak is cooking if you have two grill pans. When cooked, keep warm with the beef.

While the spring onions are grilling, peel and coarsely grate the beetroot. Dress with the vino cotto or vinegar, and enough olive oil to glaze the beets and season with salt and pepper to taste.

Crush the garlic used for rubbing the beef to a paste. Heat the meat juices or chicken stock to a bare simmer and whisk into the mayonnaise with the crushed garlic to achieve a soft pouring consistency. Taste and correct the seasoning.

To assemble, heat a large serving dish or four main course plates. Place the rocket on the dish and season with salt, a small squeeze of lemon juice and a drizzle of olive oil. Carefully and lightly spread the beetroot over the leaves. Carve the steak into slices, about 1cm thick, and arrange over the beetroot in an overlapping fashion. Don't hide the beetroot completely. Drape the spring onions around the beef. If there is any meat juice from the resting steaks, pop it into a small pan, bring to the boil and pour over the beef.

Finally and with a delicate hand, spoon some of the aioli over the beef. Do not feel compelled to use all of it, as any that is surplus can be passed separately in a sauce boat. Serve immediately.

Test the heat of the pan by just placing a corner of the ingredient on the heated surface. The first thing should be an immediate sizzle as the ingredient hits the heat. There will be a little smoke, but not great plumes of it.

Pan-grilling and pan-frying

A perfectly grilled steak with a mustard and herb butter, a lamb chop with a roast garlic mayonnaise, a golden fillet of fish with lemon and a herb salsa, a juicy hamburger with roast mushrooms – the sort of food that we love to eat either on a wet Monday or a celebration Sunday. What they all have in common is the technique of pan-grilling or pan-frying.

Being able to grill or fry successfully, whether fish, meat, poultry or vegetables, is a crucial technique for all cooks. It is a technique you should be able to approach with no fear, and if you are not always happy with your results it is worth thinking about the process involved. The reason I have put the two techniques, pan-grilling and pan-frying, together is because the process is exactly the same for both techniques, just using a different pan. When I see the word 'grilled' or 'pan-fried' in a recipe title, it says that the dish being served will have a rich and flavoursome colour, ranging from golden brown to mahogany. It is also worth remembering that grilled or pan-fried foods do not need to be greasy and fatty, and if you are careful you can reduce the fat being used to a minimum. The main difference in the results from the two cooking pans is appearance and texture. The grill pan with its raised ridges will give richly coloured lines on the ingredient being cooked, so the resulting colour tends to be two-tone and a slightly crispier result, whereas the frying pan gives a more even and single-colour result with not as much texture as the grill pan. The grill pan also produces a slightly deeper flavour.

Whether you are grilling meat, poultry, fish or vegetables, there are rules and guidelines that apply to all.

A heavy cast-iron grilling pan

Keys to success

Use a heavy cast-iron grill pan, an invaluable piece of kit; if you have a chargrill that gets good and hot, that is perfect too. Either way, the equipment needs to be spotlessly clean.

All ingredients should be dry. Dab them gently with a small piece of kitchen paper to remove surface moisture. This makes them much less likely to stick during the cooking.

Lightly glaze the ingredient in fat. Oil can be brushed or hand-massaged on, and butter, which should be soft, I spread on meanly with a blunt knife. Use just enough fat on the surface of the ingredient to colour it when it comes into contact with the pan. Excess fat is just wasteful and causes unnecessary burning.

Preheating the pan to the correct level of heat is essential. If the grill is too cold or too hot the ingredients will stick to it. You want a level of heat that will start to seal the ingredient the second it hits the pan, but not so hot that it burns it at the same time.

Test the heat of the pan by just placing a corner of the ingredient on the heated surface. The first thing should be **an immediate sizzle** as the ingredient hits the heat. There will be a little smoke, but not great plumes of it.

Once the correct level of heat has been achieved, **don't play with the food too much.** Resist the temptation to keep moving it around or turning it over. It will of course need to be turned at some stage, but don't be too hasty. If you are not sure what colour has been achieved on the underside, just lift it at the edges and have a close look. That will show you accurately what is going on and whether it is ready to be turned or not.

Generally when grilling, I prefer to wait until the food being cooked has been turned over once before seasoning it. There are some exceptions to this rule, such as when fish is dipped in seasoned flour before cooking.

A crucial part of the skill of grilling is testing to see how cooked the ingredient is. Experienced cooks will be able to tell by a combination of touch and sight. Less experienced cooks combine touch and sight with a temperature probe or, as I do, a fine skewer. **The tip of the skewer is inserted into the cooking ingredient, left there for 5 seconds (count it in your head), then removed.** The temperature of the tip of the skewer, tested on your fingers, tells you exactly to what point the ingredient is cooked.

I like to **rest grilled poultry or meat in a warm oven for at least 5 minutes and up to 15 minutes before serving.** This allows the juices to stabilise in the flesh, and makes for a more evenly juicy result.

Place the resting meats on an upside-down plate sitting on top of a bigger plate. This way any juices that are released from the resting meat are saved, and it also prevents the resting meat from 'stewing in its own juices', which can make it soggy.

Grilled fish does not need resting and should be served immediately it is cooked.

Is it cooked?
To judge if meat, poultry or fish is cooked, there are three words worth remembering. These are appearance, texture and temperature.

Appearance: does the ingredient look cooked? With beef and lamb, your preference as to how cooked you like your meat will of course be a determining factor. **With chicken there is no grey area. The meat needs to be cooked all the way through,** not overcooked, but cooked through, so it should look cooked – in other words, no trace of pink at all in the cooked meat. With pork, it is worth mentioning that there is a fashion now to eat pork slightly underdone. Personally, I don't enjoy or recommend pork served in this way. As with chicken, I prefer it cooked through, not dry, but cooked. With fish, I also like it cooked through, again, I stress, not overcooked, but with the flesh firm and still juicy.

Texture: as we are talking about pan-grilling and pan-frying, we will assume that a good colour has been achieved with no sign of rawness on the surface of any of the cooked ingredients. But what exactly is happening at the centre of the ingredient? Here is a general rule that I find helpful. Touch the surface of the meat or fish with your index finger and the firmness of the ingredient will tell you how cooked it is. The firmer or harder it feels, the more cooked it is. The softer it feels the more undercooked it is. Being able to judge these stages by touching the ingredient comes with practice and experience, and it is well worth practising the 'finger touch test'.

Temperature: if after checking the appearance and texture you are still unsure, you can check the internal temperature. Insert a fine metal skewer or even a darning needle into the thickest part of the meat, poultry or fish and count out 5 seconds. Remove the skewer immediately and test the temperature of the tip of the skewer on your hand. **The hotter the skewer feels, the more cooked or well done the ingredient will be; the cooler it is, the less cooked or rarer it is.** You can of course use a thermometer but I find these cumbersome, especially on the smaller pieces of meat or fish that one generally uses when grilling or pan-frying, and in some models the probe can leave a visible hole in the meat.

If all the above instruction sounds a bit complicated, I promise you it really is not. Once you have performed these tests several times, you should be able to approach the task of determining how cooked your ingredients are with confidence.

Keys to success for pan-grilling or pan-frying fish
Really fresh fish is essential for successful grilling.

Use a **heavy pan** and have it almost smoking hot before putting in the fish.

Lightly **pat the fish dry** before adding the fat.

Lightly butter or oil the surface of the fish that is going to hit the pan first and place the fish, flesh or skin side down, your choice, in the hot pan.

Always introduce the side of the fish that you want to be visible on the serving plate to the pan first, as it will have the advantage of hitting the clean pan and as a result a smarter appearance when cooked.

Heat control is crucial when grilling, so keep a eye on the pan and adjust the heat accordingly. If the heat is too high the fish will burn. If the heat is too low, the fish will stew.

Try to turn the fish only once during the cooking.

Firm-textured fish grill or fry more successfully than softer-textured ones.

Mackerel, salmon, red mullet, grey sea mullet, monkfish, hake, herring, John Dory, brill, turbot and trout all grill beautifully. Cod, haddock and whiting are possible but a bit more difficult.

Fish with noticeable scales, such as salmon, red and grey mullet, hake, herring and trout, should be descaled before cooking. This is done by making sweeping movements with the blunt side of a knife along the surface of the fish, moving from tail to head.

Grilled fish should be served immediately it is cooked.

Smearing just enough butter on the fish to add flavour and prevent sticking

Grilled sea bass
with nam jim, tomato mayonnaise and rocket

A wild sea bass, with its firm texture, flavoursome white flesh and with a slight hint of oiliness, is a fabulous fish. Grey sea mullet, with characteristics similar to the lauded bass, is less adored in general, but when fresh and caught in clean waters, it too can be wonderful and is perfect in this dish.

Both these fish have large scales that need to be removed before grilling, so ask your fishmonger to do that for you. Sea bass is now farmed extensively, but personally I prefer to wait for the less frequently available wild fish. The firmness and oiliness of the flesh of these two fish work well here with the vibrant Asian flavours of the nam jim. Nam jim, a dressing you will find all over south-east Asia, is hot and piquant. It should be hot with chilli, but on the other hand there is no point in having it so fierce that we timid Westerners can't actually enjoy it. As a result you will need to choose your chillies carefully. If you find the heat of a bird's-eye chilli is too strong, use a milder variety, such as an ancho or serrano, but don't dumb this dish down too much or the integrity and charm of the flavour combination will be lost.

This fish is just perfect with the leaves and nam jim dressing, but the tomato mayonnaise completes the picture and is great with the other flavours and textures.

The ingredients
Wild sea bass, a fish that accepts myriad flavours, is firm, white-fleshed, silky and flavoursome. The mullet is similar, but not quite so refined in flavour and texture. Both fish have a couple of fierce pin-bones at the top or head end of the fillet, so make sure these are removed before cooking, and the skin will need to be descaled before grilling.

If you can get coriander roots for the dressing, they add a delicious depth of flavour. Scrub them well before chopping or crushing.

The chilli, preferably green, as green chillies have a fresher greener flavour than the riper red ones, can be as hot as you like or mild if that is your preference. However, there should be an obvious presence of chilli in this dressing when you taste it.

Palm sugar is rich in flavour and has a creamy sweetness. More often than not when we buy it it is rock-hard, so having removed the wax seal you can scrape the sugar out with a sharp spoon or fork. If palm sugar is unavailable, use soft light brown or unrefined caster sugar.

Nam pla, or fish sauce, is an essential ingredient in the cooking of south-east Asia. Made from fermented fish, it is on first encounter strange in aroma and taste, but as you get accustomed to the taste you will find its flavour essential, so that if omitted from a dish the result will seem lacklustre and unauthentic.

Shallots, of which there are several varieties, are part of the onion family and are more delicate in flavour and less pungent than their larger cousins, so are highly suitable when just crushed raw.

Search out organic tomato purée for the mayonnaise. I make my own – please don't hate me.

Serves 4   4 x 175g pieces of sea bass or mullet, with the skin on
A little plain white flour, seasoned with salt and pepper
1 tablespoon olive oil or 1 teaspoon butter,
    at room temperature
Maldon sea salt and freshly ground black pepper
4 handfuls of small rocket leaves, carefully washed
    and dried

NAM JIM DRESSING

2 cloves of garlic, peeled
4 tablespoons coriander leaves and stalks, and if possible
    some of the roots, all chopped
Maldon sea salt
1 green chilli, seeds removed and chopped
2 tablespoons palm sugar
2 tablespoons fish sauce (nam pla)
3 tablespoons lime juice
2 shallots, peeled and finely chopped

TOMATO MAYONNAISE

1 egg yolk
¼ teaspoon Dijon mustard
1 tablespoon thick tomato purée or paste
1 teaspoon white wine vinegar
Maldon sea salt and freshly ground black pepper
50ml olive oil
50ml sunflower oil

To make the nam jim dressing, place the garlic, coriander and a pinch of sea salt in a pestle and mortar and pound until well crushed. Add the chilli and continue to pound. Add the palm sugar, fish sauce, lime juice and chopped shallots and mix. Pound again, until the consistency is slushy. Taste and adjust the seasoning as necessary.

To make the tomato mayonnaise, place the egg, mustard, tomato purée, vinegar and a pinch of salt and pepper in a small bowl and mix together. Mix the oils in a jug and pour in a thin slow stream on to the egg mixture while continuously whisking. Gradually the sauce will begin to emulsify and thicken. Keep adding the oil at the same slow pace until it is all incorporated. Taste and correct the seasoning.

Place a grill pan or heavy-based non-stick frying pan over a medium heat and allow to get quite hot. You don't want it smoking madly, but you should see a light haze, almost like vapour, arising from the pan. Lightly pat the fish dry with kitchen towel. Dip both sides of the fish in the seasoned flour and shake off the excess. Brush the flesh side of the fish fillets lightly with olive oil or butter.

Place the fish pieces, oiled side down, in the hot pan. The fish should sizzle immediately it hits the pan – if it doesn't, the pan wasn't hot enough and you need to crank up the heat immediately or remove the fish and allow the pan to get sufficiently hot. If you have difficulty determining if the pan is hot enough, take one of the pieces of fish, hold it above the pan, and just place a corner of the oiled side in the pan. It should sizzle. If it doesn't, allow the pan to get hotter.

Let the fish cook, still on a high heat, until it is well coloured. This takes about 5 minutes. There should be a bit of smoke coming from the pan, but not great clouds of it, so adjust the heat accordingly. Lift the fish at one corner to check if it is golden and getting crisp. When you are confident this stage has been reached, turn the heat down a little, then, with the help of a fish or egg slice, turn the fish over on to the skin side. Let it continue to cook for about 10 minutes, until the skin is crispy and the fish is cooked through. You will know the fish is cooked when the flesh appears white and creamy in colour and no longer looks translucent.

To serve the fish, toss the rocket leaves in just enough of the dressing to glaze them lightly. Place the cooked fish on hot plates and put a handful of the rocket leaves beside each piece of fish. Drizzle a little of the remaining dressing over each piece of fish, with a little of the tomato mayonnaise.

Serve immediately, passing any extra dressing and mayonnaise separately.

Grilled cod with roast cumin and tomato and coriander simple butter sauce

The sweet, nutty and lemony flavour of lightly roasted cumin pairs beautifully with the fish and light butter sauce in this recipe. The tomato in the sauce, which as always should be really ripe, adds a touch of acidity that helps to balance the flavours in the dish. The late addition of the coriander freshens it all up.

The sauce here, a simple butter sauce, variations of which I use several times in this book, is a really useful one and can be used in many different dishes. The flavours can be varied as often as there are weeks in the year. It is well worth mastering, and when you can make it with confidence, you will, I predict, find it invaluable. I also use it as a light sauce for asparagus, the sprouting broccolis and seakale. Chopped herbs, appropriate to what you are serving it with, can be added at the last moment to give you myriad variations.

The ingredients
Any fish for grilling should be spanking fresh, in which case the job is much easier and the flavour sweet and superior.

Try to find cod that has been caught by fishermen practising sustainable fishing. Good fishmongers will flag these initiatives in their shops.

Roasting the cumin seed adds a lovely nuttiness and richness to its flavour.

Really ripe tomatoes make all the flavours in this dish more interesting as a combination.

Serves 4   4 x 175g portions of cod, skin still attached
A little plain white flour, seasoned with salt and pepper
1 tablespoon olive oil
4 teaspoons cumin seeds, roasted and coarsely ground
Maldon sea salt and freshly ground black pepper

TOMATO AND CORIANDER SIMPLE BUTTER SAUCE
2 tablespoons water
50g butter, chilled and diced
2 ripe firm tomatoes, peeled, deseeded and cut into
    1cm dice
Maldon sea salt, freshly ground black pepper and
    a pinch of sugar
A few drops of lemon juice
1 tablespoon chopped coriander leaves

Place the pan over a medium heat and allow it to get quite hot. Dip the fish in the seasoned flour to coat both sides, shaking off the excess. Brush the flesh side of the fish fillets with olive oil. Sprinkle the ground cumin on to the oiled side of the fish and press in with your fingers.

Place the fish pieces, spiced side down, in the hot grill pan. The fish should sizzle immediately it hits the pan – if it doesn't, the pan wasn't hot enough and you need to crank up the heat immediately. Let the fish cook, still on a high heat, until well coloured. There should be a bit of smoke coming from the pan, but not great clouds of it, so adjust the heat accordingly. Lift the fish at one corner to check if it is golden and getting crisp. When you are confident this stage has been reached, turn the heat down a little, then, with the help of a fish or egg slice, turn the fish over on to the skin side. Let it continue to cook until the skin is crispy and the fish is cooked through. You will know the fish is cooked when the flesh appears white and creamy in colour and no longer looks translucent.

While the fish is grilling you can be making the simple butter sauce. Put the water into a very small pan and bring to a simmer. Pull the pan off the heat and vigorously whisk in the cold butter, two pieces at a time. The butter should start to emulsify and look slightly creamy. Continue adding the butter and whisking at the same time. Replace the pan on a low heat if the butter is not melting into the sauce. When all the butter is added and the sauce has a light yet creamy consistency, remove from the heat.

Season the tomato pieces with salt and pepper and a small pinch of sugar, and add to the sauce. Add a few drops of lemon juice. Place the pan back on the heat and bring to a bare simmer, just to warm the tomato through. You don't want it to collapse. Add the chopped coriander. Taste, correct the seasoning, and keep in a warm place while you are plating the fish.

Place the cooked fish on hot plates or a large serving dish. Drizzle a little of the sauce and tomato over the fish, but leaving some of the cumin crust exposed and not drowning the fish.

Serve immediately, with the rest of the sauce separately in a hot sauce boat.

Grilled mackerel with beetroot and vino cotto, horseradish cream and rocket leaves

Mackerel is a wonderful fish, beautiful to look at and beautiful to eat. Its elegant and streamlined shape, beautiful markings and flashing silvery colouring make it a sight to behold. The most important thing, though, is the freshness of the fish. In East Cork, where I live near the fishing village of Ballycotton, there is an expression that goes: 'The sun should never set on a mackerel.' Regardless of your closeness to the source of the fish, do try to ensure that you are bringing home a really fresh fish.

Mackerel responds very well to many different cooking techniques. It can be poached, baked, roasted, pan-fried, or as in this case grilled. I also like to souse and pickle it. Mackerel is one of the busiest fish in the sea and is constantly moving through the water as it feeds non-stop. Its athletic lifestyle is fuelled by the omega oil that it stores in its body, and which is regarded as highly beneficial for us all. So how can you go wrong with a fish that looks that good, tastes that great and is cheering our bodies up as well, and not forgetting that it is still great value for money.

The ingredients
The ruby beetroot can be replaced with the golden variety or the rippled Chioggia, all of which are delicious prepared in this way.

Fresh horseradish root is sweet and fiery and completely different from the pre-grated type, which is usually preserved in vinegar. The vinegar bullies its delicious flavour. Store fresh horseradish in a sealed bag in the fridge, where it will be happy for months.

Vino cotto, also known as 'agro dolce', is an acidulant made from underripe fruit such as apples and grapes. Like mild vinegar, it is delicious as here with the beetroot but also on salads, grilled meats and with chips. It can be replaced with balsamic vinegar.

Serves 4 2 teaspoons vino cotto or balsamic vinegar
1 teaspoon lemon juice
5 tablespoons olive oil
Maldon sea salt and freshly ground black pepper
200g raw beetroot, peeled and coarsely grated
4 mackerel, filleted
A little white flour, seasoned with salt and pepper
4 handfuls of rocket leaves, gently washed and
    carefully dried
1 tablespoon finely chopped chives

HORSERADISH CREAM
1 tablespoon finely grated fresh horseradish
2 tablespoons very softly whipped cream
Pinch of sugar
Pinch of dry English mustard
2 teaspoons lemon juice
Maldon sea salt and freshly ground black pepper

Mix the vino cotto or vinegar and lemon juice with 4 tablespoons of olive oil and season with salt and pepper. Add the grated beetroot and mix through gently. Taste and correct the seasoning. Cover and keep at room temperature.

Mix all of the ingredients for the horseradish cream together gently. Taste, correct the seasoning and chill.

Heat a heavy-based grill or frying pan until quite hot. Dip each fillet of fish in the seasoned flour on both sides and shake off the excess flour. Brush the flesh side of each mackerel fillet with the remaining tablespoon of oil. A tablespoonful should be sufficient for all of the fish. Place the fish fillets, flesh side down, in the hot pan, and cook until golden brown, being careful to control the heat properly. Turn each fillet and season with salt and pepper. Continue cooking until the skin is crisp and richly coloured.

To serve, gently fold and pull the rocket leaves through the dressed beetroot and divide between the hot plates. Place the mackerel fillets, straight from the pan, on top of the beetroot and rocket, criss-crossing them if you wish, for dramatic effect. Place a generous teaspoon of the horseradish cream on top of each serving, sprinkle with chives and serve immediately.

Pass the extra horseradish cream separately.

Grilled beef with
green mustard, shallot and tarragon butter

Mustard and beef is a combination that has been enjoyed by carnivores for ages. This highly flavoured butter can be prepared ahead of time and then simply sliced on to the beef as you are ready to eat. The mustard I like to use for this is laden with herbs, mainly tarragon, to give it a moss green colour and a sweet taste. If you can't find the green mustard in the shops, you can purée some tarragon into yellow Dijon mustard for a similar result or just add a bit more chopped tarragon to the butter. The flavoured butter keeps well in the fridge for a week, or you can pop it into the freezer for use later.

The ingredients
Steaks cut from dry-aged beef will be superior in flavour and texture to the wet-aged option. The rib-eye steak is further up along the back of the animal than the sirloin, so will have a bit more fat attached, which I don't mind. It is more flavoursome than the sirloin, as a result of its closer proximity to the hard-working forequarter of the animal.

It is worth always having a few shallots in the kitchen. Their flavour, milder and more delicate than an onion, comes into its own in a butter like this.

The tarragon in this robustly flavoured butter will remind you instantly of the food and taste of France. If tarragon is out of season, you can replace it with parsley and the result will be excellent, though not as 'French' as when made with tarragon.

Serves 4

4 x 225g rib-eye or sirloin steaks
1 cut clove of garlic, for rubbing on the uncooked steaks
2 teaspoons olive oil, for rubbing on the uncooked steaks
Maldon sea salt and freshly cracked black pepper

GREEN MUSTARD, SHALLOT AND TARRAGON BUTTER
1 shallot, peeled and finely chopped
4 tablespoons red wine
1 tablespoon port
110g butter, at room temperature but not soft and oily
2 teaspoons green tarragon mustard
1 tablespoon chopped tarragon
Freshly ground black pepper

Place the chopped shallot in a small saucepan with the wine and port and cook at a simmer until the wine and port have evaporated completely. Allow the shallots, by now a lovely ruby colour, and richly infused with the concentrated taste of the wine and port, to cool completely. Beat the butter a little, just to make it creamy in appearance, and add the mustard, chopped tarragon, cooled shallots and a few grinds of the black pepper mill. Mix well. Taste a little to check if any further seasoning is necessary.

Place a piece of cling film on your work counter and place the butter on it in a line no longer than 8cm. Roll the plastic around it to form a neat sausage shape. Twist the plastic tightly at both ends to make a tightly sealed neat little roll or cracker shape. Chill until firmly set.

Heat a heavy-based grill pan or pans until very hot. You may just see a haze of heat coming from the pan. While the pan is heating, rub the steaks on both sides with a cut clove of garlic and then with very little olive oil, as if you were meanly moisturising them. Score the fat on top of the steaks lightly with a small knife. This allows some of it to render out and the remaining fat to become crisp and delicious.

Place the steaks on the heated grill pan, leaving at least 2cm space between them. They should sizzle immediately. Cook on one side until a rich colour has developed, and, if you want, giving the steak a 180° turn halfway through the cooking to attain a grid of marks on the cooked meat. Cook on the other side, again cooking to a rich colour, until cooked to your liking. You will need to carefully control the heat all the way through the cooking. If the pan gets too hot you will burn the steaks and if the pan becomes cool, the meat will stew and toughen. Season the cooked steaks on both sides with salt and pepper.

Place the cooked steaks, a little apart from each other, on an upturned plate sitting on a larger plate to capture any juices that run from the resting beef. Allowing them to rest for at least 5 minutes and up to 15 minutes seems to work for me. Keep them warm during the resting period in a warm oven set to 100°C/200°F/gas ¼.

Just before serving the steaks, run a clean finger along the surface of the meat and taste, just to check if any extra pinch of salt is required. Serve the steaks on hot plates, drizzling them with any cooking juices and with a slice of the mustard butter placed on top just before they go to the table.

A salad of seasonal leaves and hot crispy chips or rosemary-roasted rustic potatoes are my favourite accompaniments.

Wild garlic, chive or spring onion hamburger

A good, freshly mixed and cooked hamburger can be a treat or it can be dull, dry and disappointing. There are a few important rules to remember if you want a flavoursome, juicy, sweet and delicious burger. You will need to choose meat with about 10% fat on it. The fat will ensure a juicy texture. The meat should not be a prime cut but a lesser one like neck, chuck or flank. Raw minced meat deteriorates very quickly and the freshness of taste is quickly lost. Trust your nose here, as freshly minced beef has no smell at all. If there is even a hint of a smell from the mince, it is not fresh enough, and when cooked it will taste as it smells. It is the freshness of taste of the meat that is the secret of a really good burger. For that reason the meat must be cooked on the day it is minced.

I like to go to my butcher, point to the cut of beef I want and ask for it to be minced there and then in front of my eyes. If you are buying the mince off a supermarket shelf, have a good look at the packet, check to see that there is no discoloration around the edge of the meat and buy the packet with the longest remaining shelf life.

The other point of note in this recipe is that I use raw onion and garlic, so the burgers need to be cooked within an hour of being mixed. I find the raw onion, garlic and garlic leaves give a really zippy flavour to the meat. The wild garlic can be replaced with chopped chives or spring onion greens at another time of the year.

Personally, I like my burger cooked through to the centre, not overcooked and dry, but with no raw mince in the centre.

What sauces and accompaniments you choose to serve is up to you. For some a golden bread bun with sesame seed or poppy seeds on top is essential. I like chips, a salad of leaves and mayonnaise or, when the tomatoes are good, a Tomato Mayonnaise (see page 148).

The ingredients
Perfectly fresh mince from the neck, chuck or flank is best for sweet
    and juicy hamburgers.

The slender-leaved wild garlic, also known as three-cornered garlic,
    with its bell-like flowers, can appear in a mild spring as early as

February. If you are picking it yourself it generally prefers a sunny spot. The other later-arriving variety, sometimes called ramsons, has a wider leaf, a pom-pom shaped flower and likes a shaded place to grow. Every part of the plant can be used – the flowers, leaves and the little bulb-type roots. Farmers' markets and good shops will have wild garlic available right through the season.

Serves 2

1 small onion, about 50g
1 clove of garlic
450g freshly minced beef
2 tablespoons beaten egg
60g finely chopped wild garlic leaves or chives or
    spring onion greens
½ teaspoon thyme leaves
Maldon sea salt and freshly ground black pepper
Olive oil

Grate the onion and garlic on a Microplane or a very fine grater and put into a bowl with the meat. The onion and garlic will break down to a thick juice when they are grated. This is exactly what you want. Add the beaten egg, chopped garlic leaves, chives or greens and thyme leaves, and season with salt and pepper. Mix well. I always mix the ingredients with my hands, as I feel this keeps the mixture light and not too compacted. Fry a morsel in a pan and taste to check that the seasoning is correct. Form into 2 large or 4 small burgers.

Heat a heavy-based grill or frying pan until quite hot. Dab a little olive oil on to the surface of the burgers and place in the pan. As the meat starts to colour, turn the heat down a little. Turn regularly during the cooking, as the egg in the recipe will cause the burgers to brown quite quickly. They will take about 15 minutes to cook through.

If you want to assemble the burgers more than 1 hour in advance, you could chop the onion finely and sweat it in a little olive oil or butter to cook it through with no colour. Allow the onion to cool completely before mixing it with the raw minced beef.

Grilled pork burger with fennel and pistachios

These burgers are sweet and delicious. Belly or shoulder of pork is best here, as you are generally guaranteed a decent amount of fat from those two cuts, and fat is essential for a good burger. If the meat you are using is too lean, the burgers will be dry, hard and lacking in flavour. The other crucial point to remember for any kind of minced meat dish is that the mince needs to be really fresh, so it should be minced on the same day you are going to cook and eat it. Minced meat deteriorates faster than any other prepared meat, hence freshness is paramount.

Aromatic roast fennel seeds work beautifully here, as they do with almost any cut of pork, and the pistachio nuts add their own magical flavour and texture. I serve these with various different dishes. A plain mashed potato is good, as is the Courgette and Marjoram Mash. They also sit happily with a tomato stew or sauce. A Bramley apple sauce or the version with plums is also good here. Cook these burgers fully – this is not the time for a rare burger.

The ingredients

Belly or shoulder of pork with about 10% fat on it and freshly minced is what you need for these burgers. If the mincing of the pork is a problem, I have quite successfully ground the pork to a mince-like consistency in a food processor. Use the pulse button to control the speed of the blade, and don't process the meat too much or it will become too fine and more like sausage meat.

Choose a moderately hot chilli such as an ancho or serrano. I prefer the sweeter taste of a red chilli in this recipe.

Pistachios, preferably the green ones which have the best flavour, are a luxurious little nut, therefore expensive, so try to use them while they are in good condition and still fresh-tasting.

Fennel seeds, like most spices, are best bought whole, and roasted and ground as you need them.

Serves 4   700g streaky or shoulder of pork, minced
                  2 cloves of garlic, peeled and crushed
                  1–2 chillies, deseeded and finely chopped
                  2 teaspoons fennel seeds, roasted and ground
                  2 tablespoons chopped coriander leaves
                  40g pistachio nuts, shells removed
                  Maldon sea salt and freshly ground black pepper
                  Olive oil

Mix all the ingredients except the olive oil together in a bowl. Fry a teaspoon of the mixture to check the seasoning and adjust as necessary. Form the mixture into burgers, either 4 large or 8 small, and chill until ready to cook.

Heat a heavy grill pan until quite hot. Grease the burgers lightly with olive oil and place on the hot grill to cook. Allow to become golden brown on one side before turning. Control the heat carefully and cook the burgers, turning occasionally, until fully cooked through. This takes about 15 minutes – the burgers should feel firm to the touch.

Serve the burgers on hot plates with your sauce and vegetable of choice.

Grilled chicken with summer marjoram and lemon, and roasted almond sauce

Try to find an organic, or at least a free-range chicken for this recipe. If you buy the whole chicken, you will have the carcass for making a stock or broth and you can reserve the wings for another recipe. Chicken breasts alone can be used here, but I like to grill the legs and thighs also, as I prefer their flavour.

The chosen herb, marjoram, is my absolute favourite; however, it can be replaced with thyme, rosemary or tarragon if you wish, all of which are great with chicken. The roasted almond sauce is also delicious served with grilled lamb.

If you are worried about jointing the chicken, either buy joints or ask your butcher to do it for you.

Serves 6
1 chicken, jointed into 8–12 pieces, bones removed from thighs and drumsticks
2 tablespoons olive oil
2 tablespoons chopped marjoram
1 lemon
Maldon sea salt and freshly ground black pepper

ROASTED ALMOND SAUCE
100g unskinned almonds
Maldon sea salt
1 clove of garlic, peeled
2 tablespoons marjoram leaves
2–4 tablespoons olive oil
2–3 tablespoons water
2 tablespoons Parmesan, grated
Lemon juice, a few drops, as necessary

Start by making the sauce. To peel the almonds, place them in a small saucepan, cover them with cold water and bring to a bare simmer. Strain immediately and rinse under a cold tap. Slip off the skins. Place the almonds on a baking tray and roast in a moderate oven at 180°C/350°F/gas 4 until golden brown. Remove and set aside to cool.

Place a pinch of sea salt in a mortar and add the garlic and marjoram leaves. Pound to a paste, then add the almonds and pound again. Gradually they will start to break down and get creamy. Add a little olive oil as you go. When the ingredients have taken on a pesto-type consistency, taste and fold in the Parmesan. The almonds will be a little bit gritty and this is perfect. Correct the seasoning and consistency adding in a few drops of lemon juice and water if necessary. Cover and chill until needed.

Place a cast-iron grill on the heat. While the pan is heating, place the chicken joints in a bowl and rub with enough olive oil to glaze them. Add half the marjoram and a squeeze of lemon juice and mix well. When the pan is just smoking, place the chicken joints, skin side down, on the hot grill. Allow them to colour well, adjusting the heat under the pan as necessary. When the skin is crisp and golden, turn and cook on the other side. Season the crisp skin with salt and pepper at this point. As soon as a crisp surface is achieved on both sides, turn the heat down to complete the cooking without burning the meat. If you wish, you can transfer the pan to a moderate oven now to finish cooking.

Serve the cooked chicken sprinkled with the rest of the chopped marjoram, with lemon wedges and a little extra olive oil if you think it needs it. Pass the roast almond sauce separately. A salad of leaves and a dish of rustic roast potatoes make excellent accompaniments to the grilled chicken, as do glazed carrots.

During the cooking, baste the meat several times by spooning some of the fat and juices that render out back over the surface. This prevents the meat from drying out and adds extra flavour to the outside.

Roasting

If you were to ask a random selection of people what meal they would most like to be able to master, for many the immediate and unthinking response would be, 'a roast'. That 'roast' they are referring to is generally a piece of roast meat. Beef, lamb, chicken and pork seem to be the most popular and longed-for choices. There is no denying how delicious a good roast with the appropriate trimmings can be, and the pleasure it can bring. It somehow seems rather grown-up, and undoubtedly there is a particular calm that descends on a household in that post-Sunday roast hour or two. Monday still seems enough hours away not to bother you, family and friends are well fed, contentment, normality, and a feeling that things are and can be all right seems to cloak the sated diners.

Someone's got to do the work, though, but with roasting the technique is straightforward. The ingredient of choice is placed on a roasting tray, seasoned and flavoured according to the recipe, and placed in the oven at the appropriate temperature for the prescribed period of time. Like any technique, there are rules involved, and if you follow the rules, you have a much greater chance of success. As usual, the quality of the ingredients is key, and thinking ahead in terms of ingredients and shopping will reward you. In this chapter we will concentrate on meat and poultry. Clearly, other ingredients such as fish and vegetables also roast well, but that will have to be for another day.

Keys to success

Talk to your butcher and choose a piece of meat or poultry that is appropriate for roasting.

As roasting is a dry cooking technique, the ingredient being roasted will need **a layer of fat** on it, or introduced to it, to prevent it from drying out during the cooking. This is crucial, as a lean piece of meat with no protection from the direct heat of the oven tends to dry out. Don't be scared of the fat. You don't have to eat it, though well-crisped fat with the liquid fat rendered out can be quite delicious. Most of the fat renders out while the meat is cooking and is strained off before sauces or gravies are made. The fatty skin is **lightly scored** before cooking so that it melts and renders to a liquid, and runs down over the meat as it roasts. It is good to baste the meat with this liquid fat a few times during the cooking to keep protecting and flavouring the meat as it cooks. With the exception of fillet of beef, which is very tender to start off with and cooks very quickly, an overly lean piece of meat will not reward you with a juicy roast.

When choosing beef, the ideal is that the meat has been hung to dry-age for **a minimum of 3 weeks**. The ultimate cut of beef for roasting is the prime rib or forerib, with a nice coating of fat. The sirloin on the bone, also with a coating of fat, is excellent. The fillet, the most tender part of the animal, is generally trimmed of all its inedible tough gristle before cooking; as a result no fat remains and it breaks the rules of the longer cooking joints mentioned previously. You may still like to introduce it to a little fat in the cooking as I do, in the form of a rub of olive oil or a basting of beef fat or dripping from a previous roast. There are less expensive cuts such as the flank which also roast well when aged up to 4 or 5 weeks, but they will need a longer cooking time because of their toughness.

Leg, shoulder and loin of lamb all roast beautifully. The leg and shoulder are best roasted **on the bone** and need very little preparation. The leg roasts relatively quickly, whereas the shoulder is best slow-roasted to melt the connective tissue to an almost creamy consistency. A light scoring of the fat and a seasoning of salt and pepper is sometimes all that is needed. Herbs, spices and marinades can also be added to the skin if required. Watch out for the cut called the chump, which is at the top of the leg, heading towards the end of the loin. This small cut of meat also roasts well and is my favourite cut for grilling. The loin, which is essentially the back of the animal or the long piece between the shoulders and the legs, is usually broken into two pieces. The top end, heading towards the shoulder and with the rib bones attached, is the familiar rack. The lower end of the loin, called the centre loin, heading towards the legs, is often boned and rolled before roasting, in which case it can also be stuffed.

All cuts of pork roast well, but only if the cut of meat has **a good layer of fat** on it before you start. A lean piece of pork will generally disappoint. I like to see about 1cm of fat on the raw meat. By the time the meat is cooked, most of that fat will have rendered out to be strained off, cooled and chilled for using another day. If you want crackling, the skin must be left attached to each joint and scored so as to crisp up in the cooking. Cut the skin with a very sharp knife. A Stanley knife with its ultra-sharp blade and sturdy handle, which facilitates a good firm grip, is perfect. Always cut the skin in the same direction as you are going to carve the cooked meat. I cut in 1cm wide cuts. The shoulder, loin and belly are best. The leg is the most challenging in terms of achieving a succulent result. Both the shoulder and leg require **long, slow cooking** to release as much liquid fat as possible and to tenderise the flesh. The loin and belly cook more quickly. The loin with most of the belly left attached can be stuffed and rolled. Many flavours may be added to the pork before cooking.

Most poultry is perfect for roasting, for example chicken, duck, turkey, goose, guinea fowl and quail. A light smear of butter or olive oil may be rubbed on the skin of the leaner birds. Duck and goose are sufficiently fatty and do not need any extra. The fat that renders from any of these birds, especially duck and goose fat, should be saved and chilled and used another day for roasting vegetables, grilling meats and so on. The fat will keep covered in the fridge for at least 1 month.

Wild game birds, such as pheasant, pigeon, snipe, woodcock, grouse and partridge, and wild ducks, such as mallard, teal and widgeon, all roast well. **Casserole-roasting also suits these birds**, as that method leads to a more tender result with these wild, busy and sometimes wiry creatures. Wild birds, which tend to be leaner than domesticated ones, will generally benefit from some fat such as streaky bacon, butter or olive oil included in the cooking to help to prevent the flesh from drying out.

Weigh the meat and calculate the cooking time. Use the chart on page 550.

Season the meat before cooking and place in a preheated oven. Fatty joints such as pork, duck and goose can be placed on a sturdy wire rack to make it easier to strain off the fat that will render out in the cooking.

During the cooking, **baste** the meat several times by spooning some of the fat and juices that render out back over the surface. This prevents the meat from drying out and adds extra flavour to the outside.

When the meat is cooked to your liking, remove it from its cooking tray and **allow it to relax** in a warm oven with the temperature reduced to 100°C/200°F/gas ¼. This resting period is very important, as it allows the meat to relax and the juices to settle before the meat is carved. Large cuts of meat such as a shoulder or leg of lamb or pork, or a rib of beef, will need a minimum of 15 minutes but will happily rest for an hour before carving. Smaller cuts or birds, such as a rack of lamb or a chicken, can sit for a shorter time, though a minimum of 15 minutes is still desirable.

Fat rising to the surface of the cooking juices – ready to be skimmed off

The gravy is made while the meat is resting. There are two words to remember when making any gravy – **'degrease and deglaze'**. This is the mantra. Degrease by pouring off all of the fat. Deglaze by adding the liquid of choice to the grease-free roasting pan. The liquid, with the aid of your whisking, will dissolve the chestnut-coloured caramelised meat juices in the bottom of the pan, and that adds colour and flavour to the gravy. If you are adding alcohol to the roasting tray to deglaze, it is crucial that it goes in before the stock and that it is allowed to boil and reduce by at least half before any other liquid is added. Otherwise the gravy will taste 'winey' or 'boozy', as the raw flavour has not been boiled off. As soon as the stock has been added, I strain the liquid through a fine sieve into a smaller and more manageable saucepan. Taste the gravy and see if it requires further seasoning or cooking. If it is lacking in flavour, allow it to continue simmering to reduce and concentrate the flavour. If you like a thick gravy (I don't), whisk in a knob of roux (see page 31) to the simmering liquid and allow it to simmer for a further 3 minutes to make sure there is no taste of raw flour. If I want to add a little body to the gravy, my preferred addition is a small knob of butter whisked in. This thickens enriches lightly, and gives the gravy a silky consistency and a hint of a shine.

When you are ready to carve the meat, place it on a carving board. Sit the board in a low-sided tray to catch any juices that may escape. I use a long-bladed non-serrated carving knife for large pieces of meat such as a rib of beef or leg of lamb. I am happy to use a flexible filleting knife for a chicken or a duck, as it gives me more control when dealing with the smaller bones and joints. Remember that as a general rule, when carving, you **carve straight down on to the bone or towards the board**. This is to follow the grain of the meat. So the knife is generally going south. If you are going east or west, you are probably cutting the meat in the wrong direction and will end up with stringy and tougher slices or joints.

Roast meats are best served not too hot, as this can toughen the meat. Hot plates and bubbling gravy make up for any lack of temperature the meat may have.

Roast leg of spring lamb
with salt and pepper and mint relish

A leg of lamb can be roasted like this at any time of the year but is best with spring lamb, which in this part of the world appears at Easter time. Spring lamb for the table, coming from lambs born around Christmas, is sweet, mild and subtle, hence the absence of flavourings other than sea salt and freshly ground pepper. The skin on spring lamb when roasted gets particularly crisp and delicious, so don't be tempted to trim any of it off before roasting the meat. Strongly flavoured herbs and spices will overpower the delicate flavour of the early or new season lamb, so I wait until a bit later in the season before introducing those. Ask your butcher to remove the aitchbone from the lamb to facilitate easier carving. The leg bone is best left in and brings a delicious sweetness to the meat. A light and simple gravy and a relish made with new tender and sweet mint leaves are the best sauces to show it off.

The ingredients

A leg of spring lamb is an expensive treat, so order it from your butcher in advance to ensure it will be properly hung, and ask to have the aitchbone removed. Calculate the cooking time accurately and rest it for at least 15 minutes before carving.

Flaky Maldon sea salt and a little freshly ground black pepper are the only seasonings needed to enhance the flavour of the lamb.

The mint in the relish should be fresh and bright green and is one of the first of the herbs to re-emerge after winter in the spring garden. Chop the mint just before you are ready to mix it with the other ingredients, as it will oxidise and become bitter very quickly if left chopped and exposed to the air.

The chicken stock for the gravy should not be too strong, so as not to overpower the flavour of the lamb.

A knob of butter added to the gravy gives a little richness and body as well as a silky consistency.

Serves 6–8   1 leg of spring lamb, about 2.7kg
Maldon sea salt and freshly ground black pepper
300ml chicken stock
20g butter

Preheat the oven to 180°C/350°F/gas 4. Put the lamb into a roasting tin and season it with salt and pepper. Place it in the oven and roast for 1–1¼ hours for pink, 1¼ hours for medium, 1½ hours for well done. Baste the meat several times during the cooking.

Remove the lamb from the oven and reduce the oven temperature to 100°C/200°F/gas ¼. Put the lamb on a platter and replace it in the warm oven to rest for at least 15 minutes.

While the lamb is resting, make the gravy. Degrease the roasting tray by pouring the liquid lamb fat into a Pyrex jug. Place the jug in the freezer. There will be a little of the meat juices mixed with this fat, and as it sits and chills, the fat will rise to the surface and the dark-coloured juices will be visible at the bottom. The fat can be removed and these juices can be added to the gravy later. Place the roasting tin on a low heat and pour in the stock to deglaze the tin. Whisk vigorously to encourage the caramelised meat juices on the bottom of the roasting tin to dissolve into the stock. Add a pinch of salt and pepper and allow to come to a simmer. Strain the gravy through a sieve into a small saucepan and bring back to a simmer. Lift the fat off the chilled meat juices and add the juices to the tin.

Taste the gravy now to check the flavour. If it tastes a little light, allow it to continue simmering for a few minutes longer, so that it will reduce and concentrate the flavour. You will have less gravy, but more flavour. Taste again, and if you are happy with the taste, add the butter and gently whisk it into the sauce at a simmer. As soon as it is incorporated, remove the gravy from the heat and set it aside to be reheated when you need it.

Serve the lamb on a hot platter with the bubbling gravy and pass the mint relish separately.

Mint relish

Serves 6–8   1 tablespoon caster sugar
4 tablespoons boiling water
2 tablespoons lemon juice or verjuice
4 tablespoons mint leaves

Dissolve the sugar in the boiling water and add the lemon juice or verjuice. Chop the mint finely and add. Mix well.

Slow roast shoulder of lamb
with aioli and salsa verde

A few years ago, butchers had some difficulty selling shoulder of lamb, as it was considered inferior to the leg and loin. Now all that has changed, and the cooking world realises that the shoulder is every bit as good as the more 'prime' cuts and in some ways actually better. The hard-working and muscular shoulder has marvellous flavour but needs long and slow cooking to gently tenderise it so that the flesh becomes sweetly succulent. The cooked lamb in this dish should be soft and melting and will be gently pulled apart for serving rather than being carved.

This recipe needs time. You can't rush the cooking of a shoulder of lamb, but once it is in the oven, there is plenty of time to prepare sauces and vegetables to accompany it. I suggest two sauces here, a garlicky mayonnaise that is thinned with some of the lamb cooking juices and a fresh-tasting and piquant herb salsa. The two combine really well with the soft flavoursome meat.

The ingredients

Shoulder of lamb is easily available and here the shoulder is cooked whole, with just a sprinkle of sea salt and freshly cracked pepper. If the shoulder is excessively fatty, as may be the case later on in the lamb season, trim some of it off, or ask your butcher to do it for you.

The aioli to serve with the lamb is based on mayonnaise. I urge you to make your own mayonnaise, either by hand or in a food mixer or processor. Good mayonnaise is one of the cornerstones in any good cook's repertoire.

Salsa verde has become something of a cliché in the last few years and as a result the quality has suffered. That doesn't mean that when made with fresh herbs and good ingredients it can't be as exciting as the first time any of us tasted it. It is a wonderfully refreshing foil for the sweet lamb and rich aioli.

Search out best-quality anchovies and capers for the salsa; they vary enormously in quality, so what seems like a bargain when you are buying them may disappoint at a later stage. Salted anchovies and capers are best, and they will need plenty of rinsing in cold water to remove the excess salt.

The herbs for the salsa should be chopped just before being added to the other ingredients.

Serves 8–10 1 whole shoulder of lamb on the bone, weighing about 3.6kg
Maldon sea salt and freshly ground black pepper

AIOLI
6 large tablespoons mayonnaise
2 cloves of garlic, peeled and crushed to a paste
4–6 tablespoons lamb cooking juices

SALSA VERDE
See page 39

Preheat the oven to 180°C/350°F/gas 4.

Place the lamb shoulder, skin side up, in a wide roasting tin or oven tray. Score the skin several times to encourage the fat to run out during the cooking and to crisp up the skin. Season with salt and pepper. Place in the oven and roast for 30 minutes, then turn the temperature down to 160°C/325°F/gas 3 for a further 3½ hours.

While the lamb is cooking, make the salsa verde.

The crushed garlic can be mixed into the mayonnaise for the aioli, but this sauce cannot be finished until we have the juices from the cooked lamb. To test if the lamb is cooked to a melting tenderness, pull the shank bone – some of the meat should come away easily from the bone.

When the lamb is cooked, remove it from the oven and lower the oven temperature to 100°C/200°F/gas ¼. Put the lamb on a platter and replace it in the warm oven to rest for at least 15 minutes. There will be plenty of fatty cooking juices. Strain these off the roasting tin through a sieve into a bowl.

When the fat has risen to the surface of the lamb cooking juices, skim it off carefully and thoroughly with a large spoon. Thin out the garlic mayonnaise with 4–6 tablespoons of the degreased juices to achieve a consistency similar to softly whipped cream; or, in other words, the mayonnaise should now just lightly coat the back of a spoon. Bring the remaining juices to a simmer and taste and correct the seasoning.

The best way to remove the meat from the bones is to use tongs or a serving fork and spoon. Prise largish pieces off the bones and serve on hot plates, with some of the hot cooking juices, the salsa and aioli.

Roast chicken with bread and thyme leaf sauce and redcurrant sauce

Roast chicken is many people's desert island dish: crisp and golden skin, juicy and tender flesh, and the bits that go with it to complete the picture, such as gravy, roast potatoes, maybe a bread stuffing and so on. The quality of the chicken will be immediately obvious in this dish, so try to get a free-range bird and, if you wish, an organic one. The basic roasting of the bird is simplicity itself. A little seasoning, a few herbs in the cavity, into the oven in a roasting tin and off you go. I am going down the bread sauce route here, not the tepid, thick and gloopy type but a warm, slightly softer, more flavoursome one that I hope will appeal to all. Let's face it, bread sauce has as many sworn enemies as friends, so this is an attempt to convince a few more of its detractors that this sauce is worth a chance. A simple sauce of redcurrants, which is delicious served with most poultry, is a sweet and sharp finishing touch.

The ingredients

The chicken should be the best you can find. A free-range and organic chicken will be significantly more expensive than a factory-reared one, so if you can extract a second meal from the bits left on the carved carcass, all the better. The carcass, picked clean, can be made into a chicken stock.

Thyme and lemon pair beautifully with chicken. Use fresh thyme here, and pierce the lemon a few times before putting it into the chicken cavity.

The breadcrumbs for the sauce can be fresh or frozen. Freeze slices of stale leftover white bread for this purpose, or make it into breadcrumbs and freeze.

The redcurrants for the sauce can also be fresh or frozen. This sauce will keep in your fridge for up to a month in a covered jar.

Serves 4–6   10g soft butter

1 free-range chicken, about 2kg

Maldon sea salt and freshly ground black pepper

1 lemon

1 large sprig of thyme

500ml chicken stock

BREAD AND THYME LEAF SAUCE

450ml full-fat milk

110g white breadcrumbs

1 onion, studded with 2 cloves

1 large sprig of thyme

50g butter

50ml regular or double cream

REDCURRANT SAUCE

110g redcurrants, fresh or frozen

170g caster or granulated sugar

120ml water

Preheat the oven to 180°C/350°F/gas 4. Smear the soft butter over the chicken skin and season with salt and pepper. Prick the lemon a few times with a skewer or a needle and push into the chicken cavity with the sprig of thyme.

Place in a roasting tin, put into the oven, and roast for 1½ hours. Check to ensure that the chicken is fully cooked before removing it (see page 25). Lower the oven temperature to 100°C/200°F/gas ¼. Put the chicken on a platter and replace it in the warm oven.

While the chicken is cooking, prepare the two sauces. For the bread sauce, place the milk, breadcrumbs, onion, thyme and butter in a small saucepan and bring to a simmer. Cover and cook on a very low heat for 30 minutes. Give it a stir two or three times during the cooking to prevent it from sticking to the bottom of the saucepan. Remove from the heat. The sauce can be made up to this point several hours ahead and will be reheated and finished just before serving.

Place the redcurrants, sugar and water in a small saucepan and bring to a simmer. Stir gently to dissolve the sugar and continue to cook on a gentle heat for 5 minutes more. The sauce will look quite thin, but thickens slightly as it cools. This sauce can also be made several hours or indeed days ahead.

To make the chicken gravy, degrease the roasting tin by straining off the fatty liquid into a small bowl. Place the bowl in the freezer to encourage the fat to set on top, so that you can remove it and get at the chicken juices for adding to the gravy. Deglaze the tin with chicken stock, scraping the bottom of the tin with a whisk or wooden spoon to dissolve the caramelised meat juices into the gravy. Season with salt and pepper. Strain the gravy into a small saucepan and bring to a simmer. You could squeeze a very little of the juice from the collapsed lemon inside the chicken into the gravy if that appeals to you. Taste, and if the flavour is thin and light, continue to cook to reduce the liquid and concentrate the flavour.

To serve, carve the chicken on to hot plates or one large hot platter and keep warm. Place the bread sauce back on the heat and remove the onion and the thyme stalk. Many of the leaves will have fallen off the thyme into the sauce. That's perfect. They are exactly where you want them to be. Add the cream and about 4 tablespoons of the chicken gravy and stir to mix well. The consistency of the sauce should be neither too thick nor too thin but like softly whipped cream. Bring to a simmer, taste and correct the seasoning and place in a heated sauce boat. Finally, remove the fat from the chilled chicken juices and save for roasting potatoes or vegetables another day. Add the juices to the gravy. Bring to a simmer.

Serve the carved chicken with the bubbling gravy and the two sauces on the side.

Roast duck with spiced and pickled peaches

Duck is one of my favourite meats and I like it best when it is roasted whole, on the bone, in the old-fashioned way. Cooking the duck this way means it will be cooked through – not pink, not overcooked, just cooked through with a crisp skin and delicious juicy flesh. Ducks are fatty little creatures and if you cook them at the correct temperature you will have a lovely bonus in the shape of duck fat, which when strained and cooled will keep in your fridge for months. This fat can be used for roasting vegetables, sautéing potatoes, cooking sausages and so on.

The rich dark meat calls out for a little fruit of some description to eat with it. Think of some of the classic combinations such as duck with orange, duck with blackcurrants, and duck with apples; here I am suggesting lightly spiced and pickled peaches. These peaches are also very good with ham or bacon. The duck in this recipe is simply roasted with a little seasoning and some citrus rind in the cavity to lightly perfume the flesh. The gravy is light and similar to all the gravies in this chapter on roasts.

The ingredients
A free-range duck is much more delicious and less greasy than its unfortunate factory-raised cousins.

The peaches should be quite ripe but not necessarily as ripe as if you were going to eat them raw. Nectarines are an excellent substitute.

Remember to use cold water when making the spiced syrup for poaching the peaches. The cold water draws the flavour out of the spices and into the syrup, and that is where you want it.

The spices – star anise, cloves, cinnamon and ginger – should gently flavour the pickling liquid, rather than being too strong and forthright, so don't be tempted to add more than the recipe suggests.

The gravy should not be too thick and syrupy.

Serves 4   1 free-range duck, about 1.8kg
Maldon sea salt and freshly ground black pepper
4 thin strips each of orange and lemon rind
500ml chicken or duck stock

SPICED PEACHES
4 cloves
5cm piece of fresh ginger, peeled and thickly sliced
450g sugar
250ml cold water
125ml white wine vinegar
½ a cinnamon stick
1 star anise
1 red chilli
450g peaches, halved and stoned

Preheat the oven to 180°C/350°F/gas 4. Place the duck on a rack in a roasting tin and season it with salt and pepper. Using a wire rack when roasting the duck will make it easier to strain off the fat. It is a good idea to strain off the fat a couple of times during the cooking so that it doesn't burn. Place the citrus rinds in the duck cavity and put it into the preheated oven. Roast the duck for 1½ hours, or until cooked through.

While the duck is cooking, prepare the spiced peaches. Stick the whole cloves into the sliced ginger. Place the sugar, cold water and vinegar in a small, non-reactive saucepan. Add all the spices and the chilli and bring slowly to the boil. Add the peaches and simmer gently until the fruit is nearly tender. Use a skewer to check. Remove the saucepan from the heat, cover, and allow the peaches to finish cooking in the heat of the pan. Their size and hardness will determine the cooking time. It can take between 10 and 20 minutes.

When the duck is cooked, remove it from the rack and place it on a platter. Lower the oven temperature to 100°C/200°F/gas¼ and return the duck to the warm oven. Strain off any remaining fat from the roasting tin, then place the tin on a low heat and add

4 tablespoons of the peach pickling syrup. Allow it to bubble up and change colour to a light caramel. Do not let it burn. Add the stock and bring back to a simmer. Stir well and season with salt and pepper.

Strain the gravy into a small saucepan and taste. If necessary, simmer the sauce for longer to reduce it slightly and concentrate the flavour.

When ready to serve, carve the duck on to a hot platter and coat lightly with some of the bubbling gravy. Garnish the dish with a couple of the peaches if you wish. Pass the rest of the gravy in a hot sauce boat, and the peaches and their juices in a pretty bowl.

Roast fillet of beef with roast peanuts, Asian dressing, mint and coriander salad

This is a great mixture of flavours and textures to combine with an extravagant fillet of beef. The amount of beef is scant, but there is so much else going on that I find it sufficient.

The sauce, dressing and salad leaves can be prepared in advance, so the final assembly is pretty straightforward. The tingling tastes in this dish are both delicious and refreshing.

The ingredients
Fillet of beef is the tenderest cut of beef and is best served somewhat rare. It dries out considerably if cooked to well done, but you must have it just as you like it.

The salad should include one crisp type of lettuce such as 'Little Gem'.

If possible, get peanuts with their skins on for the peanut sauce, as the skins add a depth of flavour. Please do not be tempted to use roasted salted peanuts for the sauce. It will be disgusting.

The chilli in the Asian dressing should be quite hot, such as a serrano, but taste a tiny bit before using it in the dressing, and add it according to the preferences and heat threshold of your guests. When tasting a raw chilli, taste a tiny bit from the fat middle of the chilli. This is the part of the chilli that gives an accurate indication of the overall heat. Chillies of the same variety can vary in heat, so tasting is really the best way to find out what the true heat is. Chilli fiends might like to use a bird's-eye chilli here.

Serves 4–6
500–600g fillet of beef, trimmed of all gristle
1 tablespoon olive oil, for rubbing on the beef fillet
Maldon sea salt and freshly ground black pepper
3 handfuls of mixed greens such as rocket, mizuna,
    Little Gem and watercress
1 handful of mixed mint and coriander leaves
4 spring onions, finely sliced at an angle

ROAST PEANUT SAUCE
100g unskinned peanuts
1 teaspoon cumin seeds
4 tablespoons water
1 tablespoon peanut or sunflower oil
80ml chicken stock
Maldon sea salt

ASIAN DRESSING
2 tablespoons white wine vinegar
1 tablespoon very finely chopped ginger
1 level tablespoon very finely chopped garlic
2 fresh chillies, seeds removed and very finely chopped
1½ teaspoons soft dark brown sugar
1 level teaspoon freshly ground black pepper
1 tablespoon toasted sesame oil
Maldon sea salt, to taste

Preheat the oven to 200°C/400°F/gas 6. Place the peanuts on a baking sheet and roast for about 25 minutes, until golden brown. Shake the pan occasionally to ensure that the nuts are browning evenly. Remove from the oven and allow to cool completely. Blissfully, they do not need to be peeled.

While the nuts are roasting, dry roast the cumin seeds briefly in a small frying pan and grind to a fine powder. Place the cold peanuts in a food processor with the ground cumin and purée to a thick consistency with the water and oil. Bring the chicken stock to a simmer and add to the peanut purée. The consistency should be similar to pouring cream. Taste and correct the seasoning. Reserve for later.

Mix all the dressing ingredients together, then taste and correct the seasoning.

To assemble the salad, turn the oven up to 220°C/425°F/gas 7. Heat a heavy ovenproof grill pan or roasting tin on the hob. The pan should be nearly smoking hot before you add the beef. Rub the fillet of beef with the olive oil and put it into the pan. Allow it to brown all over, turning it occasionally to achieve an even colour. Season it with salt and pepper, then place it in the oven and roast for 15–20 minutes. Use the 'skewer test' to check how cooked it is. Remove from the tin and place it on a small plate which you have turned over so it is the wrong way up, and this plate should sit on a larger plate. This allows any juices that escape from the meat to drain off and be saved for later. Lower the oven temperature to 100°C/200°F/gas ¼ and put the meat in to rest for 15 minutes.

When ready to serve, toss the salad leaves and herbs in a large over-sized bowl with just enough dressing to make the leaves glisten lightly. Place on hot plates or a platter. Slice the beef into 1cm thick slices and lay over the leaves. Drizzle a little of the peanut sauce over the beef, but not too much. Add any meat juices from the resting plate as well. Add a final flourish of sliced spring onions and serve immediately, passing the extra peanut sauce in a sauce boat.

Roast sirloin of beef
with red wine, tomato and gherkin

Sirloin of beef on the bone is a lovely cut and somewhat easier to carve than the more traditional wing rib. This is another of those cuts of meat that will be best if ordered from your butcher a little time in advance, so as to give him time to put aside a piece of properly hung beef for you. Like most cuts of meat, especially the larger ones, this will sit quite happily after cooking for at least half an hour before you serve it. You can make a simple gravy, which would be lovely, or you can pull out all the stops and make the very grown-up sauce that I am suggesting here. This is serious cooking, not difficult but serious, and when you pull off this sauce, you should clap yourself thunderously on the back.

The sauce takes about an hour to cook. Most of that time, though, it is simmering away on its own and you just have to give the saucepan the odd glance to make sure everything is OK. The sauce can be made a couple of days ahead if you wish.

The combination of flavours in the sauce may seem unusual, but it is delicious. The tomato and gherkin, which are added at the last minute, cut through the richness and are surprisingly successful. I am recommending a 'roast chicken stock' for the sauce (see page 60); that is to say, the bones either raw or from a cooked chicken are roasted before being made into a stock. This gives a deeper flavour and colour, which is excellent and a very good alternative to the 6–8-hour cooked beef stock that a restaurant cook might use here. The sauce is also excellent with a roast fillet of beef or a grilled steak.

The ingredients

Sirloin of beef, here roasted on the bone, is a 'prime' cut and as a result is expensive. Ideally, the meat should have been dry-aged in the traditional way and hung for at least 3 weeks.

The red wine sauce can be made ahead, as it is independent of the roasting of the beef. The sauce will keep for several days in the fridge, or can be frozen.

The gherkins should be the little ones mostly sold as 'cornichons'. Avoid large ones, as they tend to be watery and flabby.

The tomatoes should be really ripe and firm to ensure a good flavour and texture.

Serves 6–8   2.5kg sirloin of beef, on the bone
Maldon sea salt and freshly ground black pepper

THE SAUCE
20g butter
3 shallots, peeled and finely chopped
325ml red wine
2 tablespoons port
2 tablespoons Grand Marnier
900ml roast chicken stock
2 ripe and firm tomatoes, peeled, deseeded and
    cut into 1cm dice
60g gherkins, cut into 3mm dice
50g butter, chilled and diced, for enriching the sauce
Maldon sea salt

The sauce is a bit unusual in that we don't season it until the very end of cooking. If you season it early on, the seasoning will become too concentrated as the liquids reduce and intensify in flavour. In a medium-sized, low-sided, heavy-based saucepan, melt the butter and allow it to foam. Add the shallots and stir to coat in the butter. Cover with a piece of greaseproof paper and the saucepan lid and sweat on a gentle heat for 5 minutes. Remove the lid, add the wine, then bring to a simmer and cook uncovered until the wine is almost completely reduced. The contents of the saucepan will look oily, ugly and unlikely, and like a red shallot purée by now. That's exactly how it should look. Add the port and Grand Marnier and simmer until reduced by half. Add the stock and continue to cook at a simmer until the stock has reduced or evaporated by two-thirds of its original volume.

Strain the shallots from the sauce through a sieve, pressing them to extract every last drop of flavour. Taste the sauce – though it will be still quite thin in consistency, it should have lots of flavour, though it won't be dazzling just yet. That doesn't happen until you add the butter at the end. This is the basic sauce and this is what you can make ahead of time to store in your fridge or freezer. The finishing of the sauce, which takes only a matter of minutes, should be done just as the beef is ready to go to the table.

Preheat the oven to 240°C/475°F/gas 9. Lightly score the fat on the surface of the beef and place it in a roasting tin. Season the beef with salt and pepper and place in the preheated oven. Roast for 15 minutes, then reduce the oven temperature to 180°C/350°F/gas 4 and continue to roast the beef to your liking. When the beef is cooked, remove it from the oven, lower the temperature to 100°C/200°F/gas ¼, then put it back in and leave it to rest for at least 15 minutes and up to an hour.

To finish the sauce, bring back to a simmer. Add the tomatoes and gherkins and the cold diced butter. Swirl the contents of the saucepan to incorporate the butter while still just simmering. It is not until this point that the sauce really reveals its magic. The sauce will be thickened slightly by the butter, though not too much. The consistency should be similar to light pouring cream. Taste and add a pinch of salt if necessary.

Serve the sauce hot, with the carved sirloin of beef.

Roast loin of pork with fennel seeds, chilli and garlic, Bramley apple and plum sauce

A loin or belly of pork, roasted on the bone, with the rind transformed to a crispy burnished golden crackling, is a lovely sight and makes a delicious meal. When buying a piece of pork there needs to be some fat on the meat. A lean piece of pork will lack the juiciness, sweetness and succulence of a fattier joint. Look out for about 7mm of fat on the loin of the pork, and a belly piece should be generously streaked with fat. The excess fat will render out during the cooking, so you won't be eating it all, but if it isn't there to start with you have little chance of success. You can strain the liquid rendered fat, allow it to cool and store it in the fridge for roasting vegetables or frying. It will store happily for at least a month when chilled. Specialist butchers or farmers' markets are probably the best shopping route to a good piece of pork. It can be very dry and disappointing or it can be a proper treat. The pork definitely needs to be free-range to guarantee a delicious result.

To achieve a good crackling, apart from the fat on the pork, you will need to score the rind before the pork is cooked. A very sharp small knife or a Stanley knife will work perfectly. The meat is scored at 1cm intervals, in the direction that you will be carving it.

The added flavourings here of fennel seeds, chilli and garlic work brilliantly with the sweet pork meat. The traditional apple sauce with the addition of plums pairs really well with these southern European flavourings. The gravy is simple and light.

The ingredients
Watch out for pork from old breeds such as Gloucester Old Spot, Saddleback, Red Duroc and Black Berkshire for juicy and flavoursome meat.

Fennel seeds have a sweet and aniseed-like flavour and are lovely with pork.

Dried chillies, with their deep and slightly smoky heat, enliven this dish.

Bitter Bramley-type cooking apples and dark red plums are best for the accompanying sauce.

Star anise is a beautiful, sweet and aromatic spice but needs to be used with restraint. Too much can result in an over-the-top, pot-pourri-type flavour.

Serves 6–8   2.25kg loin or belly of pork, on the bone, with the rind on
1 tablespoon fennel seeds
2–4 cloves of garlic, peeled
2 dried chillies or 2 teaspoons chilli flakes
Maldon sea salt and freshly ground black pepper
500ml chicken stock
2 tablespoons finely chopped flat-leaf parsley

Preheat the oven to 190°C/375°F/gas 5.

Score the pork rind at 1cm intervals, running with the grain of the meat. If you are worried about this, ask your butcher to do it for you. Grind the fennel seeds to a coarse powder with a pestle and mortar. Add the garlic and chilli and a pinch of sea salt and continue to grind to a paste. Season the pork with a pinch of salt and black pepper. Place it on a wire rack in a roasting tin and roast the loin for 1 hour or if using belly for 40 minutes. Remove from the oven and spread on the spice paste. Replace in the oven and roast for a further 40 minutes. By now the juices should be running clear, and if you do the 'skewer test' on the pork, the skewer will be hot. Baste the pork several times during the cooking.

Remove the pork from the oven and place it in another roasting tin. Increase the oven temperature to 230°C/450°F/gas 8 and return the pork for a further 10 minutes to give the rind a final crisping. Remove from the oven and lower the temperature to 100°C/200°F/gas ¼. Put the pork on a plate and return it to the oven to keep warm and rest for at least 15 minutes before carving.

To make the gravy, degrease the first roasting tin thoroughly, saving the fat if you wish. Deglaze the tin with the chicken stock, scraping the tin to dislodge any caramelised meat juices. Strain the liquid through a sieve into a small saucepan. Taste and correct the seasoning, and if necessary continue to cook the gravy to reduce and to concentrate the flavour. Add the parsley just before serving.

Carve the pork into neat slices and serve on hot plates, with the bubbling gravy and the apple sauce on the side.

Apple and plum sauce

Serves 6–8   450g Bramley apples
                 4 plums
                 2 tablespoons sugar
                 2 tablespoons water

Peel, quarter and core the apples. Cut each quarter in half. Place in a small saucepan with the sugar and water. Quarter the plums and remove the stones and add to the apples. Cover the saucepan with a tight fitting lid and cook on a very low heat. The apples and plums will collapse to a frothy fluff. Allow to cool a little and then lift the skins off the pieces of plum. Stir gently to mix the apples and the plums, taste and if necessary add another pinch of sugar.

The benefit of this method of cooking is that the juices that the bird releases are trapped in the covered and sealed pot, and you end up with the purest-tasting liquid.

Casserole-roasting

This cooking technique is invaluable. The aim is to cook the main ingredient in a tightly sealed casserole so as to achieve succulent flesh and trap all the precious cooking juices. These richly flavoured juices then become the basis for the sauce. Chicken, guinea fowl, quail, turkey, pheasant, grouse and partridge all cook beautifully in this way.

There is much to be learned from the process and it is worth pulling the two words apart to understand what is going on. 'Casserole' suggests a heavy pot with a lid, and 'roasting' suggests no liquid, and that is basically what happens here. The ingredient of choice – in this instance we will concentrate on fowl – is cooked dry, in a heavy pot with a tight-fitting lid. The result and benefit of this method of cooking is that the juices that the bird releases are trapped in the covered and sealed pot, and you end up with the purest-tasting juices. This liquid then becomes the basis for your sauce, or in fact sometimes can simply be the sauce. Flavourings of your choice can be added to the bird before cooking or can be added to the juices at the end. The other benefit is that by cooking the bird whole one also maximises the flavour of the flesh, with the flavour from the skin and bones imbuing both the meat and the juices. The texture of the bird cooked whole is also generally superior to that of jointed portions, and another advantage is having the leftover carcass for stock. If you are lucky enough to be able to scrape enough leftover flesh from the cooked carcass for a sandwich, all the better.

The range of flavours that can be added when using this cooking technique are many, and some of them are explored in the following recipes.

A chicken browned to a golden colour – ready for covering and casserole-roasting

Keys to success
Choose **a heavy casserole with a tight-fitting lid.**

Heat the casserole over a gentle heat and **carefully brown the main ingredient,** for example chicken, making sure neither the casserole nor the ingredient burns. If the casserole does burn at this stage, cut your losses and clean it before proceeding. This is not ideal, as you will have lost some of the precious caramelised meat juices, but at least the sauce will not taste burnt at the end.

Season and cover with a tight-fitting lid. If your lid is not quite securely sealed, place a sheet of greaseproof paper or foil underneath to act as another layer of insulation.

Cook the ingredient as directed and check to ensure that it is fully cooked.

Remove the ingredient and keep warm in the oven with the temperature reduced to 110°C/225°F/gas ½, bearing in mind that most meats and poultry are best served quite warm rather than red hot.

Degrease the cooking juices by using a degreaser or carefully spooning off the fat. Add any additional ingredients and finish the sauce. If the sauce is a creamy one, avoid having it too thick.

Casserole-roast chicken with French tarragon

Tarragon is a wonderful herb and pairs beautifully with chicken. The sauce here will be rich and scant and should not be too thick.

The ingredients
Use best-quality chicken for this recipe. There is a world of difference between the flavour and texture of a happy free-ranging organic chicken and that of a trapped battery bird.

Justify the extra cost of the organic or free-range bird by not wasting a scrap and by saving the carcass for stock.

Try to find French tarragon, especially if you are going to plant it in your garden – it has a far superior flavour to its cousin Russian tarragon, which is the wild form of the plant. The French version is low-growing and can only be grown from a root cutting, whereas the tall Russian tarragon can be grown from seed.

The cream in this recipe adds richness and essentially makes this dish into a classic French tarragon chicken.

Serves 6
1 free-range chicken, about 1.3kg
20g butter, softened
2 heaped tablespoons tarragon leaves
225ml regular or double cream
Maldon sea salt and freshly ground black pepper

Preheat the oven to 180°C/350°F/gas 4. Put a heavy casserole on a gentle heat.

Rub the breast of the chicken dry with kitchen paper, then smear it with half the butter. Place the chicken, breast side down, in the heated casserole. The butter should sizzle a bit and that tells you the casserole is hot enough. If it doesn't sizzle, whip out the chicken immediately and allow the casserole to get hotter. Allow the chicken breasts to become golden brown, making sure the casserole doesn't get so hot that it actually burns the butter. This will involve a bit of manoeuvring, perhaps sitting the chicken on its side and so on. Season the coloured chicken breasts with salt and pepper. Chop half the tarragon, then mix it with the remaining butter and smear it over the browned chicken breasts. Stuff any tarragon stalks into the cavity of the chicken and sit the chicken, breast side up, in the casserole. Cover with a sheet of greaseproof paper and a tight-fitting lid. Place in the preheated oven and cook for 90 minutes.

Remove the casserole from the oven and check to ensure that the chicken is fully cooked. Lower the oven temperature to 110°C/225°F/gas ¼. Take the chicken out of the casserole, place it on a dish, cover with the greaseproof paper and put it back into the oven to rest for at least 15 minutes.

Strain all the cooking juices into a bowl and allow them to settle for a minute or two. The butter and chicken fat will rise to the surface. Spoon off the fat, saving it for other uses, and pour the degreased juices back into the casserole. Chop the remaining tarragon leaves and add with the cream. Allow to come to a simmer again and let the sauce thicken slightly, just enough to lightly coat the back of a spoon. This will take only a matter of minutes, so watch it carefully. If the sauce is on the heat for too long and becomes too thick, add a little chicken stock or water to correct the consistency. Taste and correct the seasoning.

Carve the chicken and place on a heated serving dish. Serve with some of the hot sauce poured over. Do not drown the chicken in sauce – pass any extra in a hot sauce boat.

Serve with Glazed Carrots (see page 280) and new potatoes. Save any leftover chicken for a sandwich on White Soda Bread (see page 375) with mayonnaise and chives.

Casserole-roast chicken with Indian spices

Sometimes when I want a spiced chicken dish I want a no-holds-barred, hot and spicy experience. Other times, I am in the mood for tender and succulent slices of chicken with a lightly spiced, thin cream or juice to accompany it. This recipe is the latter. The chicken is casserole-roasted with a light sprinkling of spices and fragrant green chillies. The spiced cooking juices with the addition of cream become the light sauce. The chillies will collapse in the cooking, but infuse the sauce with their own special flavour. Some people will want to eat the cooked chillies, others will avoid them.

The ingredients

Green chillies, when left on the plant, will eventually ripen and become red – or, in some varieties, yellow or orange. I suggest using a cayenne, jalapeño or serrano chilli here.

The underripe green chilli can have the same intensity of heat as a ripened red one, but has quite a different, somehow greener and more refreshing flavour.

The particular variety of chilli you choose will determine the level of heat it has, but even specific chillies will vary in heat from time to time. The best way to ensure you have the level of heat that you like is to taste a tiny bit of the chilli before you use it. Cut a tiny piece of the raw flesh from the middle of the chilli, no bigger than a cumin seed, and taste. This way you will know exactly what amount of heat you are dealing with and can decide how much is appropriate for you and your guests.

Use whole spices for this recipe and roast and grind them, as directed on page 23. This combination of spices is a mild and aromatic one.

Serves 6

1 heaped teaspoon lightly toasted and ground
   coriander seeds
1 heaped teaspoon lightly toasted and ground cumin seeds
¼ teaspoon ground turmeric
Pinch of chilli powder
Maldon sea salt and freshly ground black pepper
20g butter, softened
1 free-range chicken, about 1.3kg
4 green chillies
2 tablespoons lemon juice
225ml regular or double cream
2 tablespoons chopped coriander leaves

Preheat the oven to 180°C/350°F/gas 4.

Mix the ground coriander, cumin, turmeric and chilli powder with a pinch of salt. Stir this spice mix into half the butter.

Heat a heavy casserole on a gentle heat. Rub the breasts of the chicken dry with kitchen paper and smear the whole chicken with the remaining butter. Place it, breast side down, in the heated casserole. The butter should sizzle a bit and that tells you the casserole is hot enough. If it doesn't sizzle, whip out the chicken immediately and allow the casserole to get hotter. Allow the chicken breasts to become golden brown, making sure the casserole doesn't get so hot that it actually burns the butter. This will involve a bit of manoeuvring, perhaps sitting the chicken on its side and so on. Season the coloured chicken breasts with a pinch of salt and pepper. Allow to cool for a few minutes and then smear the spiced butter all over them.

Put the chicken back into the casserole, breast side up. Pop the chillies around the chicken and sprinkle over the lemon juice. Cover with greaseproof paper and a tight-fitting lid and place in the preheated oven. Cook for 90 minutes.

Remove the casserole from the oven and check that the chicken is fully cooked. Reduce the oven temperature to 110°C/225°F/gas ½.

Take the cooked chicken and the chillies, which by now will be collapsed and a bit sad-looking, out of the casserole and put them on a dish. Cover them with greaseproof paper and put them back into the oven to keep warm for at least 15 minutes.

Strain all the cooking juices into a bowl and allow them to settle for a minute or two. The butter and chicken fat will rise to the surface of the liquid. Spoon off the buttery fat, now full of the flavour of the spices, and save it for roasting vegetables. It is particularly good with parsnips or for tossing into crushed new potatoes. Place the degreased juices back in the casserole and add the cream. Bring to a simmer and cook until the sauce is lightly thickened. Add the chopped coriander leaves, then taste and correct the seasoning.

Carve the chicken neatly and serve with the sauce. The chillies should be used to garnish the dish and heat fiends will find them delicious to eat. Serve with plain boiled rice or boiled new potatoes.

Casserole-roast chicken with watercress

I have a strong affection for watercress. I love its fresh peppery and green taste when eaten raw in a salad and I love it when it is lightly cooked to release even more of its generous flavour. It is high in vitamin C, has more calcium than full-cream milk and has more iron than spinach. When I first started cooking in the kitchen at Ballymaloe House, I was offered an extra daily task of collecting watercress to supplement my minimalist apprentice wages, so the cress and I go back a long way. I got to know every little stream it grew in, within a ten-mile radius of the hotel. A clean and fast-running stream with no sheep in sight was always the goal. Some of the streams were obvious, some were well hidden. Some were easy to access, others required an almost trapeze-artist-like balance to reach the quarry. I got to recognise its purple-tinged colour after a frost and how at certain times of the year it looked practically identical to its growing companion,

wild celery. I could tell from fifty yards if it was tough or tender. I came to know that, maddeningly, cattle or cows would clear a patch in no time, if allowed access to it, leaving the previously abundant crop looking as if a scythe had been pulled through it. I knew when its little white flowers were pleasant to eat and when they were just too big and bitter. I got to know how a dry spell would wilt and toughen it and make the leaves fade, and how a mild and wet spell would have it leaping out of the ground, the colour of hay barn green.

If you decide to go foraging yourself, make sure you find a really clean source, the ultimate site being a spring. There are many stories in Irish folklore about holy wells and the value both mental and physical of the watercress that sometimes flourished there. Probably the most well known of these wells is St Brendan's Well, at Birr Castle in Co. Offaly. Perhaps you could make a watercress pilgrimage there.

Of course you can also buy cultivated watercress, which when fresh is excellent, and that will be the realistic option for most cooks. Look for vibrant and fresh-looking bunches and wash it several times in plenty of cold water.

The ingredients
Watercress, while peppery when eaten raw, becomes sweet and aromatic when lightly cooked.

If you go foraging for wild watercress, it is essential to ensure you have found a clean source.

The top leaf on sprigs of watercress is always the biggest, whereas the top leaf on wild celery, which often grows beside it in the wild, is the smallest.

After removing the tender leaves from the watercress, save the tough stalks and stuff them into the chicken cavity.

Watercress is delicious eaten raw, but it really releases its sweet, peppery and pungent flavour when heated.

Serves 6   1 free-range chicken, about 1.6kg
               10g butter, softened
               Maldon sea salt and freshly ground black pepper
               110g watercress leaves, weighed after removing the tough
                    stalks (reserve these for stuffing into the chicken cavity)
               2 cloves of garlic, peeled
               225ml regular or double cream

Preheat the oven to 180°C/350°F/gas 4.

Heat a heavy casserole on a gentle heat. Rub the breasts of the chicken dry with kitchen paper and smear them with the soft butter. Place the chicken, breast side down, in the heated casserole. The butter should sizzle a bit and that tells you the casserole is hot enough. If it doesn't sizzle, whip out the chicken immediately and allow the casserole to get hotter. Allow the chicken breasts to become golden brown, making sure the casserole doesn't get so hot that it actually burns the butter. This will involve a bit of manoeuvring, perhaps sitting the chicken on its side and so on. Season the coloured chicken breasts with salt and pepper. Stuff any watercress stalks into the cavity of the chicken and sit it, breast side up, in the casserole. Add the peeled cloves of garlic and cover with a sheet of greaseproof paper and a tight-fitting lid. Place in the oven and cook for 90 minutes.

Remove the chicken from the casserole and check that it is fully cooked. Place on a dish and cover it with greaseproof paper. Reduce the oven temperature to 110°C/225°F/gas ¼ and put the chicken back in to keep warm for 15 minutes.

Chop the watercress leaves. Strain all the cooking juices from the casserole into a bowl. Place the empty casserole back on a medium heat and add the chopped watercress and the garlic that has been cooked with the chicken. Crush the garlic, which by now will be soft, into a paste and add a pinch of salt. Cook until the watercress starts to wilt and you smell it starting to release its sweet aroma. This only takes about 3 minutes. Remove the fat from the chicken juices with a spoon and add the juices to the watercress. Allow to come to a simmer, then add the cream. Allow to come to a simmer again and let the sauce thicken slightly, just enough to lightly coat the back of a spoon. If you prefer a sauce with a smoother consistency, you can give the sauce a quick purée with a hand-held blender. Taste and correct the seasoning.

Carve the chicken and serve with the hot sauce. Accompany with boiled new potatoes with mint and Glazed Carrots (see page 280).

Casserole-roast chicken
with shallots, garlic and marjoram

This is so easy and so good, and sometimes that is the thrill of cooking. I hope if you cook this, using a good chicken, you will be delighted by the simplicity of the dish and the purity of taste of the cooking juices. The joy here is that when you take the lid off the casserole, the job is done.

Marjoram is perhaps my desert island herb. I would miss lots of the others for sure, but if marooned, and only allowed one, this would be it. There is a bit of confusion around marjoram, and the one I like best is called sweet, knotted or annual marjoram. If you are buying seeds or plants to grow, which I encourage, this is the one you want. You need to be specific, as some of the varieties, like pot marjoram, are coarser and while they certainly have their uses, are not what is called for here.

Follow the recipe carefully and you will have a master technique that you can use year round. French tarragon can replace the marjoram with wonderful results. The buttery, marjoram-infused, allium-flavoured chicken juices are the sauce. The cloves of garlic and the shallots are the vegetable. There won't be a lot of sauce, but it has that 'cooked on the bone' intensity of flavour which, when tasted, seems as though it is entering your veins rather than your stomach. All you need to accompany this are some boiled potatoes and maybe some carrots or spinach.

It sounds like a lot of garlic and shallot in the recipe, but when you cook both of these members of the allium family in this way, they are transformed from being sharp and aggressive to being mild, timid and delectable. The cooked garlic and shallots should be soft, slightly collapsed but still vaguely holding their shape. Don't try to be clever here and have them all firm and cheffy. That would really miss the point. There is a time for firmness, and this is not it.

The ingredients
Shallots are more delicate in flavour than onions and will cook to a 'melting' consistency. However, the sweet and mild new season onions are excellent here instead of shallots. Leave about 10cm of the onion greens attached.

The garlic cloves are left unpeeled. You just squeeze out the melting soft flesh when eating the dish.

Marjoram, like tarragon, should be mixed into a dish immediately it has been chopped. If left exposed to the air after chopping, it oxidises and gets bitter almost immediately.

Serves 6

1 free-range chicken, about 1.3kg
10g butter, softened
2 sprigs of marjoram
Maldon sea salt and freshly ground black pepper
2 heads of garlic, cloves separated and unpeeled
12–16 shallots, peeled, or 12–16 new season onions, cleaned and with 10cm of greens attached
2 heaped tablespoons chopped marjoram

Preheat the oven to 180°C/350°F/gas 4.

Heat a heavy casserole on a gentle heat. Rub the breasts of the chicken dry with kitchen paper and smear them with the soft butter. Place the chicken, breast side down, in the heated casserole. The butter should sizzle a bit and that tells you the casserole is hot enough. If it doesn't sizzle, whip out the chicken immediately and allow the casserole to get hotter. Allow the chicken breasts to become golden brown, making sure the casserole doesn't get so hot that it actually burns the butter. This will involve a bit of manoeuvring, perhaps sitting the chicken on its side and so on. When the chicken is properly coloured, place it breast side up, season with salt and pepper and place the sprigs of marjoram in the cavity.

Scatter the garlic, shallots or onions and chopped marjoram around the chicken. Season with salt and pepper and turn them with a spoon to mix in the herbs. Cover with greaseproof paper and a tight-fitting lid. Place in the preheated oven and cook for 90 minutes. Test to ensure that the chicken is properly cooked.

When the chicken is cooked, remove it from the casserole and place on an oven tray. Reduce the oven temperature to 110°C/225°F/gas ¼ and put the chicken back in to rest for at least 15 minutes. Taste the chicken juices and with a tablespoon remove any excess fat. Correct the seasoning if necessary and keep warm.

Carve the chicken and serve with the hot juices, shallots or onions and garlic.

Serve with Summer Courgette, Potato, Olive Oil and Sweet Marjoram Mash (see page 314) and a Winter Salad of Organic Greens (see page 124).

Casserole-roast guinea fowl with marjoram

Guinea fowl, sometimes referred to as 'the Bohemian Pheasant' or 'the bohemian of the farmyard', is a delicious bird. Native to Africa and now domesticated in this part of the world, this beautiful bird with its speckled plumage and busy nature makes a horrendous racket, and as a result was often included in a farmyard poultry flock, as a noisy deterrent to vermin. They need fencing in well, as they are very inquisitive by nature and will bolt if given the slightest chance. Not nearly as well known as the chicken or turkey, this richly flavoured bird makes wonderful eating. Roasted, grilled, braised or, as in this case, casserole-roasted, it is versatile and accepts lots of different flavours. Somewhat more slender than a chicken and with less fat, this bird needs careful cooking, so as not to cause the flesh to become dry. The birds generally feed just two people, so I have allowed two birds here, to feed four. The marjoram in the recipe can be replaced with tarragon or lemon thyme, but really the marjoram is the stand-out herb for this handsome creature. The cream gives the sauce a silky consistency, but feel free to eat this dish just with the cooking juices as they come from the casserole.

The ingredients

Four ingredients here, six if you count the salt and pepper, but enough going on to create a most delicious dish.

Try to get a free-range or organic guinea fowl.

Guinea fowl are less fatty than chicken, and for that reason casserole-roasting them helps to keep them juicy and prevents them drying out during the cooking.

Marjoram and guinea fowl is a heavenly combination of flavours.

Don't allow the sauce to become too thick and heavy.

Serves 4   2 guinea fowl
10g butter
2 tablespoons chopped marjoram
Maldon sea salt and freshly ground black pepper
225ml regular or double cream

Preheat the oven to 180°C/350°F/gas 4.

On a gentle heat, heat a casserole that the two birds will fit snugly into. Smear half the butter over the breasts of the guinea fowl and place, breast side down, in the preheated casserole. The buttered breasts should sizzle gently the moment they hit the bottom of the casserole. If this doesn't happen, whip out the birds and allow the casserole to get hotter. Continue to cook on a moderate heat until the breasts are golden brown. It is vital that neither the birds nor the bottom of the casserole burn at this stage, as this will taint the birds and the sauce at the end of cooking. In the event of the casserole burning, cut your losses and wipe out the bottom of the casserole with a clean towel. The problem with wiping out the casserole is that you are removing some of the lightly caramelised juices that contribute to the flavour of the sauce at the end of cooking. However, we all know that black is burnt, but don't be too depressed, as you will learn from this and will be more careful the next time.

Turn the guinea fowl breast side up in the pot. Add half the chopped marjoram to the remaining butter and smear it over the coloured breasts. Push any marjoram stalks into the cavities. Season with salt and pepper, cover with a sheet of greaseproof paper and the tight-fitting casserole lid and place in the preheated oven for about 45 minutes.

Test the birds in the same way as you would a chicken to determine that they are cooked. As soon as they are ready, take the casserole out of the oven and lower the temperature to 110°C/225°F/gas ¼. Take the guinea fowl out of the casserole, put them on a plate, cover with greaseproof paper and put back into the oven to rest for at least 15 minutes.

Degrease the cooking juices by carefully spooning off the buttery fat from the surface of the liquid or by passing the juices through a mais-gras. Add the cream to the degreased juices, bring to a simmer and cook on a gentle heat to thicken the sauce slightly. The sauce should just lightly coat the back of a spoon. This doesn't take too long, a matter of minutes really. If the sauce becomes too thick, thin it with a little chicken stock or juices that may have gathered under the resting birds, or failing that, some water. Add the remaining marjoram to the sauce and stir in. Taste and correct the seasoning.

Carve the guinea fowl neatly, and if any juices have collected on the plate the birds were resting on, spoon those over the meat. Serve on hot plates, with the hot sauce and chosen vegetable.

Casserole-roast pheasant with red wine and bacon

Pheasant is a delicious meat and generally speaking excellent value for money. The lean birds can be a little dry though, so I like to casse-role-roast them, finding the result juicier than a traditional roast, and with the addition of a few robust flavours the bird is almost self-saucing. When buying a pheasant, have a good look at what is on offer and choose the plumpest-looking bird. The addition of cinnamon may seem a little odd, but it adds a delicious scent to the cooking juices.

Serves 2
100g rindless fat streaky bacon
1 tablespoon olive oil
1 plump pheasant
150ml red wine, e.g. Cabernet Sauvignon
100g tinned or bottled tomatoes, finely chopped
½ a cinnamon stick
1 sprig of rosemary, about 6cm long
Maldon sea salt and freshly ground black pepper
25g butter (optional)

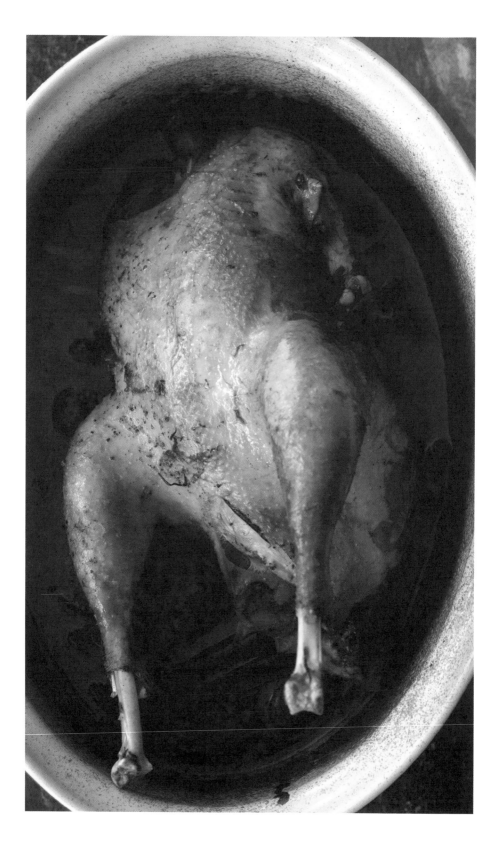

Preheat the oven to 180°C/350°F/gas 4.

Cut the bacon into fine lardons, about 3cm long and 5mm thick. Heat a heavy casserole on a gentle heat until quite hot. Add the olive oil and then the bacon, stirring it regularly with a wooden spoon and allowing it to become slightly crisp and golden. Remove from the casserole and leave to drain on kitchen paper.

Dry the breast of the pheasant and place it, breast side down, in the fat remaining in the casserole. Cook gently until the breast is a golden colour. Do not try to rush this stage of the recipe, otherwise you may burn the casserole, in which case the flavour of the sauce at the end will be spoiled. Remove the pheasant from the pan and pour off the excess fat. Replace the casserole on a low heat and add the wine, tomatoes, cinnamon, rosemary and bacon. Place the pheasant on top and season with salt and pepper. Place a piece of greaseproof paper and a tight-fitting lid on the casserole and cook in the oven for 1 hour.

When the bird is cooked, remove the casserole from the oven and reduce the temperature to 100°C/200°F/gas ¼. Put the pheasant on a dish, cover it with greaseproof paper, and put it back into the oven to keep warm. Place the casserole on a gentle heat and bring the juices to a simmer. Taste and decide if the liquid needs to reduce a little to concentrate the flavour. If it already tastes delicious, you are ready to go. I sometimes swirl a little butter into the juices at this stage, just to give the sauce a little more body – however, the sauce should not become too thick and strong.

Carve the pheasant neatly and serve with the bubbling sauce, and either Savoy Cabbage Purée (see page 266) or Brussels Sprouts with Brown Butter and Almonds (see page 265).

To be sure that the fish is cooked, pull back a little of the skin at the thickest point and with a small knife check that the flesh lifts away easily from the bone.

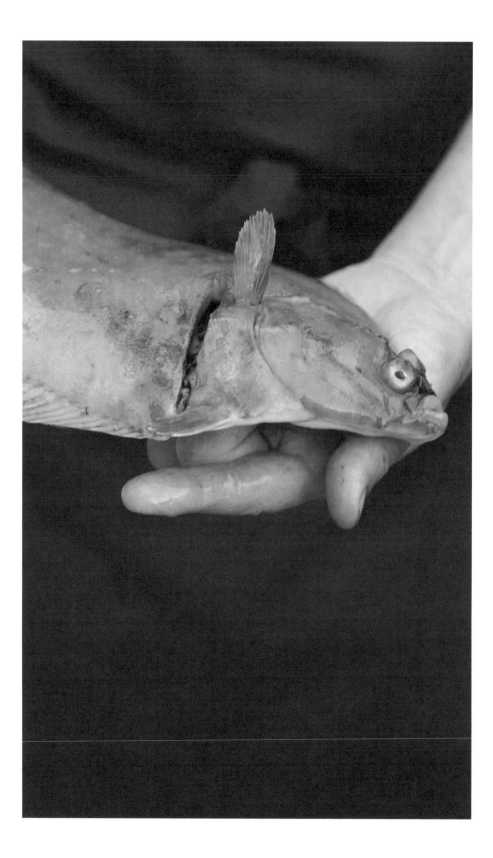

Baked fish

In this chapter, there are several different methods for baking fish.

Whole flat fish baked on the bone
Baking fish on the bone is a lovely technique that is particularly suitable for flat fish such as summer plaice, turbot, brill, and Dover and lemon soles. The resulting flesh is moist, tender and flavoursome, benefiting greatly from the skin and bone of the fish as it is cooking.

Fish fillets baked in foil parcels or 'en papillote'
Baking fillets of fish in foil parcels is easy. The hermetically sealed parcels trap and accentuate the flavour of the fish and its seasonings, and yield delicious juices to make this dish self-saucing.

Fish fillets baked on baking parchment
Baking fish on baking parchment is again easy and quick, and ideally suited to oily and firm-fleshed fish such as mackerel, bass, mullet and salmon.

Fish fillets baked 'au gratin'
Thicker fillets of round fish such as hake, pollock and cod are ideal for a gratin. The suggested recipe can be conveniently assembled ahead of time, chilled and cooked later. The use of the word gratin suggests a dish with a comforting bubbling sauce and a golden topping.

Whole flat fish baked on the bone

This is a great technique for cooking flat fish. Myrtle Allen, at Bally-maloe House, came up with the method and it was in her kitchen that I learned how to do this.

Ideally, a large fish is required for this cooking technique, one that will feed 4 people. Failing that, smaller fish can be used, but the bigger fish have rather more meaty and succulent flesh.

My favoured fish for cooking in this way is plaice. You might be a bit surprised by that choice, especially if you have only ever tasted watery and roe-filled plaice whose flesh is thin and tasteless. How-ever, when plaice are big and fat during the summer months, it is a revelation. When I was cooking at Ballymaloe, our fish came from the local fishing village of Ballycotton, where day boats landed fabu-lous mixed boxes of fish. Large plaice, so fresh they curled at the head and tail end, decorated on their upper side by fingerprints of the deepest tangerine colour and with perfectly white underbellies, were always a thrilling sight to me. They remain so to this day, and I still get my fish from Ballycotton.

Any of the other flat fish are also splendid cooked like this. The grand and expensive turbot, many people's favourite fish, and the quite similar brill both work perfectly. Dover sole, once allowed to relax for a day after being caught, and its relation the lemon sole are particularly good. The Dover sole is quite unusual in that it is too tough to eat the day it is caught, hence the need for it to tenderise for a day before eating.

There are a variety of different sauces to serve with fish cooked this way, from a very simple herb butter to a more complex Bretonne or beurre blanc sauce.

The fish, carefully cleaned, and with its head attached or removed, is scored on the top side through the skin. This cut continues all the way around the edge, just above the frill. The fish is then baked in a shallow pool of water in the oven. The advantages are obvious, in that by cooking the fish on the bone and with its skin still intact, you really capture the flavour of the fish, the skin and bone adding a tre-mendous amount to the taste of the cooked fish. The peripheral scoring of the fish facilitates easy removal of the skin after cooking.

The skin of the fish, cut through all the way round and crossing
at the tail to form an X

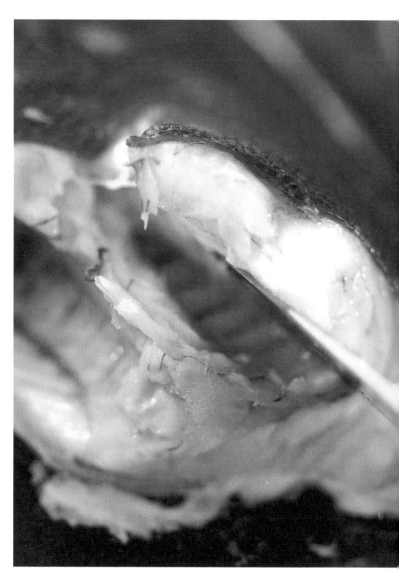

Checking that the flesh lifts away easily from the bone, to be
sure that the fish is cooked

Generally, the skin, both top and bottom, is discarded, but I have certainly in the case of brill and turbot received requests for the soft, white underskin during my restaurant cooking days.

Even though I specify which type of flat fish to cook for each recipe, these are my personal choices, so feel free to change around the combinations of fish and sauce. Once you have mastered the technique involved in preparing the fish, you will approach the cooking of flat fish in this manner, with no fear.

Keys to success

When preparing the fish, make sure you **wash out any trace of blood**, otherwise the cooked flesh may taste a little bitter.

When cutting the skin of the fish before cooking, make sure your knife actually **cuts through the skin** rather than just marking it.

Don't drown the fish on the baking tray, but use just enough water as directed to prevent it from sticking to the tray.

To be sure that the fish is cooked, pull back a little of the skin at the thickest point and with a small knife check that the **flesh lifts away easily** from the bone.

Do not remove the skin of the cooked fish until you are ready to serve it.

Baked brill with Bretonne sauce

Brill is a very fine fish, flat and broad, with a smooth stone-coloured skin on top and a white underside. It is expensive, so therefore a treat, and as a result the sauce being served with it should reflect this. If the sauce is a simple olive oil, it should be really good extra virgin olive oil; if it is butter it should be real butter. The firm-textured and flavoursome flesh will accept all sorts of flavours. It bakes beautifully, revealing, when the cooked skin is lifted off, glossy and juicy, pearl-coloured flesh.

If making a hollandaise sauce strikes fear into you, then maybe this sauce, which is easier, will give you more confidence. The sauce, apart from being delicious with flat fish, is also great for prawns and shrimps and is surprisingly good with oily fish like mackerel and salmon. It is an immensely useful sauce that I predict you will use over and over again. It is rich, so should not be too thick when being served. I usually stir a few tablespoons of the fish cooking water into the sauce before serving. This thins the sauce to the consistency you require and also adds a little of the flavour of the skin and bones of the fish.

The ingredients
Brill, with its firm texture and fine flavour, handles this sauce beautifully.

Free-range eggs and good butter will make this sauce delicious.

The green tarragon-flavoured mustard which gives this sauce a particular flavour and colour can be replaced quite successfully with a yellow Dijon mustard.

The last-minute addition of the herbs to the sauce ensures their bright green flavour and colour.

Serves 4   1 large brill or other flat fish, weighing about 1.4kg
Maldon sea salt

BRETONNE SAUCE
2 egg yolks
1 teaspoon green tarragon-flavoured mustard or
    Dijon mustard
½ teaspoon vinegar or lemon juice
110g butter
1 generous tablespoon mixed chopped herbs:
    chives, parsley, chervil, tarragon and a small pinch
    of thyme leaves

Preheat the oven to 180°C/350°F/gas 4.

Place the fish, dark side up, on a sturdy chopping board. With a sharp knife, remove the head if you wish. Starting at the top of the fish, near where the head was, cut through the skin, into the flesh, just inside the 'frill' and continue all the way around the fish. The cuts on either side of the edge of the fish should meet and overlap at the tail, forming an X. This facilitates the easy removal of the skin after cooking. Give the fish a good wash, being particularly careful to remove the little blood clot at the top of the backbone.

Put 5mm of water into a shallow baking tray or roasting pan and slide in the fish. Sprinkle a pinch of salt over the skin. Place the fish in the preheated oven and cook for 20–30 minutes. To test if the fish is cooked, insert a knife into the thickest part of the flesh at the head end. The flesh should be white and firm, with no trace of pink, and willing to come away easily from the bone. Watch the water level in the tray during cooking, topping up the water a little if the pan looks like it might go dry.

When the fish is cooked, you can leave it on the tray in the oven with the temperature lowered to 100°C/200°F/gas ¼, for up to 30 minutes.

While the fish is cooking, make the Bretonne sauce, which is what is known as a warm emulsion sauce. What happens here is that when you whisk the hot melted butter into the egg yolks, an emulsion is formed. The two disparate ingredients blend together to form a sauce with a creamy and smooth consistency, and that is the way you want to keep them. The sauce is served warm, not hot. It cannot be reheated over a direct heat, so you need to keep it warm. So when the sauce is cooked, transfer it into a Pyrex jug and sit the jug in a small saucepan of water which you then place on the lowest heat you can manage on your cooker. It will sit quite happily like this for an hour.

Place the egg yolks in a small bowl with the mustard and vinegar or lemon juice and whisk to mix. Melt the butter and bring to the boil. Remove from the heat. Now, in a very slow drizzle, pour the hot melted butter on to the eggs, whisking all the time. The sauce will gradually begin to thicken. This does not mean you can add the butter more quickly – there is only a certain speed at which the eggs can absorb the butter and emulsify. Continue until all the melted butter, including the creamy and sometimes salty bits at the end, have been added. The sauce should be the consistency of pouring cream. If it is a bit too thick, add a little of the fish cooking water from the baking tray to achieve the correct consistency. Keep warm as directed above. Add the chopped herbs to the sauce just before you are going to serve it.

Serve the fish on the bone or filleted, on hot plates with the warm sauce. Garnish with a relevant herb of your choice and pass lemon wedges.

Baked turbot with shrimps and wild garlic leaves

Turbot fits many people's idea of the ideal fish. Similar in appearance to brill, but with distinctive little sharp lumps on its upper side acting as a mild form of armour, firm-textured, highly flavoured and white-fleshed, it is certainly one of the best fish to eat. As with any fish, freshness is key. If you are buying a turbot, it will be expensive and you need to be sure it is of the best quality so that you get value for the money you are spending.

The shrimps and garlic in this recipe combine well with the robustly flavoured and textured fish. The sauce is light but the ingredients all pack a punch.

The ingredients
The wild garlic leaves in the recipe can be replaced with chives when the garlic is out of season.

For this dish the olive oil should be a good one and not too peppery.

The shrimps should smell sweet and fresh.

Serves 4
1 turbot, about 1.4kg in weight
Maldon sea salt

SAUCE
8 tablespoons fish cooking water
100g cooked and peeled shrimps
1 clove of garlic, peeled and crushed
4 tablespoons finely chopped wild garlic leaves or chives
zest and juice of ½ a lemon
4 tablespoons olive oil
Maldon sea salt and freshly ground black pepper

Preheat the oven to 180°C/350°F/gas 4.

Place the turbot, dark side up, on a sturdy chopping board. With a sharp knife, remove the head if you wish, being economical in removing just the head and not too much of the lovely flesh that surrounds it. Have a look at the fish now and note where the skin meets the 'frill' all the way around the edge of the fish. Starting at the top of the fish, near where the head was, cut through the skin, into the flesh, just inside the 'frill' and continue all the way around the fish. The cuts on either side of the edge of the fish should meet and overlap at the tail, forming an X. This facilitates the easy removal of the skin after cooking. Give the fish a good wash, being particularly careful to remove the little blood clot at the top of the backbone.

Put 5mm of water into a shallow baking tray or roasting pan and slide in the fish. Sprinkle a pinch of salt over the skin. Place the fish in the preheated oven and cook for 20–30 minutes. To test if the fish is cooked, insert a knife into the thickest part of the flesh at the head end. The flesh should be white and firm with no trace of pink, and willing to come away easily from the bone. Watch the water level in the tray during cooking, topping up the water a little if the pan looks like it might go dry. You will need 8 tablespoons of water for the sauce.

When the fish is cooked, you can leave it on the tray in the oven with the temperature lowered to 100°C/200°F/gas ¼, for up to 30 minutes.

To make the sauce, place 8 tablespoons of fish cooking water from the baking tray in a low-sided saucepan. Bring to a simmer and allow to reduce by half. Add the shrimps and crushed garlic and simmer for 1 minute to heat through. Add the wild garlic or chives and allow to wilt. Add the olive oil, and then the lemon zest and juice to taste. Stir gently and warm through again to a simmer. Taste, adding a little salt and pepper as necessary.

Remove the skin from the turbot and with a fish slice remove the fillets to a hot serving dish or plates. Using your fish slice, flip the fish over. Remove the soft white underskin, and continue to remove the flesh as neatly as you can. Coat the fish with some of the warm sauce and serve immediately. Serve any surplus sauce in a warm sauce boat.

Baked plaice
with broad beans and their leaves

When I was growing up in Laoise, in the midlands of Ireland, most of the sea fish we ate came on the bus every Friday morning to the local shop. This regular delivery was in place to satisfy the needs of the mostly Catholic community, who did not eat meat on Friday. We thought the fish was rather good, but it was not until I tasted the fish in Co. Cork, which had come from the sea that day, that I realised what the real thing was about. In fact, when I tasted a baked plaice with hollandaise sauce for the first time, that was the point in my life when I realised that I would need to spend some time in a restaurant kitchen. It was fantastic, one of the best things I had ever tasted, an eye-widening moment of revelation. I knew then that I absolutely had to learn how to cook fish like that and I had to learn how to make hollandaise sauce. At the time, the only place to learn such a skill was in a good restaurant kitchen.

Plaice is a marvellous fish and I cook it in many different ways. I like it pan-fried or the more grandly titled 'à la meunière'. I grill it, fry it in batter for fish and chips and, as here, bake it on the bone. Try to get a large and spanking fresh fish with thick-looking fillets. Without doubt the best time of the year to eat plaice is during the summer months. I don't bother with it at any other time.

The broad bean butter sauce is simple. If you can get some of the broad bean leaves they add a lovely silky consistency to the sauce, but if not, just proceed without them. What we are making here is a simple butter sauce, to which we add the cooked and shelled beans and the leaves if we have them. Keep this recipe up your sleeve for other situations where you need to make a little sauce in a hurry. Asparagus would be a very good alternative to the broad beans, and summer peas or even a few really soft green lettuce leaves, with a sprinkling of small mint leaves, would also be great.

The ingredients
Plaice are at their best during the summer. Check to see there is no roe in the fish you are buying, as the flesh of a roe-filled fish will be thin and watery.

Broad beans are a summer treat, but you have to do a bit of work to release these treasures from their pods and skins.

The broad bean leaves are delicious, but if you can't get them the sauce is still good without.

Serves 4 1 large plaice, weighing about 1.4kg, or 2 smaller fish
Maldon sea salt

SIMPLE BUTTER SAUCE
4 tablespoons fish cooking water
115g butter, chilled and diced
4 tablespoons podded, cooked and shelled broad beans and a handful of broad bean leaves
Lemon juice
Maldon sea salt and freshly ground black pepper

Preheat the oven to 180°C/350°F/gas 4. Prepare the fish for baking as directed on pages 234.

Put about 5mm of water into a shallow baking tray or roasting dish. Lay the fish on top and season the skin with a sprinkle of salt. The purpose of the water is to prevent the fish from sticking and to create a steamy atmosphere for the fish to cook in. Bake in the preheated oven for 15–30 minutes, depending on the size of the fish. To test if the fish is cooked, insert a knife into the thickest part of the flesh at the head end. The flesh should be white and firm with no trace of pink, and willing to come away easily from the bone. Watch the water level in the tray during cooking, topping up the water a little if the pan looks like it might go dry.

When the fish is cooked, you can leave it on the tray in the oven with the temperature lowered to 100°C/200°F/gas ¼, for up to 30 minutes.

To make the simple butter sauce, place 4 tablespoons of the fish cooking water from the baking tray in a small saucepan. Bring it to a simmer and allow it to reduce to 2 tablespoons. Turn the heat down quite low and whisk in a few lumps of the cold butter. The sauce will start to emulsify and will thicken lightly. Whisk in the rest of the butter to achieve a light, thin and silky butter sauce. Remove the sauce from the heat and keep warm.

Just before serving, place the sauce on a low heat, add the cooked broad beans and let them heat through. Finally, add the leaves and allow to melt into the sauce. Taste and correct the seasoning, adding a little lemon juice if necessary.

To serve, remove the fish from the baking tray to a hot serving dish. Peel off the skin from the surface of the fish and sauce the fish lightly. Garnish the dish with sprigs of fennel or chervil and serve the surplus sauce in a sauce boat.

Fish baked in foil parcels or 'en papillote'

Cooking fillets of fish in a tightly sealed parcel of cooking foil is a quick, easy and effective way to trap flavours and create self-saucing fish dishes with exquisite light juices.

Keys to success
Use good-quality heavy cooking foil.

Season and flavour the fish with great care, so that once it is cooked and the parcel is cut open, it is ready to serve there and then without requiring any further intervention.

Be generous with the size of the piece of foil you use, leaving **lots of space around the fish** so as to allow plenty of steam to build up inside the parcel, ensuring a quick and accurate cooking time.

Use a **double thickness of foil** to avoid leakage of the precious cooking juices in the event of a hole being accidentally made while moving the parcels.

Always put the foil parcels into a **preheated oven**.

I like to put the parcels on to **a hot oven tray**, as this starts the fish cooking immediately and shortens the cooking time.

Time the cooking of the parcels carefully.

Salmon ready to be wrapped in its foil parcel and baked

Salmon in a foil bag
with lemon, chilli and mint

The trick to cooking fish in this way is to make sure your parcels are tightly sealed and that no holes are made in the foil that might allow steam or delicious cooking juices to escape. The parcels can be conveniently assembled several hours ahead and chilled for cooking later. The mint in this simple recipe is not introduced until the fish is about to be eaten, thereby adding a lovely last-minute freshness to the dish.

I serve this dish with boiled new potatoes and peas, and sometimes with a tomato and basil salad.

Serves 2

40g butter, softened
2 x 150g fillets of salmon, skin removed
Maldon sea salt and freshly ground black pepper
Pinch of chilli flakes
Grated zest of ½ a lemon
1 tablespoon lemon juice
1 tablespoon mint leaves
2 lemon wedges, to serve

Preheat the oven to 200°C/400°F/gas 6 and put a baking tray in to heat up.

Cut a piece of foil about 80cm long and lay it on your worktop. Fold it in half from the top down, just to crease the centre line crossways, and open it out again. Rub the lower half of the foil, where the fish will be sitting, with some of the soft butter.

Place both pieces of fish on the foil and season with salt and pepper, chilli flakes and the lemon zest. Pour the lemon juice over and dot the remaining butter on top of the fish. Fold the top of the foil down and seal the sides with two sharp and definite folds. Seal the mouth of the bag with two more tight folds – there should be plenty of space around the fish inside the bag to allow for steam to build up during cooking.

Place the parcel on the heated tray and cook for 15 minutes, by which time the bag should be inflated like a balloon.

While the fish is cooking, coarsely chop the mint leaves. Slash open the bag along the top of the foil and sprinkle the chopped mint all over the fish. Serve immediately, on hot plates with lemon wedges, making sure you spoon the buttery juices over the fish.

Fish fillets baked on baking parchment

Keys to success
A hot oven and a quick cooking time are essential for this technique, which could also be correctly described as roasting.

Parchment or non-stick cooking paper makes the task really easy and will ensure that the fish does not stick to the cooking tray.

Try to leave a little space between the fish fillets when placing on the paper, as they will cook more quickly and colour at the edges, adding a richer flavour.

Mackerel baked
with courgettes and harissa

Mackerel is one of my favourite fish, and this is a simple and effective way to cook it. The firm and oily flesh combines beautifully with the strong and hot flavour of the harissa. I serve these with a harissa-flavoured mayonnaise, though a plain mayonnaise would be perfectly good too. A green salad and boiled new potatoes would be the perfect accompaniments.

The ingredients
Mackerel needs to be spanking fresh to show off this wonderful fish at its best.

The courgettes need to be no longer than 12cm so that they will remain firm and nutty after cooking.

Serves 4 4 teaspoons harissa
4 tablespoons olive oil
4 small courgettes
8 mackerel fillets
Maldon sea salt and freshly ground black pepper
4 teaspoons coriander leaves
4 teaspoons small mint leaves

TO SERVE
4 lemon wedges
Drizzle of olive oil

HARISSA MAYONNAISE
2 tablespoons mayonnaise (see page 40)
1 teaspoon harissa (see page 47)
Maldon sea salt and freshly ground black pepper

Preheat the oven to 230°C/450°F/gas 8.

Place the harissa and olive oil in a large bowl and mix well. Slice the courgettes, at an angle if you wish, into 3mm thick slices and add to the harissa oil with the mackerel fillets. Toss gently with your fingers to coat the fish and vegetables completely. Add a good pinch of salt and pepper and toss again.

Line a flat oven tray with a sheet of baking parchment and place the mackerel and courgettes on it in a single layer. Bake in the preheated oven for about 8 minutes, until the mackerel and courgettes are just cooked. The fish and vegetables should be well coloured.

While the fish is cooking, mix together the mayonnaise and harissa. Taste and correct the seasoning.

Serve the fish immediately it is cooked, sprinkled with the fresh coriander and mint leaves, with lemon wedges and a drizzle of olive oil. Pass the harissa mayonnaise separately.

Fish fillets baked 'au gratin'

Keys to success

Measure all the ingredients accurately, so as to ensure the correct amount of sauce and flavourings for the amount of fish being cooked.

The cooked gratin should be a rich golden colour and bubbling hot when ready to be served.

Gratin of hake with tomatoes, basil, olives and Parmesan

The firm texture of hake is perfect for this dish, although cod, pollock and salmon are also good here. Really ripe tomatoes are essential to add sweetness and depth of flavour to the sauce.

The final addition to the dish of the strong-tasting chopped olive and basil pulls the flavours together. The cooked gratin should arrive at the table bubbling hot, with a rich golden colour.

The ingredients

Hake is a firm-textured, white-fleshed fish with great flavour. Freshness, as ever, is the key to a delicious result.

Fat, black and briny Kalamata olives are the preferred choice for this dish.

Serves 4

2 teaspoons olive oil, plus 2 tablespoons
600g ripe tomatoes, peeled and sliced 5mm thick
Maldon sea salt and freshly ground black pepper
1 large clove of garlic, peeled and very thinly sliced
4 x 150g pieces of hake fillet, skin removed
10 basil leaves
100ml regular or double cream
50g Parmesan
16 fat black olives, such as Kalamata, stones removed and
   finely chopped
8 small basil leaves, for serving

Preheat the oven to 180°C/350°F/gas 4.

Rub an ovenproof gratin dish with the 2 teaspoons of olive oil. Place the sliced tomatoes in the dish and season with salt and pepper. Sprinkle with the sliced garlic. Lay the pieces of fish on next. Tear the basil leaves and scatter over the fish. Whisk the cream and Parmesan together and season to taste with salt and pepper. Spoon the cream directly over the fish.

The dish can now be cooked immediately or covered and refrigerated for up to 2 hours. To cook, place in the preheated oven and bake for 20–25 minutes, until the fish is just cooked through and the cream and tomatoes have become a bubbling light sauce with a golden hue.

Mix the chopped olives with the remaining 2 tablespoons of olive oil and drizzle over the dish.

Scatter the small basil leaves over and serve.

For green vegetables, rapidly boiling water in large quantities and enthusiastic salting of that water are crucial.

Green vegetables

Green vegetables are an essential part of the ingredient basket for all cooks. At any time of the year there will be something green in season. From the profusion of the spring, summer and autumn months to the relative scarcity of winter, there is always a green vegetable that is bang in season and ready for the table. Not everyone gets excited about green vegetables, and they are generally seen in this part of the world as something to be served as an accompaniment to a main course. We will concentrate here on relatively simple preparations, and for the purpose of this particular chapter will cook our vegetables in the traditional way with a view to serving them with a main course of fish, meat or poultry, but where appropriate I will suggest when and how they can be served on their own as a separate course.

Generally speaking, I like to cook my green vegetables in boiling, salted water. Some cooks like to steam their vegetables and that's fine, but I never feel the flavour is as good as the boiling water and salt method.

The key to a delicious and nourishing bowl of green vegetables for the table is seasonality and freshness. So if you decide you want to eat French beans in December – well, I'm afraid there is nothing I can do or say that will magically make them taste like they taste in July and August. The same goes for asparagus. Fantastic and worth waiting for when at its best here in April and May, but a rather pale imitation of that brilliance when eaten after a long voyage in other months of the year. So it is for all vegetables – buy them when they are at their freshest and you will get the very best results, and vegetables that you might have hitherto considered as rather humble, when at their best, can become a revelation. Where before you might have considered only the haughty asparagus worthy of being elevated on to a slice of buttered toast or olive-oil-drenched grilled bread, now you might begin to realise that the lowly kales or sprouting broccolis can be just as heavenly and worthy of that lofty position, and that they too are deserving of a grating of Parmesan or a drizzle of hollandaise sauce.

The other important point to make is that when your particular vegetable of choice is in season, it will also be at its cheapest. So it's a win-win situation. Great taste and great price.

There are subtleties involved in cooking the suggested green vegetables listed here but there are rules that are common to the cooking of all of them.

Keys to success

The vegetables must be **really fresh** to get a great result.

The fresher the vegetables are, the **more quickly they cook**.

The quicker the vegetables cook the more delicious they will be to eat and the more beautiful they will be to look at.

Rapidly boiling **water in large quantities** and **enthusiastic salting** of that water are crucial.

Green vegetables should **never be covered** when being cooked.

Serve the cooked vegetables **immediately** they are cooked, if possible.

Measuring in the salt

Cooking French, flat or runner beans to serve 'plain'

The bean recognisable to most will be what we call the French bean or haricot vert. Thin, green, slender and pencil-shaped, ideally not more than 10cm long, these can be delicious and I eat lots of them when in season in July and August and into September. However, for the rest of the year they are imported in vast quantities from distant parts of the planet at great expense, and really I can't countenance eating them after such a long voyage.

The French bean has yellow, purple and black relations that you treat in exactly the same way.

The ingredients
The beans should be really fresh, not too big, and should be kept cool until you are ready to use them.

These beans take more salt in the cooking water than any other vegetable I cook.

Serves 4–6 1.2 litres water
Maldon sea salt and freshly ground black pepper
900g beans, topped and tailed and cut into 5cm pieces on the bias
25g butter or 2 tablespoons olive oil

Bring the water to a rolling boil, then add 2–3 teaspoons of salt. Add the prepared beans and cook uncovered for about 6 minutes, then taste one of the beans. The texture should be slightly firm, but not in any way tough or 'squeaky'. 'Yielding' is perhaps the best word to describe the texture. Strain the beans immediately through a sieve or colander.

Place the beans back in the empty but still hot saucepan and add the butter or olive oil and a few grinds of black pepper. Stir to glaze the beans and taste one to see if a little more salt is required. Serve immediately in a hot serving dish.

Cooking broad beans to serve 'plain'

Broad beans, of all the beans, require the most commitment from the point of preparation. They are grown especially for the beans inside the pod. The pods are large and have a spongy lining, like nature's eiderdown, in which the beans are snugly nestled. These pale green beans are removed from their cushioned environment and then cooked like the others, in boiling, salted water, but generally they are not eaten before another soft leathery skin is removed to reveal the glamorous and vibrant green beans inside. I think they are worth every bit of the labour involved. When the pods are particularly small, the extracted beans can be eaten raw and still in their skins, with a little sea salt and olive oil.

The beans should be really fresh as above, not too big, and should be kept cool until you are ready to cook them.

Serves 4–6   600ml water
Maldon sea salt and freshly ground black pepper
500g broad beans, weighed after removing the beans from their pods
10g butter or 1 tablespoon olive oil

Bring the water to a rolling boil, then add a good pinch of salt. Add the beans and cook uncovered for about 5 minutes, by which time you should notice the leathery skin starting to crack to expose the bright green bean inside. Taste one of the beans to ensure it is tender. If so, strain the beans through a colander, reserving about 6 tablespoons of cooking water for reheating the beans later. If you don't mind the skins on the broad beans, you can toss the beans in a little butter or olive oil now and serve them immediately. Unless the beans are really tiny, I prefer to proceed as follows: with the beans still in the colander, hold them under a cold running tap to stop them overcooking. Spread them out on a flat tray to cool. Now pinch the beans out of their skins. Discard the skins unless there is someone in the kitchen who likes them. The peeled beans can be reheated for serving now or kept cool until later.

Broad beans, removed from their rubbery skins and ready for eating

To reheat the beans, bring the reserved cooking water to a gentle simmer in a small wide saucepan. Add the beans and just warm them through. This will take only a matter of minutes. Broad beans should never be served red hot, as they will overcook and spoil. Finally and quickly, add the butter or oil and a little black pepper and mix. By now the water will have evaporated and the beans will have a light shiny glaze. Taste to check the seasoning and serve immediately in a warm serving dish.

Broad beans and their leaves

The ingredients are as above, but with 1 large handful of broad bean or pea leaves.

Proceed as above to the point where you are reheating the peeled beans. Add the leaves to the simmering cooking water in the saucepan with the beans and continue. The leaves will wilt, taking on a lovely melted consistency. Add the oil or butter, taste and correct the seasoning and serve immediately in a warm serving dish.

Cooking peas to serve 'plain'

Fresh peas are truly a treat, but they need to be moist, juicy and tiny so they have not become hard and starchy.

The peas should ideally be fresh and recently podded; however, it must be said that best-quality frozen peas are a remarkably good product, although I do feel quite naughty any time I use them. Chopped mint, coriander or chervil, may be added to the peas just before serving.

Serves 4 225ml water
Maldon sea salt and freshly ground black pepper
450g podded peas
10g butter or 1 tablespoon olive oil

Bring the water to a rolling boil and add a good pinch of salt. Add the peas and cook uncovered for about 5 minutes until tender. Drain in a sieve or a colander and replace in the warm saucepan. Add the butter or olive oil and stir in gently. Taste and correct the seasoning, adding a little black pepper if you wish. Serve immediately in a warm serving dish.

Add 1 tablespoon of the freshly chopped herb of choice to the peas with the butter or olive oil. Taste, correct the seasoning and serve.

Green, white and purple sprouting broccoli with lemon and Parmesan

I feel sorry for the poor children whose loved ones are to be seen with arms tensely folded over a heaving chest, watching said child trying to swallow the dreaded green because 'it's good for you'. Please, mums, dads, minders all, do yourselves and the little darlings a big favour – put a little dab of butter on it or a lick of olive oil and the path of the green goodness will be much quieter, smoother and even enjoyable.

The broccoli that I like to cook is not the type with large and uniform-looking heads that is for the most part commercially grown and available year round in the shops. These look bland and they taste bland. I prefer the varieties that do better during the cold growing season, and in autumn, winter and spring I am happy to cook any of the sprouting green, white or purple varieties. These varieties require just a little more time in the preparation but have a much better flavour than the forced and rather crude large broccolis, though a cleanly produced head of calabrese can be very good indeed. Another member of this varied and complicated vegetable family to watch out for is romanesco, which looks like a cauliflower that has become fused with a fantastic sea-shell. Its pale green florets have a pointy tip, and overall it looks like the work of a sculptor rather than a gardener, but then we always knew that nature was the real genius. It has a really good flavour and will be perfect in this recipe.

The ingredients

Whichever broccoli you choose to use, make sure it is as fresh as possible. The general appearance and feel of the vegetable will tell you most about its freshness, so the colour should be good and vibrant, the stalks firm and there should be no sign of yellowing regardless of the variety you are choosing. When choosing these types of vegetables, turn them upside down and look at where the stalk has been cut from the plant. The fresher-looking the cut, the more recently harvested the vegetable will be and the better it will be to eat.

The amount of olive oil used here is scant and should be of a lovely quality.

The amount of Parmesan in the recipe is also scant and ideally should be just freshly grated.

Serves 4–6   600g sprouting broccoli
1.2 litres water
Maldon sea salt and freshly ground black pepper
2 tablespoons olive oil
1–2 tablespoons grated Parmesan
Zest and juice of ½ a lemon

Broccolis will vary in appearance and shape, depending on what time of the growing season it is when you are cooking them. So each time you prepare them there may be slight changes to be made. In any event, the object of the exercise is to remove any really tough stalks or skin on the stalks, and to cut the heads or florets into even-sized pieces that will cook quickly and uniformly with the trimmed stalks.

If necessary, separate the florets from the stalks in even-sized pieces. If there are any particularly tough-looking ends on the broccoli stalks, carefully trim them off. Peel the remaining stalks with a sharp vegetable peeler, just to remove the tough skin. Bring the water to the boil and add salt, a generous teaspoon or so. Taste the water; it should taste really quite salty. Add the peeled stalks and cook for 1 minute before adding the florets. Continue to cook uncovered and at a rolling boil. Using a skewer or a small knife, check one piece of the broccoli after about 4 minutes to see if it is cooked. When it is tender, carefully strain off all the water using a sieve or a colander.

Allow the broccoli to sit in the strainer for 1 minute to be sure all the water has drained away. Replace it in the still warm but now empty saucepan and drizzle on the olive oil. Sprinkle on the Parmesan, lemon zest and juice, a pinch of sea salt and a few grinds of black pepper. With a light hand, shake and rotate the pan to mix the oil, cheese and lemon through the broccoli. Taste a little, correct the seasoning and serve immediately in a hot serving dish.

Brussels sprouts with brown butter and almonds

The particular look of disgust that creases some faces at the very mention of Brussels sprouts is an indication of how horribly badly cooked this vegetable has been in many people's formative experience. When overcooked, they are like soggy little miniature cabbages with that unique overcooked flavour. But they can be fresh-tasting, nutty and delicious and will sit happily with lots of different flavours. If you consider how many flavours you can combine with cabbage, then Brussels sprouts are no different.

The sprouts themselves need to be small, tight and with dark green outer leaves, and like many winter vegetables seem to taste more delicious after the first few frosts. I sometimes make a purée with the sprouts to serve with a peppered steak, which I think is heaven, though the nay-sayers think that is even more torturous than the plain old sprout. They also sometimes end up in the winter salad bowl, raw and sliced as thin as paper, where with other winter leaves they will be enlivened with a few roast hazelnuts and some jewel-like pomegranate seeds.

The ingredients
Brussels sprouts should be small, firm, dark green and fresh-looking and not in any way yellowing on the outside.

Watch out for the purple variety – pretty, though it turns green when cooked.

Buy almonds with their skins still on, as the skins keep the flavour of the almond intact.

Serves 4–6 40g whole almonds
450g Brussels sprouts
1 litre water
1 teaspoon Maldon sea salt
25g butter
Freshly ground black pepper

Preheat the oven to 200°C/400°F/gas 6.

Chop the almonds coarsely and place them on a baking tray. Roast in the oven for about 15 minutes, or until golden brown. Remove from the oven and they will crisp up as they cool.

To prepare the sprouts, remove the darker and sometimes damaged outer leaves. Cut each sprout straight down through the middle with a vertical cut to achieve perfect halves. The sprouts cook more quickly when prepared like this, and retain their bright green colour and nutty flavour.

Bring the water to a boil and add the salt. Add the sprouts, bring back to the boil and cook uncovered for 6–8 minutes. Test with a skewer to check that they are tender. Strain the cooked sprouts well, allowing all the cooking water to drain off. Keep them warm.

Melt the butter in the saucepan, then let it cook until it turns to a hazelnut brown colour. Keep a close eye on the butter, stirring it from time to time. You will smell the nutty aroma when it has reached the colour of a hazelnut. Put the sprouts and almonds back into the pan and toss gently. Taste, correct the seasoning and serve immediately in a warm serving dish.

Savoy cabbage purée

I could bore you to tears extolling the virtues of cabbage. It is a wonderful vegetable and in my opinion much undervalued. It is generally regarded as a very poor relation to supposedly smarter vegetables like French beans or sugar snap peas, and you know by now that I have no interest in beans and peas that have been flown from the other side of the world when I can get a crisp, sweet and peppery cabbage which has been grown locally.

There are many lovely varieties of cabbage and I particularly like the crinkly green leaves of the Savoy. Essentially, the important thing is to buy the cabbage that's in season when you are making this purée. I also love the elegant shape of greyhound cabbage, so called because the head looks like the long elegant nose of a greyhound. Dark green spring cabbage is also a favourite. I avoid white cabbages, especially the cannonball-like 'Dutch' cabbage. In my opinion it would be better used for target practice than in the kitchen. I don't understand why the 'Dutch' cabbage is the cabbage of choice for coleslaw, which is often revolting but can be quite delicious. In this country we have so many good green cabbages that look and taste so much better. Cabbage is spectacularly good value, and if you slice it as thin as you can bear to, it is a good addition to a salad bowl and again will have so much more flavour and crisp texture than something that's been cranking up the air miles on its way to your kitchen.

This purée is good with most meats and poultry. I sometimes serve it with venison and wild duck, and it has also been successful with roast and grilled fish.

The ingredients
The cabbage, fresh, crisp and green, is the easy secret to success here.

The cream and butter can be scant or plentiful here, though there is no point making the dish too rich, otherwise the green charm of the cabbage will be lost under the cream and butter.

Serves 4–6 1 head of Savoy cabbage
1.75 litres water
Maldon sea salt and freshly ground black pepper
25–40ml regular or double cream
25–40g salted butter

Remove any damaged outside leaves from the cabbage. However, don't remove any more of those nice green outside leaves than is necessary, as they are full of flavour and will give lovely bright green flecks to the finished purée. Place the cabbage on a chopping board and cut directly down through the middle of the head, then quarter and remove the hard core. Slice the cabbage against the grain, nice and thinly.

Bring the water to the boil and salt well. Add the cabbage and cook uncovered at a simmer until it is just tender. Strain the cabbage well, reserving 100ml of the cooking water. In a blender or using a hand-held blender, blend to a coarse purée, adding cream and butter as you see fit. The consistency should be like that of a soft mashed potato. If the purée is a bit firm, add a little of the reserved cooking water to soften it and blend briefly again. Taste and correct the seasoning and serve in a hot dish.

The purée can be made ahead of time and gently reheated later. A non-stick pan is perfect for reheating it, and a little of the reserved cooking water can be used here as well if the purée has thickened in the meantime.

Summer spinach
with garlic, chilli and lemon

Spinach is such a versatile vegetable and is used in cuisines all over the world. It ranges in size from small baby leaves, which can be eaten raw or cooked with the stalks attached, to large leaves, which generally have the stalks removed. The removed stalks on the medium and large leaves can also be cooked and eaten, though they will only taste really delicious if they have come from tender spring or early summer spinach. The stalks of really fresh spinach should be crisp, and the leaves regardless of size should be glossy, firm and a rich green colour. The central rib or stalk of medium and large spinach leaves is easily removed. Fold one side of the leaf over the stalk to rest on the other piece of leaf and gently pull the stalk away.

Spring and summer spinach cooks quickly, so you need to be vigilant. Winter spinach will need more cooking.

The ingredients

Try to use spinach as soon as you can after buying or picking. It deteriorates quite quickly, and is immeasurably better when fresh.

Spinach requires less salt than most vegetables, so season with caution here.

The chilli in this recipe is dried rather than fresh, to impart a flavour that is less harsh, and a texture that is less fleshy, than a fresh chilli.

The garlic is thinly sliced and cooked slowly so that it turns golden, becomes nutty and releases its flavour. Be careful not to allow the garlic to become too dark or it will be bitter and spoil the dish.

The lemon juice and zest are the final addition to the dish. They should be added with caution and to taste. They are there to enliven the dish and to pull all the flavours together.

Serves 4–6   1kg spinach leaves, stalks removed
2 tablespoons olive oil
2 large cloves of garlic, peeled and very thinly sliced
1 dried chilli, crushed into small pieces, or a pinch of
   chilli flakes
Maldon sea salt and freshly ground black pepper
1 lemon, zested and juiced

Wash the spinach in several changes of cold water and allow to drain in order to remove as much of the water as possible. Place a wide low-sided heavy-based saucepan or frying pan on the heat and add the olive oil. Immediately add the garlic and cook gently until the oil gets hot and the garlic colours slightly. Add the chilli and cook for a few seconds. By now the pan should be very hot and the garlic golden. Add the spinach, being careful as it will hiss and spit a bit. Continue cooking the spinach, turning it constantly. Season with a little salt and pepper. Add the lemon juice and zest and stir in. Pull the pan off the heat and taste. Correct the seasoning and serve immediately in a hot dish.

The spinach can be removed from the pan when cooked, spread out flat to cool, and served later at room temperature.

Winter spinach

Follow the recipe above, but instead of sautéing the spinach in the pan, cook it in a large saucepan of boiling, lightly salted water until tender. Drain, removing as much water as possible, then proceed exactly as above, replacing the raw spinach leaves with the cooked spinach.

Curly kale
with anchovy and marjoram

Kale is another of those vegetables that is not regarded as being glamorous, but when cooked properly is as delicious and stylish as anything. I love it in the winter months, when the availability of fresh green vegetables is scarce. With tightly curled crisp green leaves, it stands brave and tall in the garden, surviving winter chills, and is a beautiful sight sparkling in the sunlight on a crisp and frosty morning or when covered with a dusting of snow. Its more stylish cousins, such as the ragged-leaved and purple-tinged Red Russian or the long, dark and plume-leaved Nero di Toscano, otherwise known as Black Tuscany or cavolo nero, can also be cooked in the manner suggested here.

Any of the kales are great in soups and broths, in purées, folded through mashed potatoes, in gratins, as a topping for grilled bread, as a simple accompanying vegetable to poultry, meat and fish and so on. Tiny pinched pieces of raw kale can also be added to the winter green salad bowl. So you can see it is tremendously versatile.

The key to the success of any kale recipe is to cook it really well until it is quite tender, and it takes quite a bit of cooking to get it to this soft and comforting stage, so be a little patient and hopefully you will be amazed by its versatility and deliciousness.

The ingredients

Curly kale is the easiest of all of the kales to find, but any of the kales will work perfectly in this recipe. The kale should look fresh and vibrant and the tough stalks should always be removed before cooking.

The small amount of anchovy gives a very savoury flavour to the kale. Buy the best quality you can, either salted or packed in oil, and store any excess anchovies in a covered container in the fridge, where they will store perfectly for at least a month.

Sweet or annual marjoram, as it is known, is a marvellous herb and works beautifully here. I have also used rosemary in this recipe with excellent results.

Serves 4–6   3 litres water
3 teaspoons Maldon sea salt
500g kale, with stalks removed to yield about
    350g kale leaves
4 anchovies
1 heaped tablespoon marjoram leaves
5 tablespoons olive oil
1 lemon
Freshly ground black pepper

Bring the water to a boil in a large wide saucepan and add the salt. Add the kale leaves and cook uncovered at a good simmer for about 8 minutes. Taste a small piece of the kale to ensure it is really tender. Drain the kale and allow to sit in a sieve or colander to lose as much of the cooking water as possible. Press it gently with your fingers to encourage a little more of the water to be expelled, but don't manhandle it otherwise it will become compacted and less pleasant to eat. Lay the drained kale out flat on a wide dish and allow it to cool slightly.

While the kale is cooling, chop the anchovies and marjoram together until they look like a coarse purée. Transfer to a small bowl and blend in the olive oil. It is unlikely that this mixture will take salt, as the anchovies are already salty. Sprinkle this oil over the still warm but not hot kale and gently massage it into the leaves. If the kale is still hot it may 'cook' away the fresh taste of the olive oil and the marjoram. Grate the zest of half the lemon over the kale, then cut a quarter out of the lemon and squeeze the juice from that over as well. Mix again gently. Add a few grinds of black pepper and taste to check the seasoning. If necessary, add a little sea salt and perhaps another splash of olive oil.

Serve the kale at room temperature, not chilled, as an accompaniment to a grilled steak or oily fish such as mackerel. It is also excellent on warm grilled bread which has been rubbed lightly on one side with a cut clove of garlic. A soft poached egg sitting on top of that would be a feast.

Gratin of chard and Gruyère

Big and leafy, looking like an exceptionally healthy leaf of spinach and with several colourful varieties, chard is great. The most well-known variety, with its thick white stalk and glossy leaves, is sometimes called Swiss chard. The colourful members of the family are the red-stemmed Ruby chard and the variety known as Bright Lights or Rainbow chard, which has a range of multi-coloured stems varying from white, yellow and orange to pink, purple and red.

Generally, unless the leaves are tiny, the stalk is removed from the leaf and cooked separately. The cooked leaves and stalks can be served together or as individual dishes. The flavour of the leaf is similar to spinach, but somewhat stronger and earthier in flavour, though the two greens are pretty much interchangeable in any recipe. I like to cut out the stalks or stems from the leaves with a sharp knife to achieve a neat finish. This is another vegetable that needs to be well cooked, and there is no flavour or texture advantage to having to chew it. The tiniest leaves, no more than 8cm long and including the stems, colourful or otherwise, sometimes end up in the salad bowl.

This recipe combines the vegetable with Gruyère cheese in a gratin and is finished with a crisp bread topping. This dish can be prepared ahead and reheated later. It will make a delicious vegetarian supper dish or accompaniment to a roast shoulder of lamb or a grilled lamb chop.

Serves 4–6
1kg chard
3 litres water
3 teaspoons Maldon sea salt
60g coarse sourdough breadcrumbs
3 tablespoons olive oil
30g butter
30g plain flour
300ml full-fat milk
100ml regular or double cream
Freshly ground black pepper
160g Gruyère cheese, coarsely grated
1 tablespoon marjoram leaves, chopped

Preheat the oven to 200°C/400°F/gas 6.

Remove the stalks from the chard with a sharp knife. Cut the stalks against the grain into 2cm pieces. Bring the water to a boil and add the salt, then add the stalks to the boiling water and cook at a simmer for about 6 minutes, or until nearly tender. Add the leaves to the pot and cook for a further 3 minutes, until the leaves and the stalks are both cooked. Strain off all the water and allow the chard to sit in the strainer so that the rest can drain away.

Toss the breadcrumbs in the olive oil, then spread out on a baking tray and place in the preheated oven for about 15 minutes, or until toasted and golden. The crumbs tend to cook unevenly, so you will need to move them around on the tray a couple of times while they are cooking. When ready, remove from the oven and reserve for later. Melt the butter in a small saucepan, then add the flour and stir to mix. Cook on a gentle heat for about 3 minutes, then stir in the milk and cream and bring the mixture to the boil, whisking constantly.

The sauce will by now have thickened. Turn the heat down low and allow it to simmer for a further 2 minutes. Remove from the heat and season with salt and pepper. Give the drained chard a further gentle squeeze, then add to the sauce with 110g of the grated Gruyère and the chopped marjoram and mix gently but thoroughly. Taste again and correct the seasoning.

Place the mixture in an ovenproof gratin dish and sprinkle with the remaining Gruyère and finally the roasted breadcrumbs.

The gratin can be put aside for later or reheated now at 180°C/350°F/ gas 4 for about 15–20 minutes, until bubbling and golden. If you are reheating it from cold it will need 30 minutes.

Root vegetables are immeasurably better when sold with the soil still on them rather than washed. The soil creates a seal around the skin of the vegetable which helps retain nutrients and flavour and keeps the vegetables fresher for longer.

Roots and alliums

This is a rather random collection of vegetables, all of which I love to cook, and in fact you could make a rather wonderful vegetable dish with a carefully proportioned mixture of the lot of them.

Carrots, parsnips, turnips and beets are root vegetables. Jerusalem artichokes are tubers and are also classed as a stem vegetable, and leeks, onions, shallots and garlic are all members of the allium family.

This selection of vegetables provides a year-round bounty for the cook, though it is not until the chilly autumn and winter months that some of them come into their own. Like all vegetables, the fresher these vegetables are from the ground, the better they will taste. The root vegetables are immeasurably better when sold with the soil still on them rather than washed. The soil creates a seal around the skin of the vegetable which helps retain nutrients and flavour and keeps the vegetables fresher for longer.

Keys to success

If at all possible, buy these vegetables **unwashed and unpeeled**, as the flavour is generally vastly superior.

Cook the vegetables listed here until **tender**, as serving any of them 'al dente' is no advantage at all. Many of them taste delicious when served raw but that is a different discussion.

Where appropriate, **use a vegetable peeler** rather than a knife for peeling.

Try to chop the vegetables evenly to ensure an even cooking time.

Glazed carrots

Carrots are now regarded as a year-round vegetable, but for lovers of home-grown carrots, and I number myself as one of those, there will be a gap in their availability in late winter and early spring. The arrival of the first of the new season carrots in late spring is always a treat, and if they come in time to serve with the first of the spring lamb for Easter, all the better. The early carrots, usually sold with their green leaves attached, are delicious raw or cooked. The leaves, which are also edible, are best removed if the carrots are being stored for a few days.

I recently came across the expression 'infant carrot', to describe a tiny carrot being served on a restaurant menu. Well, call me old-fashioned, but I think this is taking vegetable-picking and menu-writing too far. Poor little carrot, plucked from the ground before it was much more than a tiny root. There seems to be a movement towards serving some vegetables in such a state of 'infancy' that, as slender as a knitting needle, a magnifying glass will soon be required along with the normal cutlery at one's place setting to identify the particular micro-organism being served. I don't buy into the 'small-est is best' approach when it comes to choosing vegetables. Clearly, there is an optimum size for different vegetables. We have all strug-gled with peas and beans that have outgrown their best showing and become too big, tough and starchy, courgettes that have gone from being petite, firm and nutty to fat, flabby and watery, parsnips with woody cores, tough and stringy celery and so on.

I have picked many a tiny baby carrot straight from the ground with great expectations of taste only to decide that it would be con-siderably more flavourful a couple of weeks hence. You can of course make up your own mind. For me, the carrot picked from the ground to be consumed as soon as possible in its raw state needs to be as thick as my little finger, but for this method of cooking carrots, they need to be at least as fat as your thumb. These small carrots can be cooked whole. Larger ones, which need to be sliced, also work per-fectly here.

This technique is interesting, and it is fascinating the way a rather common and readily available vegetable like the carrot can be

elevated to something special when thoughtfully cooked. Carrots roast successfully and can be delicious. They can also be steamed, but I find those deadly dull. Here the carrots are cooked in a small amount of water with seasoning and a knob of butter or a drizzle of olive oil. The quantity of water may look like it is too little. It is not. The objective is to have perfectly cooked carrots just as all the liquid in the saucepan has evaporated, and the hope is that by then the carrots will be coated in a shiny and highly flavoured glaze. There are several variations to the master recipe and I think this method for cooking carrots can open your eyes as to how good carrots can be.

One or two words of caution here. Choose a saucepan the carrots fit neatly into, in other words, neither too big nor too small. Really fresh small carrots only need scrubbing; larger older ones need peeling with a fine swivel-top peeler.

The ingredients

Try to find carrots that have been grown in your own country. Spring and summer carrots will have their green leaves still attached. If you are storing the carrots in a cool place for a couple of days before use, remove the green leaves, since interestingly they store better like this. With winter carrots the leaves will have died back. Watch out for some of the more interesting varieties of carrots that are starting to make an appearance in farmers' markets and good vegetable shops. Purple Haze, for example, has the most beautiful purple skin and a clashing orange interior. Parmex is golf-ball shaped and quite delicious. Nantes is conventional in shape and appearance and also very good to eat.

Serves 4   450g carrots, peeled and sliced 1cm thick if large,
 or left whole if small
15g butter or 1 tablespoon olive oil
Pinch of fine sea salt and freshly ground black pepper
Large pinch of sugar
110ml water
1 tablespoon finely chopped parsley

Place the carrots, butter or olive oil, salt, pepper, sugar and water in a low-sided saucepan and bring to the boil. Cover the pan and cook for 10 minutes at a simmer, then remove the lid and continue simmering until the carrots are tender. Keep an eye on the level of liquid in the pan and if it is evaporating too quickly before the carrots are cooked, add a few more tablespoons of water.

If the water has not all evaporated by the time the carrots are cooked, remove the cooked carrots, boil the remaining liquid further to achieve a shiny glaze, then put back the cooked carrots and shake the pan to coat the vegetables in the glaze. Add the parsley and slide the carrots into a hot serving dish. Serve as soon as possible.

Carrots with watercress

This is a lovely combination of flavours. The greenness of the lightly cooked watercress is terrific with the sweet carrots, adding a freshness and vibrancy to the dish. Watercress is high in vitamin C and has more iron than spinach. It is delicious either as a salad green or, as in this case, added to the sauce at the end of cooking.

Serves 4 450g carrots, peeled and sliced 1cm thick if large, or left whole if small
15g butter or 1 tablespoon olive oil
Pinch of Maldon sea salt and freshly ground black pepper
Large pinch of sugar
110ml water
50g watercress leaves, finely chopped

Prepare the carrots as above. As soon as you are happy that the carrots are properly cooked and glazed, add the chopped watercress and place over a low heat. The watercress will probably release some water, but don't worry – this will evaporate and a glaze will be formed again. Add a pinch of sea salt and stir the watercress through the carrots with a flexible rubber spatula, so as not to break up the carrots. As soon as the watercress looks wilted and releases its aroma, it is ready. This will take only a couple of minutes. Taste, correct the seasoning and serve as soon as possible.

Carrots with cream and tarragon

Ingredients as in Glazed Carrots (page 280), plus:

Serves 4   4 tablespoons regular or double cream
1 tablespoon chopped tarragon

When the carrots are cooked and glazed, add the cream and tarragon and allow to bubble to form a thin sauce.

Carrots with coriander

Ingredients as in Glazed Carrots (page 280), plus:

Serves 4   1 teaspoon roasted and coarsely ground coriander seeds
1 tablespoon chopped coriander leaves
Lemon juice (optional)

When the carrots are cooked and glazed, add the ground coriander seeds and chopped leaves and stir in. Taste to see if the dish will benefit from a few drops of lemon juice – sometimes it does.

Carrots with ginger and lemon

Ginger and lemon pair beautifully with carrots, and this dish will be an excellent accompaniment to lamb or chicken, either grilled or roasted. Fresh ginger is a marvellous ingredient, completely different from the dried and powdered form, and if you haven't previously used it, you will be opening up all sorts of possibilities in the kitchen.

Fresh root ginger is sometimes called green ginger and will keep for weeks covered in the fridge. It should be plump and shiny when you buy it.

Serves 4   450g carrots, peeled and sliced 1cm thick if large,
        or left whole if small
    15g butter
    3cm piece of fresh ginger, peeled and finely grated
    Pinch of Maldon sea salt and freshly ground black pepper
    Large pinch of sugar
    110ml cold water
    ½ a lemon, zested and juiced

Place the carrots, butter, grated ginger, salt, pepper, sugar and water in a small saucepan and bring to the boil. Cover the pan and cook at a simmer for 10 minutes, then remove the lid and continue simmering until the carrots are tender and the water has evaporated to leave a shiny glaze coating the carrots. Stir in the lemon zest and some lemon juice to taste.

Keep an eye on the level of liquid in the saucepan and if it is evaporating too quickly before the carrots are cooked, add a few more tablespoons of water. If the water has not all evaporated by the time the carrots are cooked, remove the cooked carrots and boil the remaining liquid further to achieve a shiny glaze, then put back the cooked carrots.

Taste and correct the seasoning if necessary. Serve as soon as possible.

Gratin of swede and potatoes
with thyme leaves, smoked bacon and Parmesan

Turnips can be a difficult vegetable to master and that may be because they are only good at very specific times of the year. When cooked outside the optimum season, they can be brutish, tough and bitter. The two main types that flourish in this part of the world are the white turnip and the larger and less glamorous purple-skinned and yellow-fleshed turnip, often referred to as a swede or a swede turnip. The larger swede may be less chi-chi than its paler cousin, but I like it just as much.

This is a robust, warming gratin made with the cheap and cheerful swede turnip. This brassica, the least glamorous of the turnip family, brings back happy childhood memories. I remember as a child going to our nearest farm, owned by Bill and Mary Walsh, and grabbing the raw sliced turnips from the slicer before they were taken out into the fields to be spread as winter feeding for the sheep when the grass had become scarce. We would dip the slightly muddy shards of turnip into the nearest churn of water, so cold it turned our little hands purple, give them a cursory rinse, then munch away with relish. That sweet and peppery flavour has stayed with me, and I still think this purple-skinned and golden-fleshed root is a thing of beauty.

The ingredients

Swede turnips need to be peeled before use. The greens, if they are still attached, are also edible and can be destalked, cooked and folded through the cooked root to give a really lovely earthy flavour. When buying, pick a swede that feels heavy for its size, with an unblemished skin. They will store in a cool place for several weeks.

The smoked bacon should be from the belly and be quite fatty, to ensure a succulent texture and a sweet flavour. The lardons are little strips or cubes cut not less than 5mm thick.

Serves 8–10   Maldon sea salt and freshly ground black pepper
450g swede turnips, peeled and sliced into 4mm thick slices
450g potatoes, peeled and sliced into 3mm thick slices
1 tablespoon olive oil
110g lardons of smoked or unsmoked bacon
A little butter
1 teaspoon thyme leaves
110g grated Parmesan
350ml regular or double cream or chicken stock

Preheat the oven to 180°C/350°F/gas 4.

Bring a large saucepan of water to the boil and season with a good pinch of salt. Drop in the sliced swede, bring back to the boil and simmer for 5 minutes. The swede will have tenderised slightly but will not be fully cooked. Strain, reserving the water for cooking the potatoes. Place them on a tray lined with a tea towel.

Bring the water back to the boil and add the sliced potatoes. Bring to a simmer and cook for 1 minute only. Strain, rinse under the cold tap, then place on a tray lined with a tea towel like the swede.

Heat the olive oil in a frying pan and add the bacon lardons. Cook, stirring, until the bacon is crisp and golden. Remove the bacon and place on a piece of kitchen paper to drain.

To assemble, grease a 1.5 litre gratin dish with a light smear of butter. Put in a layer of swede and potatoes, followed by a sprinkle of thyme leaves, a sprinkle of bacon and a sprinkle of grated Parmesan. Season with salt and pepper. Splash on a little of the cream or stock, then repeat the process, finishing the gratin with a final sprinkling of the cheese.

Place the gratin in a roasting tin and pour boiling water into the tin to come halfway up the sides of the dish (this is known as a bain-marie). Place in the preheated oven and cook for 60–80 minutes. After 60 minutes, test with a skewer to see if the potatoes and swede are tender. The skewer should go through the vegetables with no resistance and the top of the gratin should be a rich golden colour. The cooked gratin will sit happily in the oven for an hour before serving, with the temperature reduced to 100°C/200°F/gas ¼.

Roast Jerusalem artichokes

Jerusalem artichokes are a wonderful winter vegetable. In appearance they are somewhat similar to potatoes, but with knobbly bits which are tedious to peel. They make an excellent soup and purée, and pair particularly well with shellfish, especially mussels and scallops. They are also great with pork, duck, goose, pheasant and venison.

Here they are simply roasted with olive oil, salt and pepper. The olive oil can be replaced with duck, goose or pork fat. I strongly advise using a sheet of baking parchment under the artichokes when roasting, as otherwise the crispy cooked skin will stick to the roasting pan and will not end up on your plate, which is where you want that golden deliciousness.

The ingredients
The artichokes when really freshly harvested do not have to be peeled. This is ideal, because most of the vitamins are just under the skin, but if they are a couple of days old, you will definitely have to make that slightly purgatorial journey. 'Offer it up', as the saying goes, and if you don't know what that expression means, just disregard my rantings as those of an older generation.

The artichokes have a tendency to cook unevenly, so test several pieces when determining whether they are ready.

The choice of fat here is yours, but whichever you choose, use just enough to glaze the vegetables lightly.

Serves 4   8 artichokes, allowing 2 artichokes per person
2 tablespoons olive oil or duck, pork or goose fat
Maldon sea salt and freshly ground black pepper

Preheat the oven to 200°C/400°F/gas 6.

Scrub and if necessary peel the artichokes and cut each one in half lengthways. Dry with a tea towel and place in a bowl. Add the oil or fat and toss well. Season with salt and pepper.

Line a baking tray with baking parchment and arrange the artichokes in a single layer and if possible not touching, as this encourages the skins to colour and caramelise. Place in the preheated oven and roast for 30–50 minutes, until the vegetables are tender and very well coloured. The tips can be as dark as hazelnut skins. If the artichokes are not colouring properly, turn up the oven by 20° for the last 10 minutes of cooking. By now they will not look pretty in the conventional sense of the word, but it is amazing when something tastes good how one's eye looks at these things in a different way.

Serve immediately.

Roast Jerusalem artichokes with roast hazelnuts and rocket leaves

Prepare the artichokes as above. Add 2 tablespoons of roasted, skinned and chopped hazelnuts to the cooked artichokes, then fold in a handful of rocket leaves and allow to wilt into the hot cooked vegetables.

Spiced parsnip and coriander leaf purée

This purée is easy and has a mildly spiced flavour that is excellent with roast or grilled pork and duck. The finished purée should be smooth and with a soft but not runny consistency, like soft mashed potato.

The ingredients
Parsnips are at their best during the winter months, when they are in season and very good value for money. They become sweeter and cook more quickly after the frosts have arrived.

The curry powder should be best quality and of a medium heat. I roast and grind my own spices (see page 48).

The parsnip cooking water is an essential ingredient here, as it lightens and softens the purée without making it too rich.

Serves 4
450g parsnips, peeled and sliced
Pinch of Maldon sea salt
4 tablespoons regular or double cream
25g butter
¾ teaspoon curry powder
2 tablespoons chopped coriander leaves

Place the peeled and sliced parsnips in a saucepan and cover with cold water. Season with a pinch of salt. Bring to the boil and simmer for 15 minutes, or until the parsnips are completely soft. Strain the liquid off, reserving 8 tablespoons of the cooking water.

Place the strained parsnips in a blender and add the cream, butter, curry powder and three-quarters of the cooking water. Process to a smooth purée. Add more cooking water if the purée is too dry and firm. It should be soft and comforting. Add the chopped coriander and mix in briefly. Taste and correct the seasoning. Serve hot.

This purée can be made ahead of time and reheated later, in which case keep some more of the parsnip cooking water in case it dries out.

Beetroot, red onion, orange and mint compote

This compote is delicious served as a vegetable accompaniment to a plain roast duck or pork. I also serve it with homemade sausages or pork burgers and it is delicious on hot, olive-oil-grilled bread, which has been buttered with a soft goat's cheese.

The ingredients
Ruby, golden or Chioggia beets will do here.

The sour Bramley cooking apple works well with the beetroot, and collapses to a fluff when cooked.

Serves 6–8
- 4 tablespoons olive oil
- 100g red onions, peeled and thinly sliced
- 450g ruby beetroot, peeled and coarsely grated
- 450g Bramley cooking apples, peeled, cored and cut into quarters
- Maldon sea salt and freshly ground black pepper
- Zest and juice of ½ an orange
- 2 tablespoons chopped mint
- 1 tablespoon red wine vinegar or lemon juice

Heat 2 tablespoons of the olive oil in a stainless steel saucepan. Add the sliced onions and toss in the oil. Cover with greaseproof paper and a tight-fitting saucepan lid and sweat on a low heat for about 10 minutes, or until the onions have softened. Add the beetroot and the apples and mix well. Season with salt and pepper and continue cooking, covered as before, on a low heat until the apples collapse and the beetroot softens somewhat. This takes about 20 minutes.

Add the orange zest and juice and the chopped mint. Mix well and correct the seasoning, adding a little red wine vinegar or lemon juice to taste. The compote can be put aside to be reheated later or indeed can be served at room temperature. Reheat on a gentle heat, adding a tablespoon of water if it is inclined to stick to the pan. Finally, drizzle with the remaining olive oil and serve.

Swede purée with olive oil and Parmesan

This flavoursome purée couldn't be simpler and is delicious as an accompanying vegetable with lamb, pork or duck.

Don't forget to save some of the cooking water for adding to the purée. The purée can be prepared ahead of time and reheated later, in which case a little more of the cooking water can be added if necessary.

Serves 4   660g swede turnips, weighed after peeling and cut into
        2cm cubes
    500ml cold water
    Pinch of Maldon sea salt
    25g butter
    Freshly ground black pepper
    3 tablespoons olive oil
    3 tablespoons finely grated Parmesan

Place the swede in a saucepan and cover with the cold water. Add a pinch of salt and cook for about 30 minutes, or until the turnips are completely tender. If they are not tender, the purée will be lumpy.

Strain off the cooking water, reserving some for softening the purée. Put the turnips into a blender with the butter, adding enough of the cooking water to achieve a smooth purée. Taste and correct the seasoning.

Serve hot, in a warmed shallow serving dish, drizzled with the olive oil and sprinkled with the Parmesan.

Leeks with olive oil, Parmesan, toasted pine nuts and pangrattata

Leeks are a great vegetable and can accompany almost any meat, fish or poultry. They need to be cooked until tender, but if overcooked will become dull and watery. There is no need to add any water to them when cooking, as they already contain enough to moisten them as they cook, but you do need to be vigilant and cook them over a low heat.

The ingredients

The leeks for this recipe are best when they are not too big and thick – you want them to almost melt, so not much thicker than your thumb. Bigger leeks will work, they just won't be quite so sweet and lovely. Look out for firm, fresh-looking leeks with no trace of yellowing and verdant green leaves.

The leek's long green leaves are mostly discarded, as their flavour is strong and coarse. I sometimes use about 3–5cm of the very pale green part of the leek between the white stem and the darker leaf tops. Buy them with the roots still attached, as that keeps them fresher, and avoid any ones that have begun to shoot – they will have a tough core and be losing their delicate sweetness. You will know they are shooting if you can see the beginnings of a flower head developing near the leaf tips.

Pine nuts, the edible seeds of several species of pine tree, known to most cooks as an essential ingredient in Pesto Genovese, are one of the most expensive ingredients that come into your kitchen, so should be bought and stored with care. In an ideal world you would be able to taste some of the nuts before buying them in small quantities. In the unlikely event of that being possible, choose the freshest and most unblemished-looking nuts and store them in a cool dark place in a sealed container. Some people like to keep them frozen, which though not ideal is certainly preferable to allowing them to become old and rancid and losing them altogether.

Serves 4   450g leeks
1–2 tablespoons olive oil
1 teaspoon thyme leaves
Maldon sea salt and freshly ground black pepper
2 tablespoons grated Parmesan
1 tablespoon pine nuts, toasted

PANGRATTATA
40g coarse white breadcrumbs, such as sourdough
2 tablespoons olive oil

Preheat the oven to 200°C/400°F/gas 6.

Toss the breadcrumbs in the olive oil and spread out on a baking tray. Place in the preheated oven for about 15 minutes or until toasted and golden. The crumbs tend to cook unevenly, so you will need to move them around on the tray a couple of times during the cooking. When ready, remove from the oven and set aside, leaving the oven on.

Remove most but not all of the green leaves from the top of the leeks. I like to leave at least a couple of centimetres of the pale green. The green tops can be used in stocks or to make an excellent soup, following the green vegetable soup recipe (see page 82). Slice the leeks into 2.5cm pieces, at an angle if you wish. Wash well in plenty of cold running water to remove any sandy clay. Drain well.

Heat the olive oil in a small, heavy-based saucepan until it is moderately hot. Add the leeks and thyme leaves, season with salt and pepper and stir to coat in the oil. Cover with a butter wrapper or a piece of greaseproof paper and a tight-fitting lid. Cook on a very low heat for about 15 minutes, or until the leeks are just tender. A metal skewer will pierce the cooked leeks with no resistance. It is important the heat under the saucepan is quite low – you haven't added any water and are reliant on the moisture in the leeks to help create steam in the pan to prevent them from sticking and burning, and if the heat is too high that is exactly what will happen.

Decant the tender cooked leeks and any cooking juices into a small gratin or other ovenproof dish. Sprinkle the pangrattata, Parmesan and pine nuts over the top in an even layer and put into the oven or under a hot grill for a few minutes to create a golden gratin effect. Serve immediately.

Pumpkin or squash purée

Pumpkin was not one of the foods we ate when growing up, and as a result it took me a little time to get to know how to use them and to realise how versatile and delicious they can be. A turning point in my experience with pumpkins happened when I came across the Japanese pumpkin, Uchichi Kuri, sometimes called Red Kuri. Wow, what a revelation. This rust-and-orange-coloured, cannonball-shaped vegetable knocked me for six. Roasted, puréed as here, in soups, with pasta, spiced up with Indian or Asian spices, it produced a result that I had not previously achieved with the watery, paler pumpkins I had been using. Concentrating on sourcing not only the correct ingredient in perfect condition, but the best variety of that ingredient, was an important moment in my culinary development.

Serve this purée with roast or grilled lamb and pork, guinea fowl or turkey. I reserve some of the strained cooking liquid to add to the purée if it is a little thick.

The ingredients
The pumpkin of choice here is Red Kuri, but I have had excellent results with Golden Hubbard, Chioggia and butternut squash.

The reserved cooking water is a very important ingredient when you come to puréeing the vegetable and is also valuable if you wish to reheat the purée later.

Using a small, sharp knife to carefully peel the pumpkin

Serves 6   500g pumpkin
              Maldon sea salt and freshly ground black pepper
              25–50g butter
              50–125ml regular or double cream

Peel the pumpkin, being careful, as the skin can be very tough and your knife may suddenly skid along the slippery surface. Remove the seeds and cut the flesh into 2cm dice.

Cook the pumpkin in boiling, salted water, just enough to cover, until tender, then strain, reserving the cooking liquid. Blend the flesh with as much cream and butter as you like, to achieve a soft purée. Use some of the reserved cooking liquid as well, if the purée remains too thick. If you keep adding cream to achieve a very soft consistency, the flavour will be diluted, the purée will be too rich and the charm of the vegetable will be lost.

Taste and correct the seasoning, and serve hot.

Roast onions

We cooks would be pretty lost without onions. They are such an important part of our ingredient list. They are a good example of an ingredient that, due to its year-round availability, we take for granted and as a result may not pay enough attention to when buying. Like any other ingredient, onions vary in quality and it is well worth carefully choosing ones that are firm and unblemished.

The new season begins in spring with tender pearly white or ruby-coloured bulbs, some not much thicker than a spring onion, others expanding to fatter elongated bulbs with long green juicy and delicious stalks. The stalks are a great bonus – I use as many of them as possible when they are available and always feel I am getting double value for money. They can be cooked in exactly the same way as the onion bulb or can be elevated to a central position in a recipe such as a green onion soup or broth. Gradually the stalks wilt and dry off as the season progresses and the onions develop their papery skins in preparation for dry storage during the colder months.

This may be the simplest vegetable dish of all time. Place some small or medium unpeeled onions on a baking tray, sprinkle with salt, and roast them until meltingly tender. Serve them with roast or grilled meat or poultry. The onions need to be completely tender before you remove them from the oven, by which time all their sharpness will have evaporated. They will not be pleasant to eat if, when cut open, the flesh is not soft and melting. Once they are cut open they can be eaten as they are, with just a sprinkle of salt and pepper, or you can embellish them further with a small drizzle of olive oil, or a knob of butter, or with herbs such as thyme leaves, coarsely chopped rosemary or marjoram. The cooked skins are not eaten.

You can bring them to the table whole, in which case a few eyebrows may be raised, but all will be revealed when you cut them open to reveal the beautiful cross-sections of soft onion flesh inside.

Serves 4   8 medium red or yellow onions
Maldon sea salt and freshly ground black pepper

OPTIONAL ADDITIONS
a drizzle of olive oil
a few small knobs of butter
4 teaspoons chopped rosemary or marjoram
8 small pinches of thyme leaves

Preheat the oven to 200°C/400°F/gas 6.

Place the onions on a roasting tray and sprinkle with a pinch of salt. Roast until the onions feel really soft when pressed with a finger. This will take about 40 minutes, but the older the onions are, the longer they will take to cook.

Bring them to the table in their skins, in which case you cut off the root end and squeeze out the flesh, or cut them neatly in half and add some of the suggested seasonings.

Roast garlic

This is another really easy dish to accompany grilled and roast meats and poultry. Garlic cooked in this way is mild, and develops a light smoky flavour that is delicious. As with the roast onions, the cooked skin is discarded and it is crucial that the garlic is cooked to a soft melting consistency. I usually allow about 6 cloves of garlic per person. Some will eat more and some will have less. It usually balances out that all diners are happy in the end. The garlic in this case is roasted in individual cloves, which is both convenient and delicious, but on other occasions I roast heads of garlic whole, though that is generally if I want to use the garlic in purée form.

The ingredients
Buy whole heads of garlic and store them in a cool part of the kitchen. Avoid garlic where you can see green shoots sprouting from the heads, as this tends to be indigestible.

Serves 4
 1 tablespoon olive oil or duck fat
 24 cloves of garlic, unpeeled
 1 teaspoon thyme or rosemary leaves
 Maldon sea salt and freshly ground black pepper

Preheat the oven to 180°C/350°F/gas 4.

Put the oil or fat into a bowl, add the garlic and herbs, and stir together to lightly glaze. Season with salt and pepper and place in a small flat ovenproof dish that the cloves fit snugly into. Roast for about 45 minutes, or until the garlic feels really soft when pressed and the skins have become golden.

Serve them as they are and allow your guests to squeeze the soft flesh out of the skins.

The potatoes should be peeled and mashed immediately they are cooked – if they are allowed to cool before mashing, they tend to become gluey.

Potatoes

Potatoes hold a special place in the hearts and minds of most Irish people and I am no exception. The disastrous Great Famine of the 1840s, when the blight-affected potato crop failed with shocking results for a peasant population who had become reliant on the tuber as their staple food, is a story that is not forgotten easily in Ireland. Surprising, then, that in the immediate aftermath of those years of unspeakable misery, death and emigration, the food on whose reliance the problem was founded continued to be cultivated, and with only a cursory nod towards a diversity of crops that might prevent a repeat of the cataclysmic events of the 1840s. The most salient message from that debacle, and one which is as relevant today as it was then, is the importance of maintaining diversity of crops and of genes.

One of my favourite Irish potato stories refers to the early days of the cultivation of the crop, when suspicion surrounded it and northern Irish Protestants refused to cultivate it due to the fact that it was not mentioned in the Bible. Meanwhile, the Catholic Irish solved the problem by sprinkling their seed potatoes with holy water and planting them on Good Friday. Nice.

The thing is we grow good potatoes, very good ones. I live in an area that is famous for its potatoes. The name of my local village, Ballycotton, a fishing village where most of my fish comes from, is synonymous with good potatoes, which are grown in the surrounding area. 'Ballycotton Queens', the name affectionately given to the variety known generally as British Queens, is the single locally grown ingredient during the course of the entire year that is flagged in shops with a sign announcing its arrival. These potatoes are one of my favourite ingredients of the year, alongside the later-arriving Golden Wonder, a floury and flavoursome beauty.

The reality is that there are good potatoes grown all over the world, and different potatoes will be better at certain times in certain places. So choose the one that you think best suits the dish you are cooking, in whatever part of the world you live.

There are so many different potato dishes that it is difficult to make broad generalisations as to their cooking; however, regardless of the dish you choose to cook, the potato must be a good one.

Mashed potatoes

A bowl of fluffy and flavoursome mashed potatoes is always welcome and an essential part of any cook's repertoire. Steaming hot and with a melting lump of butter or a drizzle of olive oil, it is both comforting and sophisticated at the same time. It is amazing, though, how many cooks feel that their results with mashing potatoes are a bit hit and miss. Like most techniques, there are some rules involved and those rules are common to most variations on the mash theme. If you know the rules and follow them, you will be in a position to make a wide selection of consistently good potato dishes.

In an ideal world you would start with potatoes that still had the earth on them. This light covering of soil seals in the flavour of the potatoes and keeps them fresher while they are waiting to end up in your pot. You will have to scrub the potatoes before cooking, of course, but the resulting mashed potato will be much better. I like to cook the potatoes in their skins and peel them immediately they are cooked, though I must say I have had perfectly delicious mashed potatoes that were peeled before cooking.

In Ireland we feel that floury potatoes like the Golden Wonder make the lightest and fluffiest mash, but in other countries, like France for example, the potatoes will be of the waxy variety and there is no denying the excellence of a good bowl of French Pommes Duchesse. I like a lump-free and smooth consistency in a plain mash,

Holding the hot potato in a tea towel, and peeling

and only like the presence of bits in the dish if they have been a deliberate addition – like cabbage in the case of colcannon or spring onions in the case of champ.

This is a simple mashed potato recipe with no unusual additions, and in reality it is probably the one we want to eat most of the time. However, once you have mastered this recipe it opens up lots of other avenues for you to explore with different flavourings and additions. Sometimes there can be a bit of confusion between mashed potatoes and potato purée. Basically they are the same thing, though the potato purée tends to be smoother, richer and with a silkier consistency than a simple mash, a restaurant version of mash, if you like. The smoothness comes from the fact that the hot cooked potatoes are almost definitely passed through a potato ricer or vegetable mouli to ensure there are absolutely no lumps, and the silkiness and richness come from the extra addition of ingredients such as egg and butter.

Adding eggs to mashed potatoes has gone out of fashion, but they add a richness and colour to the mash that is undeniably good. So therefore the mash recipe here can absolutely become a super smooth pommes purée if you are happy to sieve it to ensure no lumps, and then add and beat in the egg and butter.

Keys to success

Cook the washed potatoes in boiling, salted water until **completely tender**. Undercooked potatoes will lead to a mash with hard lumps in it.

If the potatoes are floury they will probably need to be strained of 80% of their cooking water after 10 minutes of cooking and partly steamed, in the remaining water, for the rest of the cooking time.

The potatoes should be peeled and mashed **immediately** they are cooked – if they are allowed to cool before mashing, they tend to become gluey.

Any liquid additions to the mash such as milk or cream should be **boiling** when mixed with the potatoes.

Passing steaming-hot peeled potatoes through the mouli

The ingredients

Main season potatoes are best for mash. I like a floury variety like Golden Wonder. Kerrs Pink are also excellent, as are Sante and Saxon.

The egg is optional, but adds richness to the flavour and colour of the finished dish. An egg yolk or white that needs using up can also be used.

The more butter you add the more delicious they will taste.

Serves 4

900g potatoes
Maldon sea salt and freshly ground black pepper
120ml full-fat milk (approx.)
50g butter
1 egg (optional)

Scrub the potatoes really well, then put them into a saucepan, cover with cold water and salt them generously. Cover the pan with a tight-fitting lid and bring to the boil, then turn the heat down to a simmer. The variety of potato and the time of year will determine how careful you will need to be when cooking them. The more floury the potatoes are, the more likely they are to split while cooking, hence the more you need to steam them. In that case pour off most of the water after about 10 minutes, leaving just 2cm of water to steam the potatoes for the remaining time, which will be a further 20 minutes or so.

When the potatoes are nearly cooked, put the milk on to boil. Immediately the potatoes are cooked, peel them and pass them through a vegetable mouli if you have one. This will give a smoother consistency to the finished dish. If you don't have a mouli, use an old-fashioned hand masher. It is essential, however, to deal with the potatoes the minute they are cooked – if they are allowed to cool at all before mashing they may become gluey. If your milk has gone off the boil, bring it back to the boil and add it slowly. The potatoes may not take all of the milk, so be careful not to make soup. Add the butter, and the egg if using, and season well with salt and pepper. Mix well with a wooden spoon, then taste and correct the seasoning.

Mustard mash

This mashed potato is flavoured with old-fashioned English mustard powder and is perfect with beef dishes or oily fish like mackerel. This is a slightly richer version of mashed potatoes than the other ones mentioned, but you can decide if you want to cut down a little on the egg and cream. I make it according to the recipe below and just serve it in smaller quantities. It pairs really well with tomato dishes and also with a simple cabbage dish.

The ingredients
The dry English mustard powder is an essential part of the flavour of this dish.

Serves 4–6   900g potatoes
Maldon sea salt and freshly ground black pepper
60ml full-fat milk (approx.)
60ml regular or double cream (approx.)
2–4 teaspoons English mustard powder
50g butter
2 egg yolks

Follow the directions for cooking the potatoes on page 312.

When the potatoes are nearly cooked, put the milk and cream on to boil. Immediately the potatoes are cooked, peel them and pass them through a vegetable mouli if you have one. This will give a smoother consistency to the finished dish. If you don't have a mouli, use an old-fashioned hand masher. It is essential, however, to deal with the potatoes the minute they are cooked – if they are allowed to cool at all before mashing, they may become gluey. Add the mustard powder to the boiling milk and cream and whisk it in well. Add to the potatoes with the butter and egg yolks and season with salt and pepper. Mix well with a whisk or wooden spoon. Taste and correct the seasoning.

Serve the potatoes as soon as possible, in a hot serving dish.

Summer courgette, potato, olive oil and sweet marjoram mash

There are lots of green vegetables in the summer garden that are suitable for adding to a bowl of mashed potatoes. There are the obvious ones like cabbage, peas and green onions, but some perhaps more unexpected additions are broad bean leaves, pea leaves, chard leaves and stalks, and what I am going to use in this recipe, green or yellow courgettes.

Generally speaking, I prefer to use courgettes when they are very small, about 10cm, and crisp with a nutty flavour. Here they can be a bit bigger, say 15cm. If your courgettes are any bigger than that, halve them and remove the watery seeds before cooking.

The potatoes are cooked in the normal way for the mash recipes and the courgettes are coarsely chopped, sautéd in olive oil with garlic, fennel and chilli, and added with chicken stock and marjoram to the potatoes. The result should be a green- and yellow-flecked bowl of comforting potato softness with a little river of olive oil running through it.

The ingredients
Either green or yellow courgettes will work here, or a combination of both.

If your courgettes have the flowers attached, remove the stamens and little 'thorns', discard, and fold the flowers into the potatoes with the cooked courgettes.

Chilli flakes can be a source of confusion. They are basically crushed dried chillies. They are also sometimes called hot pepper or hot pepper flakes.

The sweet marjoram can be replaced with pot marjoram, which is closer in taste to oregano.

Be careful not to add too much chicken stock.

The better the olive oil, extra virgin as always, the more delicious the result will be.

Serves 4–6 700g potatoes
Maldon sea salt and freshly ground black pepper
500g courgettes, finely chopped
4–6 tablespoons olive oil
2 cloves of garlic, peeled and thinly sliced
1 level teaspoon coarsely ground fennel seeds
Pinch of chilli flakes
2 tablespoons coarsely chopped marjoram leaves
100ml chicken or vegetable stock (approx.)

Follow the directions for cooking the potatoes on page 312.

Meanwhile, cook the courgettes. Heat 2 tablespoons of olive oil in a sauté pan, then add the sliced garlic, fennel seeds and chilli flakes and allow to turn a light golden colour. Add the chopped courgettes, season with salt and pepper and continue to cook on a high heat, stirring occasionally, until the courgettes are just starting to wilt. Add half the marjoram and mix through. Taste and correct the seasoning. Remove from the heat and cover to keep warm.

Heat the stock to a simmer.

Immediately the potatoes are cooked, drain them then peel them and pass through a vegetable mouli if you have one. This will give a smoother consistency to the finished dish. If you don't have a mouli, use an old-fashioned hand masher. It is essential, however, to deal with the potatoes the minute they are cooked – if they are allowed to cool at all before mashing, they may become gluey. Add the warm courgettes and enough of the hot stock to achieve a soft but not sloppy consistency. Mix well with a wooden spoon. Add 2 table-spoons of the remaining olive oil and the rest of the chopped marjoram.

Taste and correct the seasoning, then transfer to a hot serving dish, drizzle with a little olive oil and serve as soon as possible.

Winter cavolo nero and Parmesan mash

Cavolo nero, the tall and rather stately-looking member of the cabbage family, is a favourite of mine. I sometimes think it looks a bit like a crazy Murano chandelier, with its long central stalk from which the elegant dark green, almost black leaves grow, the tips of the leaves bent over like Prince of Wales feathers. It is deliciously sweet and strong and is at its best after a few frosts. The larger leaves need to have the tough central rib removed before cooking, while the smallest leaves are tender enough to eat whole and raw.

Cavolo nero needs to be cooked until quite tender to fully appreciate its delicious taste. It combines beautifully with the potato and Parmesan in this mash.

Serves 4–6   1.5kg potatoes
Maldon sea salt and freshly ground black pepper
500g cavolo nero, weighed after removing the tough central rib
2–4 tablespoons olive oil
120g Parmesan, freshly grated

Follow the directions for cooking the potatoes on page 312.

Bring a large saucepan of water to the boil and add salt. Add the cavolo nero and cook for about 10 minutes, or until the cavolo nero is tender. Strain in a colander and reserve a little of the cooking water.

Immediately the potatoes are cooked, peel them and pass them through a vegetable mouli into a bowl. If you don't have a mouli, use an old-fashioned hand masher. Chop the cavolo nero coarsely and add to the potatoes. Add the olive oil and half the Parmesan and mix gently but thoroughly. Taste and correct the seasoning, and if necessary add a little of the reserved cavolo nero cooking water to lighten the mash. Transfer to a hot serving dish. Drizzle with the remaining olive oil, sprinkle with the remaining Parmesan and serve as soon as possible.

Roast garlic mash

Garlic is an indispensable ingredient in the kitchen. It can be hot and fiery when crushed with salt, or mild and creamy when cooked slowly in its own skin. Here, we cook the heads of garlic whole until really soft and tender, then push the soft and mild flesh through a sieve to attain a gentle purée. This is folded into the potatoes with the olive oil or butter to give a sweet and almost smoky flavour to the mash.

Don't be scared by the amount of garlic suggested in the recipe. It is not at all aggressive and the potatoes love it. The technique for roasting the garlic is simple and I use the resulting garlic purée in other dishes, one of my favourites being a roast garlic mayonnaise.

Keys to success
Make sure the little foil parcels that the garlic is roasted in are tightly sealed.

Cook the garlic until the flesh is as soft as butter.

If you have some mash left over, save it and make it into potato cakes the next day.

Reserve a little of the potato cooking water for softening the mash if it's a little firm.

Serves 4–6   900g potatoes
Maldon sea salt and freshly ground black pepper
50g butter or 6 tablespoons olive oil
1 egg (optional)

ROAST GARLIC
2–3 whole heads of garlic
olive oil
Maldon sea salt and freshly ground black pepper
2–3 teaspoons thyme leaves

Preheat the oven to 180°C/350°F/gas 4.

Cut out squares of foil big enough to enclose the heads of garlic. Place the garlic on the pieces of foil. Drizzle each one with a teaspoon of olive oil, season with salt and pepper and sprinkle over the thyme leaves. Wrap the garlic in the foil, pinching the parcel tightly closed at the top. Place in a small roasting tin and roast for approximately 1 hour. To check if the garlic is cooked, squeeze the foil parcels and the garlic inside should feel completely soft. Remove from the oven when cooked and allow to cool.

Follow the directions for cooking the potatoes on page 312.

When the potatoes are nearly cooked, remove the garlic from the foil and place it in a sieve over a bowl. Push as much of the soft garlic flesh through the sieve as you can, pressing firmly with the back of a tablespoon. You will be left with the collapsed skins in the sieve and a smooth purée in the bowl. Discard the garlic skins. When the potatoes are cooked, strain off the remaining cooking water and reserve a little of this liquid. Immediately peel them and pass them through a vegetable mouli if you have one. This will give a smoother consistency to the finished dish. If you don't have a mouli, use an old-fashioned hand masher. It is essential, however, to deal with the potatoes the minute they are cooked – if they are allowed to cool at all before mashing, they may become gluey. Add the garlic purée, the butter or olive oil and the egg, if using, and season well with salt and pepper. Mix well with a whisk or wooden spoon. If the mash is a little dry, soften it with a little of the strained cooking water. Taste and correct the seasoning, adding a little more olive oil or butter as necessary.

Serve as soon as possible, in a hot serving dish.

Boiled new potatoes

As soon as the farmers in my area start to harvest the potato crop, they will immediately appear for sale in the shops. A handwritten sign saying 'Ballycotton Potatoes' or 'Ballycotton Queens' will be posted in the shop window and will sometimes give the name of the specific potato farmer as well. Forced new potatoes will have been available for weeks before, but these local potatoes are the ones that I long to eat and I will happily wait the few extra weeks for them. With new potatoes, the longer they are out of the ground the quicker they deteriorate, so freshness is vital. The other key factor is that the potatoes should have not been washed before you buy them.

Of course you can easily grow a few potatoes if you have a little space, and nothing quite matches the pleasure of digging your own, cooking and eating them with your family and friends. The sprig of mint is optional, but adds a delicate flavour to the earliest new potatoes. If like me you are fortunate enough to live beside the sea, you can cook the potatoes in sea water. The flavour is fantastic, and with a knob of good butter they can be enjoyed as a meal on their own.

Keys to success

When it comes to new potatoes, which are relatively delicate vegetables, **freshness** or how recently they have left the ground is the key. New potatoes deteriorate very quickly after being dug up.

New potatoes are always cooked in **well-salted boiling water**.

After 10 minutes of cooking, strain off 85% of the water and finish cooking the potatoes in the steam of the covered saucepan.

New potatoes should be served immediately they are cooked.

The ingredients

Unwashed fresh new potatoes are the required ingredient.

The mint adds a delicate flavour to the early new potatoes.

Salty butter is an optional addition when serving.

Serves 4   900g new potatoes, freshly scrubbed
Maldon sea salt
Sprig of mint (optional)
Butter, for serving

Place the potatoes in a saucepan of boiling water that they fit snugly into. Add a couple of large pinches of salt and the mint, if using. The water should taste quite salty. Cook, covered, at a steady boil for 10 minutes, then strain off most of the water, leaving just 2cm of water in the pan. Replace the lid and continue cooking at a steady simmer until the potatoes are tender. They will now mostly be cooking in steam. Keep an eye on the saucepan to check that all the remaining water does not evaporate. The fresher the potatoes, the more quickly they will cook. The size of the potatoes is also a determining factor in the cooking time. Test after a further 10 minutes to see if they are tender. A skewer should pierce them easily and with no resistance. Serve with Irish or salted butter and sea salt.

Jacket potatoes

We sometimes forget how good a simple main season boiled potato cooked in its skin can be (in Ireland, what we mean by jacket potato). The potatoes can be cooked in exactly the same way as new potatoes, although the mint can be omitted and you must start the potatoes in cold water. If the potatoes are floury, a knob of butter makes the perfect sauce and a pinch of sea salt the perfect seasoning.

Gratin of potatoes, Coolea cheese and wild garlic

Coolea farmhouse cheese is a Gouda-type cheese made in West Cork. Rich, buttery and nutty, it is delicious, and a wheel in its entirety is magnificent. It is one of my favourite cheeses. The mature cheeses are wonderful as dessert cheese and I sometimes, as here, use the younger cheeses in a gratin. You can happily replace the Coolea with Gruyère. The wild garlic, a seasonal treat, can be replaced very successfully with spring onions. This flavoursome dish is excellent with roast and grilled meats.

Keys to success
Potatoes for this gratin should be **evenly cut into 2mm slices**. I use a mandoline for this job.

If you find that the gratin is colouring too much and too quickly before the potatoes are cooked, **lay a sheet of baking parchment or greaseproof paper over the dish** and continue to cook until the potatoes are tender.

The ingredients
Wild garlic leaves, sweet and gentle, are lovely here. Chop them finely with a sharp knife so they won't be stringy in the cooked gratin.

Coolea cow's milk cheese pairs beautifully with the garlic and potatoes. Gruyère makes a very good alternative.

Serves 6

1.5kg potatoes, peeled
30g butter
2 bunches of wild garlic leaves, finely chopped
170g Coolea cheese, coarsely grated
Maldon sea salt and freshly ground black pepper
450ml chicken stock

Preheat the oven to 200°C/400°F/gas 6.

Slice the peeled potatoes 2mm thick. Bring a saucepan of water to the boil, then add the potatoes and stir gently to separate the slices. Bring back to the boil, then immediately strain the potatoes and run them under a cold tap to cool down. Place the cooled potato slices on a clean tea towel to drain further. Dab them dry.

Smear an ovenproof gratin dish with half the butter. Sprinkle with half the wild garlic, one-third of the potatoes and some grated cheese. Season with salt and pepper. Repeat this process again, and finish with a layer of the potatoes, neatly arranged. Pour over the boiling stock and scatter the remaining butter and cheese over the top. Bake for 1–1¼ hours, or until the potatoes are tender and the top is crispy and golden.

Serve with grilled lamb or chicken.

Rosemarie's gratin of potatoes and Gruyère

This is a rich and comforting potato dish, so it's perhaps not for everyday eating but certainly for a special dinner for family and friends. I got this recipe from my friend Rosemarie Manning and am indebted to her. This dish will sit happily in a warm oven for 30 minutes before serving. I like to serve the gratin with roast or grilled meats such as lamb, beef or pork.

The ingredients
A waxy potato such as Nicola, Pink Fir Apple or Charlotte is best for a gratin, though I have made this with Golden Wonder and Kerrs Pink and been delighted with the result.

Gruyère, a beautiful melting cheese, combines really well with the potatoes.

Nutmeg, an aromatic spice, is best when freshly ground. Be careful though, as it has an aggressive flavour and can take over if too much is used. Treat it like a gentle seasoning.

Serves 10–12   A knob of butter
1.5kg potatoes, weighed after peeling
Maldon sea salt, freshly ground black pepper and
    freshly grated nutmeg
225g Gruyère cheese, coarsely grated
500ml regular or double cream

Preheat the oven to 180°C/350°F/gas 4. Grease a gratin dish, 28cm x 18cm, with the knob of butter.

Slice the peeled potatoes into 2mm thick slices. I use a mandoline for this task. Assemble the dish as soon as the potatoes are sliced, to prevent them from discolouring. Spread one-third of the potatoes in the dish and season with salt, pepper and nutmeg. Sprinkle on a third of the cheese and a splash of the cream. Continue building up two more layers of potato, seasoned as previously and finishing with a final sprinkling of Gruyère. You will end up with three layers of seasoned potatoes, each layer sprinkled with cheese and the whole lot moistened with cream.

Place in the preheated oven and cook for 1½–2 hours. If the potatoes are browning too quickly, cover them loosely with a sheet of greaseproof paper. Check that the potatoes are tender and cooked by inserting a skewer. The gratin can be kept warm in the oven at 100°C/200°F/gas ¼ for at least 30 minutes before eating. Turn the oven up to 180°C/350°F/gas 4 for 5 minutes before serving so that it is bubbling hot when arriving at the table.

Chips

It is hard to argue with a plate of good chips. Crisp and golden on the outside and light and fluffy in the middle, they are appealing and satisfying. Much has been written and spoken on the subject of achieving the perfect chip. I don't want to take you on that numbingly boring route or get into the complexities of the thick versus thin argument. There are, however, a couple of key factors. Good potatoes and good oil or cooking fat are essential. The variety of potato also matters, and this will vary from country to country. Here in Ireland my potato of choice is the Golden Wonder.

My preferred cooking fat for chips is the rendered fat from beef kidney suet. Sunflower oil and olive oil are also excellent options, but the oil must be of a good quality. A deep-fryer which has a built-in thermostat is the best way to cook chips, as you can control the heat accurately. I find saucepans filled with oil for the purpose of deep-frying to be dangerous and difficult to control, and I don't recommend them.

Keys to success

The potatoes should be **freshly peeled** for chips and ideally not allowed to soak in water for longer than 30 minutes.

The sooner the chips are cooked after cutting the better they will be.

The **quality of the oil or fat** being used is vital, as are the correct cooking temperatures for the two stages of cooking.

The precooking followed by the final cooking as suggested in the recipe gives a light and crisp chip.

Don't overfill the fryer with chips, as it will bring the temperature of the oil down and will result in oily and soggy chips.

The ingredients

Best-quality, freshly scrubbed and peeled potatoes such as Golden Wonder or Kerrs Pink make great chips, as do Charlotte and Royal Kidney.

Rendered beef kidney dripping or sunflower or olive oil are the fats of choice for crisp and flavoursome chips. The beef or beef kidney suet is the same fat that surrounds the beef kidney and is traditionally minced and used in Christmas puddings and mince pies. A good butcher will have this in stock, though you may need to order it.

Serves 4   6 large potatoes, e.g. Golden Wonder
               1.5 litres rendered beef dripping or sunflower oil
               Maldon sea salt

Wash and peel the potatoes. I use a swivel-top vegetable peeler. This is faster and less wasteful than using a knife and the potatoes end up a better shape. Cut the potatoes to the size and thickness of chip you require. The texture of the cooked chip will be affected by the thickness or thinness of the cut. I like a medium-sized chip, say 1cm thick and 7.5cm long. For me this gives a good balance of fluffy inside and crisp outside. Dry the cut potatoes thoroughly in a clean tea towel.

Heat the fat or oil to 160°C/325°F and add the chips. Do not overfill the basket, otherwise the temperature will come down and the chips will soak up some of the fat rather than be crisped by it, so if necessary cook the chips in batches. Cook until they are starting to tenderise and colour very lightly. Drain. At this point the par-cooked chips will sit happily for up to 30 minutes.

Increase the heat to 190°C/375°F and return the chips to the fat, cooking them for a few minutes more until crisp and golden. Lift the basket out of the fat, and if possible sit it, with the chips still in it, above the oil for a minute or two. The heat coming up from below seems to draw excess fat off the chips. Now put the chips on to kitchen paper to blot up any excess oil. Serve immediately in a hot serving dish, seasoned with salt.

Rustic oven roast potato chips

For those among you who don't possess a deep-fryer, but long for chips, these potatoes are perfect. The scrubbed potatoes are left unpeeled and cut into large wedge-shaped chips, with each wedge having its skin attached. The skin on each piece of potato is important, as it prevents them from sticking to the roasting tray, and of course it also has a delicious crispy flavour.

Serve the potatoes with roast and grilled meat, poultry or fish. They are a great accompaniment to a warm salad and you can ring the changes with the use of different herbs.

Keys to success
Cut the scrubbed potatoes into evenly sized wedges.

Use just enough fat to coat them lightly.

Place them, skin side down and ideally not touching, on the tray.
Do not season the potatoes until cooked, or the skins will stick.

The ingredients

Either a floury or waxy potato will work here. So any of the following potatoes will be excellent, such as Golden Wonder, Kerrs Pink, Charlotte, Sante or Nicola.

As the sea salt in this recipe is a last-minute addition and will be visible on the cooked potatoes, it is the ideal opportunity to showcase a flaky sea salt in all its mineral and crunchy glory.

Serves 6	900g potatoes
	4 tablespoons (approx.) olive oil, duck fat or goose fat
	Sprig of rosemary or thyme
	2-12 cloves of garlic
	Maldon sea salt and freshly ground black pepper

Preheat the oven to 220°C/435°F/gas 7.

Scrub the potatoes well – there is no need to peel them. Cut lengthways into thick chip-like wedges or, for a quicker cooking time, cut into smaller pieces. Put into a bowl and drizzle with a little olive oil or your fat of choice. Turn them in the fat to coat lightly. There should not be a pool of fat in the bottom of the bowl but the potatoes should be covered with a thin sheen of fat. Do not season the potatoes until they are cooked, as it tends to cause the potatoes to stick to the cooking tray and you may lose the lovely crispy skins.

Place the potatoes on a roasting tray in a single layer, skin side down. Add the herb of choice and the unpeeled and uncrushed garlic cloves. Place in the preheated oven and roast until the skin is crispy and the potatoes are tender in the centre, about 35 minutes. Avoid the temptation to move them on the tray, halfway through the cooking. This will only break up the potato skins. The potatoes will eventually crisp up and loosen from the bottom of the tray. Season with salt and pepper and serve in a hot serving dish with the crisped herbs and garlic cloves.

Roast potatoes

Talk to an Irish person living abroad and mention potatoes. They may become dewy-eyed and momentarily silent and possibly start muttering incoherently about their mother and home and the kitchen and 'Oh god, I miss the spuds'. Potatoes and the love of them is in our blood, mixed up in a tangle of happy and tragic emotions. Most countries of course have good potatoes; just try to find the ones with their own native soil still attached.

The potatoes here are cooked to achieve a golden brown crisp skin with a fluffy, floury interior. Bliss.

Keys to success
Peel the potatoes as close as possible to the time of cooking.

Use best-quality vegetable or animal fat.

The ingredients
Buy a floury variety of unwashed potato such as Golden Wonder or Kerrs Pink for best roast potatoes. Sante are another excellent choice for roasting.

Vegetable fat as in olive oil, or animal fat as in duck, goose, pork or beef, will give the potatoes a delicious flavour and crisp skin. I like duck or goose fat best.

Do not sprinkle on the sea salt until the potatoes are cooked – if you add it any earlier it may cause the skins to stick to the tray and for some this would be a disaster.

Serves 4   8–10 potatoes, depending on how much you like your potatoes.
2–3 tablespoons of olive oil, duck or goose fat, pork fat or beef dripping
Maldon sea salt

Preheat the oven to 230°C/450°F/gas 8.

Peel the potatoes and, if they are unevenly sized, cut the larger ones in half to have them all approximately the same. Place them in a saucepan, cover with cold water and bring to the boil. Simmer for just 1 minute, then drain – if you leave them sitting in a colander they will dry off, but you need to make sure they are quite dry, so if necessary rub them lightly with a tea towel.

Score the surface of each potato several times with a fork. This scoring encourages the skin to crisp. Put them into a bowl and toss in the fat of your choice. Transfer them to a heavy roasting tray in a single layer and cook in the oven for about an hour, until the potatoes are well coloured and crisp on the outside and tender in the middle. Season with sea salt and serve as soon as possible.

The most important thing when preparing rice is to begin by washing it to remove some of the excess starch. You will also be washing away most of the problems associated with cooking rice.

Rice

Rice is an enormous subject, and given that some estimates of the different varieties of the crop are as high as 40,000, and that half the earth's population are dependent on it as a staple food, as you can imagine we can only scratch the surface of this ingredient in terms of how we might discuss it or cook it.

We will concentrate here on savoury rice dishes and on what I consider to be the most useful and versatile ones, such as essential plain boiled rice, a rice pilaf and a risotto. Armed with the knowledge of the type of rice suitable for the specific dishes, and the relevant cooking techniques, you can expand the possibilities and have great pleasure in following the changing seasons' bounty with dozens of potential variations on each theme or technique.

Regardless of the cooking technique being applied, it is the quality of the rice itself that is the first important step. You can of course buy brands of rice that will cause you no trouble at all, such as the non-stick and boil-in-the-bag varieties, but they will pale in terms of flavour, texture and nutritional value when compared with the grains that have had no unnecessary intervention before you buy them.

I, like some cooks, was once quite scared of cooking rice. I was never fully confident that I could get perfect results every time, and so it was quite a stressful business. It was not until I started to think properly about what I was doing and actually followed the suggested rules every time that I realised that cooking rice is quite easy, and that it can be perfect each time.

Perhaps my most important lesson on the cooking and handling of rice was from the wonderful and inspirational Indian cook Madhur Jaffrey. I had the pleasure of assisting her at cookery demonstrations on several occasions, and she stressed the need to begin by washing the rice to remove some of the excess starch and to handle the precious grains with a light hand so as not to break them. As she gently washed and rinsed the rice several times, you could sense the reverence that she felt for this food, and that she was also washing away most of the problems associated with cooking rice. When cooking it she often deliberately undercooked it and allowed it to finish cooking in its own steam. I learnt a lot, perhaps most, from her respect for the ingredient, and also of course from her meticulous attention to the detail of cooking it.

It was to two other wonderful cooks, also bright stars in the culinary firmament, that I turned for assistance when I was trying to master the cooking of risotto rice: the legendary Italian cook and author Marcella Hazan, and Alice Waters, the doyenne of Chez Panisse, the ground-breaking restaurant in Berkeley, California. I devoured their words, seeking to get inside their heads via their beautifully written instructions for this essential technique. I have always found it essential and hugely helpful to read and absorb the words of other cooks that I admire.

Plain boiled rice

This is the sort of simple rice dish you will want to serve on occasions when the rice is not intended to compete with the main dish. The object of the exercise is to achieve light, fluffy, separate grains of rice. This rice is suitable for serving with meat, fish and vegetarian dishes.

The rice is gently washed in several changes of cold water, then allowed to soak for 30 minutes and drained. It is then cooked in plenty of salted water until still slightly undercooked. The drained rice is placed in an ovenproof dish, tightly covered and placed in the oven to finish cooking in its own steam. The addition of butter to the rice when it is steaming is optional but delicious.

Generally the rice is served plain, but sometimes I stir in an appropriate chopped herb just before the rice goes to the table.

Gently washing the rice

Keys to success

Wash the rice gently in several changes of cold water.

Drain the rice when there is still a little bite left in the grain.

Cover the drained rice tightly with foil to keep in the steam and heat that finishes cooking the grains of rice.

The ingredients

Basmati rice, the best of which comes from the foothills of the Himalayas in both India and Pakistan, with its long, slender, perfumed grains, is the preferred choice of rice here. Try to find rice that has been aged for a year or longer, as this maturing period improves it and increases its nutty aroma.

Serves 6–8 200g basmati rice
2 litres water
1 teaspoon Maldon sea salt
25–40g butter (optional)

Place the rice in a large bowl and cover it with cold water. Gently move the rice around in the bowl with your fingers. Drain off the cloudy water and repeat this process several times if you have time, or until the water no longer becomes cloudy. Leave the rice soaking in fresh water for 30 minutes, then drain it. The soaking allows the grains of rice to absorb water and as a result they are less likely to stick together when cooking.

Bring the water to the boil. Add the salt and sprinkle in the rice, stirring gently to separate the grains. Bring back to the boil and cook uncovered for 5 minutes. Taste the rice – it should taste a little undercooked. Strain through a sieve or colander. Don't wash it, as you will just be washing off precious flavour.

Put the rice into an ovenproof serving dish and dot the surface with a few knobs of butter, if using. Cover the dish carefully and tightly with foil and place in a low oven, 140°C/275°F/gas 1–2, for 15 minutes, for the rice to finish cooking.

Remove the foil and stir the rice gently to loosen up the grains before serving.

With herbs
Gently add 1-2 tablespoons of finely chopped flat-leaf parsley or coriander leaves to the rice just before serving.

With pomegranate and parsley or coriander
Gently add 2 tablespoons of pomegranate seeds and 1 tablespoon of chopped flat-leaf parsley or coriander leaves to the rice just before serving.

With lemon and lemon balm
Gently add 1 teaspoon of finely grated lemon zest and 1 tablespoon of finely chopped lemon balm to the rice just before serving.

Pilaf rice

This technique for cooking rice provides a rich, delicious and flavour-some result. The rice is cooked in a covered heavy saucepan with a specific amount of liquid, usually chicken stock, and occasionally, when available, turkey stock, which has a fabulously deep and rich flavour. A vegetable or a light fish stock may also be used when appropriate. By the time the rice is cooked, all the liquid will have been absorbed and the specific flavourings added to enhance the dish will all have blended to create a rice dish that is delicious and deeply comforting.

The technique can be used to create many different variations on the theme, and, depending on the additions to the rice while cooking, the pilaf can be served as a dish to accompany other meat, fish or vegetable dishes or can itself be the main event for an informal lunch or supper.

The possible additions to a pilaf are many, and you can think about those in the same way as you would a risotto – indeed, the two dishes have similarities. Try to keep vegetable additions in season.

Here I am suggesting a master recipe based on chicken stock and have listed several variations on the master recipe.

Keys to success
Rinse the rice gently in several changes of cold water before cooking.

Measure the ingredients very accurately.

Cook the rice in a heavy saucepan or casserole with a tight-fitting lid.

Cook the rice on a very gentle heat on a hob or in a moderate oven.

The ingredients
Basmati rice is the rice of choice here.

A chicken stock is the perfect liquid for this dish, though I use a turkey stock when I have it – it gives a fantastically rich and full-bodied flavour to the dish.

Turning the grains of rice in the buttery onions

Serves 4–6   15g butter
1 tablespoon finely chopped onion or shallot
250ml basmati rice, gently rinsed in several changes of
   cold water
500ml light chicken stock
1 level teaspoon Maldon sea salt

Melt the butter in a heavy-based saucepan and allow it to foam. Add the onion and stir to coat in the butter. Cover the pan and cook on a very gentle heat for 5 minutes. You want the onion to soften slightly without colouring.

Add the rice and turn the grains gently in the buttery onions. Make sure you don't break the grains of rice by being too heavy-handed while stirring. Add the stock and salt and again stir gently to mix. Bring to a simmer and cover tightly. If you think the lid of your saucepan is not a tight fit, place a layer of foil under it. Cook very gently on a low heat on the hob, or place in the oven at 180°C/350°F/gas 4, for about 15 minutes. By this time the rice should be perfectly cooked and have absorbed all the liquid. Avoid the temptation to take the lid off the saucepan before the 15 minutes have elapsed, as this allows the precious steam to escape. When the rice is cooked it will remain hot in the covered saucepan for at least 30 minutes, or for longer in the oven with the temperature reduced to 110°C/225°F/gas ¼.

With parsley
Stir 2 tablespoons of finely chopped flat-leaf parsley into the rice just before serving.

With saffron
I serve this with shellfish such as scallops or prawns. Most of the time I use chicken stock as above, but occasionally I will use a clear and clean-tasting light fish stock when I am making the dish specifically to serve with fish.

Add 1 generous pinch of saffron stamens to the onions when sautéing and proceed with the recipe.

With asparagus and chervil
To the cooked master recipe add 120g of cooked asparagus, each
spear cut into 3–4 pieces, along with 1 dessertspoon of finely chopped
chervil, just before serving.

Pilaf rice with
chanterelle mushrooms and tarragon

This is a perfect combination of flavours and could either be eaten
on its own as a lunch or supper dish, or would pair beautifully with a
simple roast or grilled chicken.

Chanterelle mushrooms are one of the best edible wild mushrooms. Much prized by that highly secretive bunch who forage for
them, they fetch high prices when they make it to the shops or markets, and are a proper treat. They taste exquisite, and while they are
great simply sautéd and served on toast, or again sautéd and folded
through soft scrambled eggs, they are wonderful with meat, fish and
poultry and in many dishes of the highest refinement.

Here the pilaf is cooked in the normal way and the cooked mushrooms and tarragon are folded into the rice just before serving.

The ingredients
Chanterelle mushrooms, in season from early summer to late autumn,
range in colour from very pale to deep yellow. Avoid very wet-look-
ing mushrooms that have been picked after a lot of rain, as you may
end up paying for the moisture they have absorbed as much as for
the precious fungus itself, and they are never as good when water-
logged as they are when firm and dry. Some rogue gatherers find it
amusing to douse the golden beauties with water to render them
heavier and therefore more financially rewarding. That excess
moisture will reveal itself as a puddle of liquid in the pan you are
sautéing them in. If they need cleaning, which they often do, avoid
the temptation to immerse them in water, but rather brush the
caps with a soft brush or wipe them clean with a damp cloth. They

will vary in size, so larger ones can be cut in half or into smaller pieces if necessary. They are generally sautéd before eating or adding to various dishes, and garlic, parsley, thyme leaves and marjoram are just some of the other flavours they combine well with.

Serves 4–6

15g butter
1 tablespoon finely chopped onion or shallot
250ml basmati rice
500ml light chicken stock
1 level teaspoon Maldon sea salt

THE MUSHROOMS
20g butter
1 clove of garlic, peeled and finely chopped
120g chanterelle mushrooms, cleaned
Maldon sea salt and freshly ground black pepper
1 dessertspoon chopped tarragon

Cook the rice as directed on page 340.

While the rice is cooking, cook the mushrooms. Melt the butter in a wide sauté pan and add the chopped garlic. Cook the garlic for 3–4 minutes on a low heat, making sure it does not colour at all. Increase the temperature and add the cleaned mushrooms. Season with salt and pepper and sauté until tender. If there is liquid from the mushrooms in the pan, remove the mushrooms to a plate and cook the liquid to a thick syrup to concentrate its flavour. Pour this over the cooked mushrooms and keep them warm.

Fold the sautéd chanterelles and chopped tarragon into the rice just before serving.

Risotto

Cooking a risotto demands your full attention. You can't be half-hearted about it. If you want to achieve a perfect result, you need to watch it, stir it, mollycoddle it, taste it and taste it again, to bring it to the stage where the rice is cooked to the perfect 'al dente' texture, while being cloaked in a creamy consistency that is slowly pourable.

Because of the commitment required, some cooks feel that a risotto is beyond them and that it can only be successfully achieved in a restaurant kitchen. This is not the case, and I hope my introduction of the dish as a demanding affair will not put you off, as with an organised approach you can easily achieve perfect risotto at home. Once you have made a risotto for the first time, a lot of the supposed difficulty evaporates and there should be no reason why it doesn't become a regular part of your repertoire.

Simply explained, it is the process of cooking a particular type of rice, with a liquid which is gradually added and absorbed, until the grains of rice are just tender and that liquid is transformed into a comfortable and flavoursome coat for the rice. It is an endlessly useful dish that can follow the new ingredients of the changing seasons and constantly bring change to your table. There are few dishes that are such a valuable vehicle for a wide variety of tastes, ranging from robust sausages and cabbage in winter, asparagus and chervil in spring, delicate peas and broad beans and their leaves in summer, and wild mushrooms and hearty pumpkin in the autumn. One could fill a book with the ingredient options or additions for what is essentially an Italian peasant dish.

The dish can be prepared to a 'pre-cooked' stage ahead of time, and I explain how to do this below. This is the way it is done in most restaurants, partly cooked and then finished just before eating. If care is taken to catch the par-cooked rice at the correct stage, the results are excellent and remove the need to be standing over the saucepan for a prolonged time close to the time of serving the meal. Five minutes should be enough time to finish the dish. This makes the dish eminently practical and useful, and I think many cooks achieve a better result this way, as it is easier to achieve correct timing and to be nice and calm when making the last-minute additions.

Barely covering the rice with simmering stock

Keys to success

A well-flavoured chicken stock or broth is the ideal liquid for most risottos. A light fish stock or even water can sometimes be used for a fish risotto. A vegetarian stock may also be used. Stock made with turkey bones is fantastic and will make a fully-flavoured risotto.

Choose a heavy saucepan with low sides, the correct size for the amount of risotto being cooked. You should not have to peer into a deep saucepan trying to see what is happening at the bottom.

Have ready your **butter diced and chilled**, for adding to the risotto at the end of cooking, and the Parmesan finely grated.

To start, very finely chopped onion, shallot, leek or other vegetables are softened without colouring in butter or oil. This is known as the '**sofrito**'.

The rice is added to this just in order to be coated in the fat and not coloured. This is known as the '**tostatura**', but don't be confused by the fact that it sounds like you should be toasting or colouring the grains of rice, because you shouldn't.

If you are adding wine, it should be allowed to evaporate completely before adding the stock.

The broth should be kept simmering while waiting to be added to the rice, a ladleful at a time. Each addition of stock should be just enough to **barely cover the rice**, so don't drown the rice, and you now need to be constantly stirring the pot with a flat-bottomed wooden spoon to prevent the rice from sticking and scorching.

The rice and broth **should bubble throughout the cooking**, so not a volcanic boil and not a sullen simmer.

Do not add more stock until the previous amount has been absorbed.

Stir the pot frequently.

Never allow the pot to go dry.

After about 15 minutes, taste the rice. It will be looking plump and will be tender but with a resistance at the core of the grain, probably a little too much resistance, but now you know how close you are to it being cooked and can react accordingly.

Start adding the stock in smaller quantities, such as a tablespoon at a time, while tasting the rice regularly to check that the perfect texture is achieved, which is tender rice with a slightly firm touch to the grain. If the centre of the grain tastes gritty, it is not cooked. The stock you have been adding should have created a sauce that is cosily wrapped around the grains and not a separate liquid. If there is a separate pool of liquid, it means you have been adding the stock either too quickly or too slowly or the heat has been too low or too high. Learn from this and it is less likely to happen to you the next time.

Taste again, and when you are happy that the rice is cooked, remove the saucepan from the heat and **allow it to cool for 1 minute before stirring in the butter and Parmesan**. This is called the 'mantecatura'. Now the finished risotto should look soft and with a hesitant ripple to the consistency if the plate is given a shake.

Correct the seasoning and serve the risotto immediately in hot but not scorching bowls. Use wide bowls such as old-fashioned soup bowls.

The ingredients
Buy best-quality risotto rice and the one which is suitable for the risotto you are preparing. There are several varieties of rice suitable for risotto, but the three main ones are Arborio, Carnaroli and Vialone Nano.

Arborio is a lovely all-purpose variety, classed as a 'superfino', which refers to the large size of the grain, and yielding a creamy result, but care needs to be taken with it to avoid a result that is too sticky and dense. It is a good medium for robust ingredients such as sausage and beans or potatoes, game and meat sauces.

Vialone Nano is a 'semifino' or small-sized rice and is the favoured rice in the Veneto region of Italy, where it features in their famous seafood and spring vegetable risottos, which are cooked to a loose consistency, sometimes described as 'all onda' or rippling.

Carnaroli, a 'superfino' with long thin grains, is a versatile rice that cooks to a lovely creamy consistency while also holding its shape, so is suitable for many risottos ranging from a delicate single ingredient saffron risotto to seafood risottos, and also for risottos where the addition of ingredients such as pea leaves or courgette flowers are last-minute.

Risotto alla Parmigiana

This is the master technique for making risotto. Once you are happy you can manage this, you can start to experiment with the endless list of possible additions to risotto.

The dish can be cooked from start to finish and eaten immediately it is ready, or it may be partly cooked ahead of time for finishing later.

The ingredients
A well-flavoured chicken stock gives the best flavour to this risotto.

Carnaroli rice is my choice here, though Arborio will do quite well too.

Grate Parmesan freshly for the risotto rather than buying pre-grated cheese, which never tastes as sweet and delicious.

Serves 6–8   1–1.3 litres chicken stock
25g butter
1 small onion, peeled and very finely chopped
400g Carnaroli or Arborio rice
150ml dry white wine (optional)

FINISHING THE RISOTTO
40g butter, chilled and diced
55g freshly grated Parmesan
Maldon sea salt

Bring the stock to the boil, then turn down the heat and keep it barely simmering. Keep a long-handled ladle ready in the stock.

Melt the 25g of butter in a heavy-based and low-sided saucepan, one that is large enough for the rice to expand by three times. Add the onion and sweat on a gentle heat until the onion is softened but not coloured. Add the rice and stir until it is well coated. Cook for a minute or so.

Increase the heat, then add the wine if using, and allow it to evaporate completely. Now, using a ladle, add enough simmering stock to barely cover the rice. It will and should splutter a little bit. Adjust the heat. Stir continuously with a flat-bottomed wooden spoon, and as soon as the liquid is just absorbed add another similar portion of the stock and continue as before. Do not allow the pot to go dry at any stage. At all times the risotto should simmer well, rather than boiling furiously. Furious boiling causes the rice to soften on the outside and remain too chewy inside and you may end up with the rice and sauce as separate entities, which is completely wrong. The cooked rice should be cloaked in its own sauce, not a mound of rice sitting in a pool of sauce. Cooking the rice too slowly will make it gluey.

If you are pre-cooking the rice for finishing later, you will need to start tasting the rice after about 10 minutes of cooking. About two-thirds of the stock will have been added. Taste a grain or two of rice between your teeth. It should be firm, slightly gritty, definitely undercooked, but not completely raw. Immediately this stage is reached, remove it from the saucepan and spread it out on a flat dish to cool as quickly as possible. At a later stage, the rice can be reheated with some of the remaining stock, again at a simmer, and the cooking and finishing of the risotto can be completed.

After about 20 minutes of cooking, when most of the broth has been added and the rice is approaching al dente, add the stock a few tablespoons at a time. The consistency should now be soft, creamy and quite loose. Taste a grain or two of the rice. The texture should now have just a gentle hint of resistance. When you are happy that this stage has been reached, remove the pan from the heat for 1 minute, before stirring in the remaining butter and the Parmesan.

Taste and correct the seasoning and serve immediately, with grated Parmesan.

Wild mushroom risotto

Ingredients as above, plus:

> 250g wild mushrooms such as chanterelles, ceps
>   or trompettes de mort
> 20g butter
> 1 clove of garlic, peeled and finely chopped
> Maldon sea salt and freshly ground black pepper
> 2 tablespoons finely chopped flat-leaf parsley

Pick over the mushrooms to ensure they are properly cleaned. Depending on the size of the variety being used, slice, chop or leave as they are. Melt the butter in a sauté pan and add the chopped garlic. Allow it to stew and soften in the butter on a low heat. Add the mushrooms and sauté on a gentle heat until tender. Season with salt and pepper, then cover until you are ready to add them to the risotto with the chopped parsley. Add to the risotto at the end of cooking, just before the addition of the butter and Parmesan.

Risotto of cavolo nero or curly kale

Ingredients as above, plus:

> 250g Cavolo nero, weighed after removing the tough stalks
> Maldon sea salt

Remove the tough central rib from the cavolo nero or curly kale and discard. Cook the leaves uncovered in a large saucepan of well-salted, boiling water until very tender. This is really important, so that the greens are both tender and vibrant and melt beautifully into the finished risotto while not tasting in any way tough. Strain the tender leaves from the cooking water and gently but thoroughly press out the excess liquid. Spread them out on a wide flat tray and allow to cool as quickly as possible. Do not be tempted to run them under the cold tap, as it dulls the flavour. Chop the cooked leaves and add to the risotto before the addition of the butter and Parmesan at the end. Make sure the greens are heated through before adding the butter and Parmesan to finish the risotto.

There is no difficulty cooking this wondrous food source, and without it you will be denying yourself myriad different recipes from all corners of the globe.

Pulses – beans, peas and lentils

Pulses, high in fibre and protein and low in fat, present endless delicious possibilities to all cooks. There is no difficulty cooking this wondrous food source, and without it you will be denying yourself myriad different recipes from all corners of the globe.

I like to buy pulses in the dried form and where necessary soak them overnight in cold water, cooking them in fresh water the next day. Tinned cooked pulses may be used, but they are more expensive and I never find them to be as fresh-tasting as the ones I have soaked and cooked myself.

Keys to success

Soak the dried peas and beans **in plenty of cold water overnight**. I usually put them into the fridge to soak.

Discard the soaking water, using it if you wish as a liquid fertiliser for your plants.

If you have forgotten to soak your pulses overnight, you can solve the problem by boiling them for 2 minutes and then allowing them to soak in that water for 1 hour. Then cook them until tender. This works, though they are not quite as good as when soaked overnight.

Lentils do not need to be soaked before cooking. I usually rinse any dust off them under a cold running tap before cooking.

Cook the pulses in **fresh water** with the suggested seasonings until tender.

The **cooking time of all pulses varies** depending on how fresh they are. The fresher they are the more quickly they will cook.

Generally pulses are **not salted** until after cooking, as salt can toughen them and cause the skins to lift off.

Always keep the cooking water. It can be used as a simple vegetable stock in soups and is quite often added in small quantities to the particular dish you are cooking with the pulses.

All pulses need quite **aggressive seasoning** and are capable of absorbing robust flavours to counteract their relative blandness.

Lentils for every day

This is a recipe for cooking lentils to serve warm to accompany meat and poultry, to serve with goat's cheese and beetroot, maybe roast pepper and basil leaves, to add spices to, or just to eat as a nourishing bowl of goodness with herbs and a knob of butter or olive oil stirred in.

The cooked lentils will keep for a couple of days in the fridge and reheat well.

The ingredients
I like to use green lentils from Le Puy in France or brown lentils from Castelluccio in Italy.

Serves 4–6   250g green lentils (such as Puy or Castelluccio)
1 carrot, scrubbed or peeled and cut into 3 chunks
1 onion, peeled and quartered
1 stick of celery, halved
1 red chilli
1 bay leaf
1 sprig of sage
1 sprig of thyme
3 cloves of garlic, unpeeled
4–6 tablespoons olive oil
1–2 tablespoons mild red wine vinegar or lemon juice
2 tablespoons chopped herbs, such as parsley, coriander, marjoram and a little tarragon (optional)
Maldon sea salt and freshly ground black pepper

Place all the ingredients except the oil, vinegar or lemon juice, chopped herbs and seasoning in a saucepan and cover with cold water. Bring to the boil, then cover the pan and simmer for about 15 minutes. The cooking time is not exact, so test the lentils regularly after 12 minutes of cooking. They should retain a gentle bite but should absolutely not be hard.

When you are satisfied that they are ready, strain off the cooking liquid and retain some of it for reheating the lentils or moistening them later. Remove the vegetables and herbs and discard. Press the garlic, which should be soft by now, out of its skin into the lentils.

While still warm, dress the lentils with the olive oil and vinegar or lemon juice, add the herbs if using, and season generously with salt and pepper.

The lentils are now ready to eat either at room temperature or gently warmed, adding a little of the strained cooking water if they appear dry.

Lentils with mustard, cream and tarragon

These lentils are good with grilled beef, chicken and guinea fowl. I also like them with lamb kidneys and liver. A slice or two of grilled bacon would be delicious with the lamb offal too.

There is a variable in the quantity of mustard in the ingredient list, to allow for your taste and also because, depending on what you are serving the lentils with, you may want more or less. I find that when I am serving lentils with grilled beef, I like them to be quite mustardy. These lentils can be prepared ahead of time and reheat perfectly.

If you can find a green French mustard with tarragon in it, that is great to use here. Otherwise use the best Dijon mustard you can find.

Serves 6–8   250g lentils
1 carrot, scrubbed or peeled and cut into 3 chunks
1 onion, peeled and quartered
1 stick of celery, halved
1 red chilli
1 bay leaf
1 sprig of sage
1 sprig of thyme
3 cloves of garlic, unpeeled
250ml regular or double cream
1–2 teaspoons French mustard
1 dessertspoon chopped French tarragon
Maldon sea salt and freshly ground black pepper

Place all the ingredients except the cream, mustard, tarragon and seasoning in a saucepan and cover with cold water. Bring to the boil, then cover the pan and simmer for about 15 minutes. The cooking time is not exact, so test the lentils regularly after 12 minutes of cooking. They should retain a little bite but should absolutely not be hard.

When you are satisfied that they are ready, strain off the cooking liquid and retain some of that for reheating the lentils or moistening them later. Remove the vegetables and herbs and discard. Press the garlic, which should be soft by now, out of its skin into the lentils.

Add the cream, mustard to taste and tarragon, and season with salt and pepper. Bring to a simmer and allow to cook for a couple of minutes for the liquid to thicken slightly.

Taste and correct the seasoning, and serve.

Gratin of lentils
with crumb and herb crust

This gratin is a handy dish that can be served as an accompaniment to grilled or roast meats, and would be perfect with cold meat, particularly ham.

The ingredients
Try to get sourdough bread for the herb crust – it has a lovely texture and flavour. I almost always have a little end or slice of a previous loaf in the freezer, and this works perfectly for these crumbs when defrosted.

Use the Lentils for Every Day recipe (see page 358) as the base for this gratin.

You will also need :

> 60g coarse breadcrumbs
> 3 tablespoons olive oil
> 2 tablespoons chopped parsley
> 1 teaspoon thyme leaves
> ½ teaspoon chopped rosemary
> 100g Parmesan, coarsely grated

Preheat the oven to 200°C/400°F/gas 6.

Toss the breadcrumbs in the olive oil, then spread them out on a baking tray and place in the preheated oven for about 15 minutes, until toasted and golden. The crumbs tend to cook unevenly, so you will need to move them around on the tray a couple of times during the cooking. When ready, remove from the oven and reserve for later.

Add the chopped herbs and half the Parmesan to the lentils. Taste and correct the seasoning if necessary, adding a little more lentil cooking water or olive oil. The mixture should be soft so that it will reheat to a comforting consistency. Place in an ovenproof gratin dish and scatter the remaining Parmesan and roasted breadcrumbs over the top.

The gratin can now be reheated in the oven for 30 minutes, until bubbling hot and with a golden crust, or can be put aside to be reheated later.

Black-eye beans with oyster mushrooms and caramelised onions

These beans are perhaps the easiest pulse of all to identify, with their cartoon-like black eyes.

The oyster mushrooms, with their silky consistency, pair beautifully with the beans, and the light spicing brings the whole dish together in a gentle way. Button mushrooms will be delicious if finding oyster mushrooms proves difficult.

This dish makes an excellent vegetarian meal when served with boiled rice, and is delicious with a plain roast chicken or grilled or roast lamb.

Serves 6

- 3 tablespoons olive oil
- 2 onions, peeled and thinly sliced
- 225g oyster or button mushrooms, thinly sliced
- Maldon sea salt and freshly ground black pepper
- Lemon juice
- 1 clove of garlic, peeled and thinly sliced
- 1 teaspoon ground turmeric
- 3 tablespoons chopped coriander leaves
- 225ml regular or double cream
- 225g dried black-eye or haricot beans, soaked in cold water overnight, then drained and boiled in fresh water until tender (reserve the cooking liquid)
- Zest of 1 lemon

Heat 2 tablespoons of olive oil in a sauté pan or low-sided saucepan and add the sliced onions. Turn the onions in the oil and cook over a moderate heat, stirring at intervals, for about 30 minutes or until the onions are caramelised to an even rich brown colour.

While the onions are cooking, heat another pan with the remaining tablespoon of olive oil and fry the mushrooms, seasoning them with salt, pepper and a few drops of lemon juice. Add the sliced garlic to the pan when the mushrooms are nearly cooked and allow to colour lightly. Stir in the caramelised onions, then add the turmeric and cook over a very low heat for 5 minutes to draw the flavour out of the spice. Add half the chopped coriander and the cream and bring to a simmer. Add the cooked and drained beans, bring back to a simmer and cook gently for just 3–4 minutes, until the cream has thickened just enough to coat the beans in a light sauce.

At this point the dish can be allowed to cool for reheating later. To serve, reheat the beans to a simmer and add the remaining coriander and the lemon zest. Taste and correct the seasoning and serve. If the sauce becomes too thick, add a little of the bean cooking water to thin it.

Chickpea and coriander purée
with mint and marjoram

This Middle Eastern chickpea purée or hummus is great served with toasted pitta bread, with super-fresh and crisp vegetable crudités or as part of a selection of hors d'oeuvres. Hummus should be kept chilled if you are keeping it overnight, and should be used within 2 days of making it.

The ingredients
Tahini is a sesame seed paste, and there are toasted and untoasted varieties available. The quality varies greatly, so try to find an authentic brand. Once the container has been opened, store it covered in the fridge.

Serves 8
175g dried chickpeas, soaked overnight in cold water, drained, and cooked in fresh water until tender (reserve the cooking liquid)
2 cloves of garlic, peeled and crushed to a paste
Juice of 1 lemon
150ml untoasted tahini (sesame seed paste)
1 teaspoon roasted and coarsely ground cumin
Maldon sea salt and freshly ground black pepper
2 tablespoons chopped coriander
2 tablespoons olive oil
Pinch of paprika
Pinch of tiny or finely chopped mint leaves
Pinch of marjoram leaves

Place the drained chickpeas in a food processor with the garlic and 4 tablespoons of the cooking water. Add half the lemon juice and purée. Add the tahini, cumin and a good pinch of salt and blend again.

If necessary, add a little more of the cooking water to achieve a smooth purée. The mixture should not be too dry. It should have a slightly creamy appearance and just hold its shape on a spoon. Taste, and add more lemon juice and salt as needed. Fold in the chopped coriander by hand. Serve drizzled with olive oil and dusted with paprika, and scatter over the mint and marjoram leaves.

Chickpea and coriander purée
to serve with roast lamb

The chickpea purée can be prepared ahead of time and kept at room temperature. Just before serving, add a little boiling gravy to the purée to warm it and soften it very slightly. Omit the mint and marjoram leaves. Serve with the roast lamb and more gravy.

Mint relish is a great accompaniment to the roast lamb and the chickpea purée.

Chickpeas with spinach, red onion, roast cumin,
tomatoes and lemon

This is a simple dish that can be enjoyed with rice for a vegetarian supper and also makes a lovely accompaniment for roast or grilled lamb or pork. The dish, which should be rich in flavour and juicy, reheats perfectly, so can if necessary be prepared ahead of time. Always remember to keep some of the liquid you have drained off the cooked pulses. It may be needed to loosen the sauce if it is too thick, or to add a little more liquid when reheating.

Pulse dishes like this sometimes need robust seasoning, so don't be too polite with it. If it seems a little dull, add another pinch of salt and sugar for the tomatoes. If it is a little watery, just allow it to bubble with the lid off for a few minutes longer. If you have a little left over it will freeze quite well.

This recipe makes enough for four people as a main course, and for eight people as an accompaniment to grilled or roasted meat.

The ingredients

Buy chickpeas in smallish quantities and store them in tightly sealed
containers. The fresher they are the more quickly they cook.

Swiss or multicoloured rainbow chard can replace the spinach, in
which case the chard leaves should be cooked in simmering salted
water before being added to the tomato sauce.

If you are using baby spinach leaves, they do not need to be destalked.

In summer the ripest fresh tomatoes can be used, while in winter
best-quality tinned or bottled ones are a better option.

Serves 4
- 600g spinach
- 2 tablespoons olive oil
- 2 cloves of garlic, peeled and thinly sliced
- 1 teaspoon roasted and coarsely ground cumin seeds
- 2 medium red onions, peeled and finely diced
- Maldon sea salt and freshly ground black pepper
- 400g ripe tomatoes, peeled and chopped, or the same
  weight of tinned or bottled tomatoes
- Pinch of sugar
- 190g dried chickpeas, soaked in cold water overnight, then
  drained and boiled in fresh water until tender (reserve
  the cooking liquid)
- Grated zest of 1 lemon

Remove the stalks from the spinach and slice them finely across the
grain. Rinse the leaves and set aside to drain.

Heat the olive oil in a wide low-sided saucepan or sauté pan and add
the sliced garlic. Allow to turn just golden and immediately add the
ground cumin seeds, diced onions and spinach stalks. Season with
salt and pepper, stir to mix and cover the pan. Lower the heat and
allow to cook very gently until the onions are tender. This takes
about 15 minutes.

Remove the lid and add the tomatoes. Season with salt, pepper and a pinch of sugar. Allow to bubble up, then put a lid on the pan and cook at a simmer for 10 minutes, or until the tomatoes have softened to a rich sauce. Turn the heat up and add the spinach leaves. You will have to work a little when adding the leaves, but gradually they will wilt down and fit in the pan. Cook until the spinach is just collapsed and tender.

Add the drained cooked chickpeas, with a little of their cooking liquid if the mixture looks a little dry. The mixture should be juicy. Allow to simmer for 5 minutes. Taste and correct the seasoning – sometimes an extra pinch of sugar can transform the dish. Remember that chickpeas need plenty of seasoning.

Serve in a large warmed serving dish, sprinkled with the lemon zest.

Measuring all the ingredients accurately goes without saying, but the level teaspoon measurement of the bicarbonate of soda here is vital.

Simple soda breads

There is a huge divide in the world of bread. At the top level, but still on a relatively small scale, breads are getting better by the day, with hungry and ambitious bakers, young and old, finding the best ingredients, often organic, and creating really fantastic food. At the other end of the scale is the mass-produced, factory-style bread that is anathema to those who care about good healthy and nutritious food.

As most bakers will tell you, particularly those who use natural starters such as sourdough, bread-making is a lifelong journey of learning. You never really know it all, and if you were to dwell on that fact, you might find it all too intimidating, and never get started. You need to start somewhere, though, and whereas a crusty loaf of sourdough bread, full of complex flavours and risen with a starter you have created yourself, may be the ultimate goal, simple and gentle soda bread is a perfect introduction to the pleasures of bread-making.

Keys to success
Always **preheat the oven** when making bread.

Measuring all the ingredients accurately goes without saying, but crucially the **level teaspoon measurement** of the bicarbonate of soda here is vital.

When adding the buttermilk to the flour, **start off by adding most of it** all in one go, and mix it into the flour. Add the rest of the buttermilk if needed.

Gently mixing to a soft dough

Soda breads need only the minimum amount of handling – you are just mixing and shaping. Kneading the dough is unnecessary and will actually toughen the bread. Make sure you bake the bread until it is properly cooked. It should have a golden brown crust and sound hollow when tapped on its base.

A simple white soda bread

'Soda bread' is so called because the raising agent used is bicarbonate of soda, also called bread soda or baking soda. You don't have to start planning this bread a week ahead. You don't need a bubbling sourdough in the cupboard, and it takes only a matter of minutes to make and not more than 45 minutes to bake. This is the least 'needy' of all breads, requiring very little handling, and no kneading at all, just a gentle mix and a simple shaping.

These Irish soda breads are generally given a cross-shaped cut with a knife before being put in the oven. This cruciform mark, with its suggestion of a blessing, is more than just a symbolic gesture. The deep fissure created by the cut of the knife allows the heat to penetrate into the thickest part of the bread, the part that takes longest to cook, thereby ensuring a properly cooked loaf. The most joyous aspect of all is when the bread is cooked and cool enough to take in both hands, and with just a little encouragement and a gasp, it breaks along the deep lines of the cross in an organised and almost biblical way.

The ingredients
Plain white flour, preferably unbleached, is used here.

Buttermilk, or what used to be called sour milk, is the liquid used to moisten the flour. If you can't get buttermilk, add 1 tablespoon plus 1 teaspoon of lemon juice to 350ml of full-fat milk, stir and proceed with the recipe.

Bicarbonate of soda is easily available and is sometimes called bread soda or baking soda. Buy it in small quantities and always seal the container it is stored in after use.

Serves 8–10   450g plain white flour
1 teaspoon salt
1 level teaspoon bicarbonate of soda
350ml sour milk or buttermilk

Preheat the oven to 230°C/450°F/gas 8.

Sieve the dry ingredients into a large wide bowl, one that seems almost too big for the task at hand. This large-sized bowl allows for gentle hand movements, which makes for a more tender bread. Take particular care when measuring the bicarbonate of soda, that it is just a level teaspoon. Adding more will not improve your bread. In fact, it will have the opposite effect, giving the bread a bitter taste and a strong smell of the soda. When sieving the soda I use a fine coffee sieve to ensure there are no lumps.

With your fingers, mix the dry ingredients really well. Make a well in the centre of the flour and add most of the milk to the bowl. This action of adding most of the milk together is important, as if you slowly drizzle in the milk as you mix, it means you will work the dough more than is necessary and end up with a tougher loaf.

Immediately, and with your hand open like a claw, mix in the flour from the sides of the bowl. The dough should be softish and not wet and sticky. If it is wet and sticky due to you adding too much milk (learn from this and use less the next time), sprinkle on a little extra flour. Add the remaining milk only if necessary. When it comes together, and this should take no longer than 10 seconds, resist the temptation to knead it and just turn it out on to a well-floured surface. Now wash and dry your hands.

Gently shape the dough into a round loaf about 18cm wide. Place it on a lightly floured baking sheet. Cut a deep cross in the top of the bread, about 3cm deep, making sure the blade of the knife goes right out over the edges of the dough. Pierce each quarter of dough with a knife, again about 3cm deep. Immediately place in the preheated oven. Cook for 15 minutes, then turn down the heat to 200°C/400°F/gas 6 for a further 30 minutes. To check that the bread is cooked, lift it up and tap the bottom. It should sound hollow and feel light. If unsure, cook for a few minutes longer.

Cool on a wire rack.

White soda scones

Makes 10   Ingredients as in White Soda Bread, above

Preheat the oven to 230°C/450°F/gas 8.

Proceed as above, flattening the dough into a round not less than 3.5cm deep. Cut with a knife into scones and place on a lightly floured baking tray.

Place in the preheated oven and cook for 15 minutes, then turn down the heat to 200°C/400°F/gas 6 and cook for a further 10 minutes. When cooked, the scones will sound hollow when tapped on the bottom.

Place on a wire rack to cool.

Rosemary and thyme herbed scones

Makes 10   Ingredients as in White Soda Bread, above, plus:
1 tablespoon chopped rosemary
1 teaspoon thyme leaves
Sun-dried tomatoes or black olives to decorate (optional)

Preheat the oven to 230°C/450°F/gas 8.

Proceed as in the White Soda Bread recipe, adding the chopped herbs to the dry ingredients just before the addition of the buttermilk. Flatten the dough into a round not less than 3.5cm deep. Cut with a knife into scones, add the sundried tomatoes or olives if using, and place on a lightly floured baking tray.

Place in the preheated oven and cook for 15 minutes, then turn down the heat to 200°C/400°F/gas 6 and cook for a further 10 minutes. When cooked, the scones will sound hollow when tapped on the bottom. Place on a wire rack to cool.

White soda bread with Indian spices

Add 2 teaspoons of curry powder (see page 48) to the sieved dry ingredients and proceed as in White Soda Bread, above.

Brown or wholemeal soda bread

This is the best known of the Irish soda breads and is best eaten on the day it is made. The dough is slightly softer than in the White Soda Bread recipe.

The ingredients
A coarse wholemeal flour is best here.

If you have difficulty sourcing buttermilk, add 1 tablespoon plus 2 teaspoons of lemon juice to 450ml of full-fat milk and proceed with the recipe.

Serves 8–10   225g plain white flour
225g coarse wholemeal flour
1 level teaspoon salt
1 level teaspoon bicarbonate of soda
450ml buttermilk (approx.)

Preheat the oven to 200°C/400°F/gas 6.

Sieve the white flour into a large bowl that seems oversized for the task. Add the wholemeal flour. Add the salt and carefully sieve in the bicarbonate of soda. Lift the flour with your fingers to mix and add air to the dry ingredients.

Make a well in the centre of the dry ingredients and pour in most of the buttermilk in one go. With your hand open like a claw, mix in a circular fashion to bring in the flour from the sides of the bowl. This will take only a matter of seconds. The dough should be soft but not sloppy. Once the ingredients come together into a soft mass, stop mixing. Put a good dusting of wholemeal flour on your work surface and gently turn out the bread from the bowl. Stop, and wash and dry your hands.

Shape the dough, resisting the temptation to knead it, into a neat round loaf about 18cm wide. Place the bread on a lightly floured baking sheet. Cut a deep cross in the top of the bread about 3cm deep, making sure the blade of the knife goes right out over the edges of the dough. Pierce each quarter created by the cross just once with a knife.

Place in the preheated oven for 35 minutes, then turn the bread over and cook for a further 5–10 minutes. When cooked, the bread will sound hollow when tapped on the bottom. Cool on a wire rack.

Cheddar cheese 'focaccia'

This is a quick, simple and delicious interpretation of the classic Italian flat bread using the white soda bread as a master recipe. Serve it cut in fingers or wedges with soups and salads, or as a sandwich bread. Olives, red onions, sun-dried tomatoes and herbs can also be added to the cheese topping.

Serves 8–10   1–2 tablespoons olive oil
450g plain white flour
1 level teaspoon salt
1 level teaspoon bicarbonate of soda
350–360ml buttermilk
110–175g Cheddar, grated on a coarse box grater

Preheat the oven to 230°C/450°F/gas 8. Brush a Swiss roll tin or baking sheet, about 23cm x 33cm, with the olive oil. The tin will look generously oiled.

Sieve the flour into a large wide bowl. Add the salt and sieve in the bicarbonate of soda very carefully. Mix the dry ingredients together, then make a well in the centre of the flour. Add 350ml of the buttermilk and mix to a soft but not sticky dough. Add the remaining buttermilk if necessary. The mixing should take no longer than 30 seconds. Further mixing only toughens the bread.

Gently flatten the dough into the prepared tin with your hands or a rolling pin. If necessary put a little flour on your fingers to aid the spreading of the dough. Scatter the cheese over the top.

Bake in the oven for 10 minutes, then turn the heat down to 200°C/400°F/gas 6 and cook for a further 20–30 minutes. The cheese should be melted and bubbly on top. If you are not sure whether the bread is cooked, lift it at one corner and have a look. The base should be well-coloured and slightly crisp. Slide the cooked bread on to a wire rack to cool. Serve cut in shapes of your choice.

Potato and rosemary 'focaccia'

Serves 8–10 Cheddar cheese 'focaccia' as above, plus:
450g potatoes, boiled, slightly cooled, peeled and
cut into 1cm slices
1 tablespoon coarsely chopped rosemary

Preheat the oven to 230°C/450°F/gas 8.

Proceed with the dough as in the Cheddar Cheese 'Focaccia' recipe and flatten it into the oiled Swiss roll tin. Carefully arrange the sliced potatoes in neat rows on top of the dough. Sprinkle on the rosemary and the Cheddar cheese.

Bake in the oven for 10 minutes, then turn the heat down to 200°C/400°F/gas 6 and cook for a further 20–30 minutes. The cheese should be melted and bubbly on top. If you are not sure whether the bread is cooked, lift it at one corner and have a look. The base should be well-coloured and slightly crisp.

Slide the cooked bread on to a wire rack to cool. Serve cut in shapes of your choice.

Cook the sugar and water to a deep chestnut-coloured caramel – be brave, as a light caramel will taste only of sugar. You rely on the bitterness of the 'burnt' sugar to add character to the sauce.

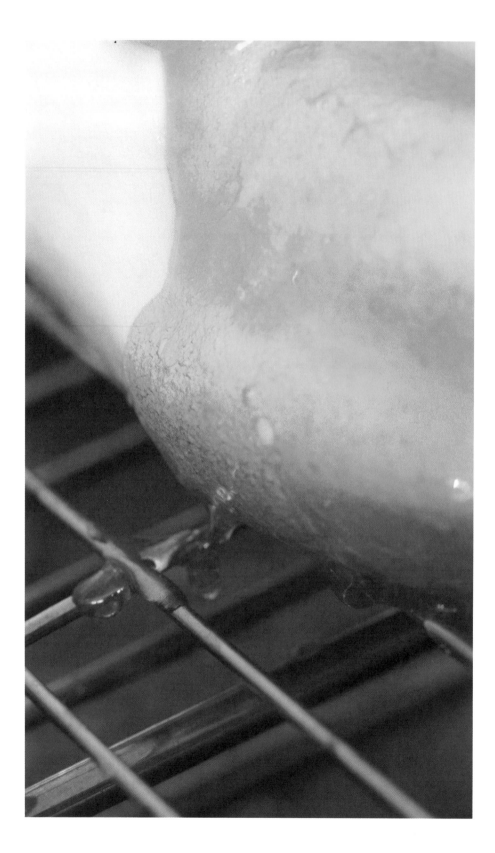

Sweet essentials

Here are a few sauces and garnishes that will accompany various desserts or puddings. Some of the sauces, such as caramel and chocolate, will keep for several weeks, while others, such as crème anglaise or whipped cream, need to be used quite quickly.

All the sauces are versatile, and for some dishes you can serve a combination of two of them to create a delicious and more complex effect. The garnishes, such as praline or candied citrus zest, are used both for flavour and, where relevant, for decoration. On occasions a sauce and a garnish will be combined, such as a caramel sauce and candied lemon or orange zest, or chocolate sauce and praline cream.

The techniques involved in some of these recipes are an essential part of the cook's repertoire.

Making a caramel sauce or praline should not fill you with fear and trepidation. Equally, a light custard like crème anglaise should not be regarded as a game of chance, but as an almost scientific exercise where you are totally in control and have the knowledge to recognise the crucial stages of the process that are involved. That is what we are aiming for here.

Chocolate sauce

Rich and dark with a lacquer-like shine, chocolate sauce is a classic and it is easy. The most important ingredient is clearly the chocolate, so search for the best quality you can find. I use Valrhona, a wonderful chocolate from France, and generally buy the 70% cocoa solid version.

I serve the sauce with ice creams and some chocolate puddings. It's best when freshly made, but will keep in the fridge for several weeks. If I have stored it for a while, I always warm it up gently before serving.

Keys to success
Never use 'cooking' chocolate – the quality is generally horrible.

Add the chocolate to the warmed cream **off the heat**.

If keeping the sauce warm, **make sure it does not get too hot**, otherwise it may curdle.

Serves 6–10 225ml regular or double cream
225g best-quality chocolate, chopped
½ teaspoon vanilla extract or 1 tablespoon rum (optional)

Put the cream into a heavy-based saucepan and bring it almost to the boil. Remove from the heat and add the chopped chocolate. Stir with a flexible rubber spatula to blend the chocolate and cream to a shiny rich sauce. Add the vanilla or rum if using.

Keep the chocolate sauce in a warm place, for example sitting in the saucepan that you melted it in, with the heat turned off.

Other flavours
Replace the rum in the recipe with whiskey or brandy or an orange liqueur, or a ¼ teaspoon of finely grated orange zest. Or try adding 2–4 tablespoons of caramel sauce to the finished sauce.

Sugar syrup

Sugar syrup, sometimes referred to as simple syrup or stock syrup is quickly and easily made by cooking equal quantities of sugar and water together .

The syrup can be flavoured with herbs such as verbena, mint, lemon balm, sweet geranium, rosemary and so on. Spices such as star anise, cinnamon and cloves are also an option when a distinctive flavour is required.

Makes 800ml   450g caster or granulated sugar
           600ml water

Place the sugar and water in a heavy-based saucepan. Place on a gentle heat and stir occasionally to encourage the sugar to dissolve. It is best if the sugar has dissolved before the water comes to the boil, as that way you are ensured of no sugar crystals remaining in the cooked syrup.

Simmer gently for 2 minutes. Remove from the heat and allow to cool.

Store covered in the fridge where it will keep for 5 days.

Caramel sauce

Caramel sauce is a very useful dessert sauce. Clear and shiny, and as richly coloured as well-polished mahogany, it needs to be cooked with care. Use a heavy saucepan with medium high sides and cook it on the heat furthermost from the edge of your cooker, so that it is safely away from an awkward elbow or a child's inquisitive reach.

It is vital to cook the sugar and water enough to achieve a deep 'chestnut brown' colour, as this 'burning' of the sugar tempers the sweetness of the sauce to achieve a balance that is neither too sweet nor too bitter.

This sauce pairs with many different flavours, for example citrus fruit, particularly orange and lemon. I serve it warm with ice-cold poached gooseberries. It also combines well with some chocolate desserts, and ice creams such as vanilla or brown bread.

The sauce will keep for months in the fridge, but will thicken as it chills. You can dilute it with a little warm water when this happens.

Keys to success

With gentle and occasional stirring, try to **ensure that the sugar dissolves** before the water comes to the boil.

As soon as the sugar and water come to the boil, **remove the spoon** you have been stirring with and do not stir the sauce again at any stage during the cooking.

The sugar and water rarely caramelise evenly. When this happens, **do not stir**, but tilt the saucepan gently to and fro to blend the darker caramel with the paler.

Cook the sugar and water to **a deep chestnut-coloured caramel** – be brave, as a light caramel will taste only of sugar. You rely on the bitterness of the 'burnt' sugar to add character to the sauce.

Be careful, as this sauce gets really hot. **Don't leave it** when it starts to caramelise.

Serves 6–10   225g caster or granulated sugar
Water in two lots:
125ml cold water for cooking with the sugar
165ml hot water for 'slaking' the caramel

Place the sugar and the 125ml of cold water in a heavy saucepan with medium high sides. Put over a moderate heat and stir occasionally with a wooden spoon to encourage the sugar to dissolve. Try to have the sugar dissolved before the mixture comes to the boil, otherwise the undissolved sugar crystals may remain in the caramel at the end of cooking and spoil the appearance and consistency of the sauce.

Once the sugar and water come to the boil, remove the spoon and do not stir again, as this can cause the syrup to crystallise and the resulting caramel may be cloudy. As the water is boiled off, the sugar will start to caramelise and most likely will colour unevenly. If this happens, tilt the pan in the direction necessary to gently encourage the coloured syrup to run into the pale syrup.

Do not be tempted to stir the syrup or it will 'block' or partly solidify, due to the introduction of a lower temperature in the form of the spoon. Do not leave the saucepan once the colour starts to change but continue cooking until a rich chestnut caramel is achieved.

Remove from the heat and add the 165ml of hot water. Be careful at this point, as the caramel sometimes spits and splutters. Using hot water here is less volcanic than using cold. You will now see two quite different liquids in the saucepan: the thick caramel, and the water you have just added. Replace the saucepan on a low heat, again resisting the temptation to stir, and cook until a single consistency is achieved. Remove from the heat and allow to cool. The sauce may look a little thin, but it will thicken further as it cools.*

Serve warm or cold. Store in the refrigerator.

*The easiest way to clean a saucepan after making caramel is to fill it to the top with hot water and allow it to soak for an hour. Any caramel that is stuck to the saucepan will eventually dissolve and the remaining chore is easy.

Salty caramel sauce
Add a pinch of Maldon sea salt to the finished caramel sauce.

Orange caramel sauce
Peel 6 thin strips of orange peel, using a sharp swivel-bladed peeler to ensure none of the bitter white pith remains attached, and add to the sugar and water at the beginning of the cooking.

Continue as in the caramel sauce recipe. Remove the orange peels before serving.

Softly whipped cream

Whipped cream is as simple as pie. All you need to remember is to keep the cream really cold and not to over-whip it. If I am whipping cream ahead of time, I under-whip it slightly, put it back into the fridge to remain chilled, then give it the last few turns of the whisk just before I am going to serve it. Softly whipped cream should always be served chilled from the fridge and only just hold its shape when lifted on to a spoon; then, full of air, it falls gently on to the food it is being served with. It should be all soft folds, no sharp peaks or grainy texture.

It is perhaps not something you want to eat every day, but when it is called for with, say, warm bread and butter pudding or a hot choc-olate soufflé, or used in just the tiniest amount on a brilliantly green soup, it is exactly correct. Its flavour is not as sharp as crème fraîche or yoghurt, and that needs to be considered when making the deci-sion to serve it. Try a blob of crème fraîche on a bowl of summer strawberries and you will know what I mean. The acidity of the crème fraîche tramples all over the berries, whereas the gentler cream, not nearly as bullying, just accentuates the berry taste. You can buy

The cream whipped just to soft folds

cream already whipped nowadays, but honestly, that is entirely unnecessary. Whipping it yourself is one of the quickest jobs in the kitchen – you can prepare exactly the amount you need and arrive at that perfectly soft and comfortable consistency with the minimum of effort.

Rose petal and cherry syrup

This syrup is great served with delicate creams such as the lemon verbena cream pots, or for adding to whipped cream to serve with meringues. It will keep for at least a year. It is also good added to a dry sparkling wine as an apéritif.

Makes 750ml
175g rose petals, the most scented you can find
1.5 litres cold water
525g caster or granulated sugar
Juice of 2 lemons
14–16 cherries

Put the rose petals and cold water into a saucepan and bring slowly to the boil. Immediately turn to the gentlest simmer and cook for 30 minutes. Meanwhile, warm the sugar in a Pyrex or stainless steel bowl in a low oven (100°C/200°F/gas ¼).

Strain the liquid into a wide stainless steel saucepan, pushing on the petals heavily to extract as much liquid through the sieve as possible. Add the warmed sugar and the lemon juice. Crush the cherries with a fork and add with their stones to the liquid. Bring to the boil, then continue to boil uncovered until the liquid looks thick and syrupy. Strain out the cherry skins and stones, then pour into sterilised bottles and store in a cool place.

Serve a little drizzle of this syrup on cream desserts and decorate with a crystallised rose petal.

Crème anglaise or light vanilla custard

Crème anglaise, a flourless, thin custard, is one of the classic dessert sauces. The classic version is flavoured with vanilla, but many variations exist. Lemon, orange, chocolate and coffee are some of the many other flavours that might be introduced. If possible use a vanilla pod or bean, but natural vanilla extract can also be used. The vanilla pod will give a superior flavour and the sauce will be flecked with the tiny vanilla seeds whose appearance in the sauce adds visual interest.

Serve the crème anglaise with fresh summer berries, with autumn blackberries flavoured with sweet geranium, with fruit compotes, meringues, chocolate desserts, bread and butter pudding and even old-fashioned baked apples.

Keys to success
The vitally important cooking tip here is that the sauce **must not boil** at any stage of the cooking. If it boils it will scramble and the silky consistency will be lost.

If your sauce does happen to scramble on you, take it off the heat and immediately whisk like crazy or blend for a few seconds with an immersion blender or in a liquidiser. Then chill quickly over a bowl of iced water. This emergency action has saved me once or twice!

The ingredients
Use full-fat milk for the sauce.

A vanilla pod and the seeds extracted from it give the best flavour and appearance to the sauce. Failing that, use an organic vanilla extract.

The quality of really good fresh eggs will shine through here in flavour and in colour.

Makes 750ml 600ml full-fat milk
1 vanilla pod or 1 teaspoon vanilla extract
6 free-range egg yolks
55g caster sugar

Put the milk into a pan, add the vanilla pod, if using, and bring almost to the boil. Remove from the heat and set aside, allowing the vanilla pod to infuse the milk. Beat the egg yolks with the sugar until thick and light. If you are using vanilla extract, add it now. Pour in the hot milk gradually, whisking all the time.

Transfer to a clean saucepan, including the vanilla pod, and cook on a low heat for 15–20 minutes, stirring constantly with a flat-bottomed wooden spoon. The custard must not boil, so keep a close eye on what is happening in the saucepan and the heat under it as well. Be patient and eventually the custard will thicken slightly – not dramatically though, and just enough to leave a light trail along the back of the wooden spoon when a finger is drawn through it. Remember that this sauce is served with a thin consistency and also remember that it thickens a little as it cools.

Immediately remove from the heat and pass the custard through a sieve into a clean, cold bowl to cool at room temperature. To maximise the flavour and appearance of the vanilla in the sauce, cut the vanilla pod in half and squeeze in the oily-looking seeds. When whisked, this thick black liquid disperses into thousands of tiny little flecks of vanilla. Stir it several times as it cools – even though it may be perfect leaving the saucepan, sometimes it can inexplicably curdle as it cools, and the occasional whisk seems to prevent this from happening.

Once the sauce is cool, it can be covered and stored for a couple of days in the fridge, though it is without doubt best on the day it is made.

Candied citrus zest

In an ideal world, I would always have these chunky batons or finer julienne strips of candied citrus zest to hand for sprinkling over ice creams and sorbets, fresh fruit or compotes, cakes and various puddings and biscuits. The candied zests keep for months when stored in sugar in a cool dry place, but are at their very best when eaten within a few days of being made. With or without the optional chocolate coating, they are one of my favourite sweets to have with coffee.

There are two recipes here, but the technique employed of blanching the fruit to remove the bitterness and then slowly candying it in syrup is similar in both recipes. I use oranges, lemons, clementines, grapefruit and occasionally limes.

I always cook the various fruits separately, as the cooking times vary.

Keys to success
Blanching the citrus rinds in cold water 5 times as directed is crucial
   to ensure a tender result that is not too bitter.

Cook the citrus very gently once added to the syrup.

The ingredients
Choose unblemished brightly coloured citrus fruit for these recipes –
   in this part of the world we receive the best citrus fruit during the
   winter months.

Makes 100   2 pink grapefruit, or 4 oranges, or 4 lemons,
                  or 6 clementines
               600ml sugar syrup (see page 390)
               200g chocolate, 60-70% cocoa solids, melted (optional)

Cut a slice of rind horizontally off the top and bottom of the fruit, just thickly enough to start exposing the juicy flesh. Cut the fruit from top to bottom in quarters. With a sharp knife, remove three-quarters of the flesh from each piece of fruit. This fruit need not be discarded, but can be lightly sugared and eaten later as a light and

Blanching strips of orange for candied citrus zest

refreshing dessert. Cut the rinds lengthways to achieve 5mm wide strips with just a little of the flesh attached. Place the strips in a saucepan and cover with cold water. Bring to a simmer and allow to cook for 2 minutes. Strain off the cooking water gently and repeat this process, always starting with cold water, 4 more times.

Drain the blanched rinds thoroughly. Place them in a clean saucepan and cover with the cold sugar syrup. Poach very gently at a bare simmer, uncovered, for about 1 hour, or until the fruit is tender and looks translucent. Do not allow the syrup to boil fast otherwise it will reduce, thicken and toughen the fruit. Remove the rinds from the syrup and place on a wire rack to drain thoroughly and become completely cold. When cold, transfer to a sheet of baking parchment and leave at room temperature overnight to dry out.

Next day, you can take either of two routes with the fruit. The strips can be rolled in dry caster sugar and stored in an airtight box, or you can dip the cooled rinds in melted chocolate. Of course you could also decide to sugar some and chocolate-dip the rest – that way you will have homemade citrus chocolates to eat straight away and candied strips to enjoy at a later date.

Dip the rinds in melted chocolate and place on parchment paper to set. Chill.

The chocolate-coated rinds will keep for weeks in a sealed container in the fridge. Roll them in best-quality bitter cocoa powder before serving.

Candied citrus julienne

The technique for making this fine candied citrus julienne is similar to that for the strips. They are more refined and suitable for dishes where a more delicate citrus garnish is required.

Makes 100　　2 lemons or oranges
　　　　　　250ml sugar syrup
　　　　　　Caster sugar, for coating

With a swivel-bladed peeler, pare the rinds off the citrus fruit from top to bottom, achieving long strips and as wide as possible to facilitate easier chopping. Place on a board and cut into fine julienne along the length of the strips. Put into a small saucepan and cover generously with cold water. Bring to the boil, and immediately strain off the water. Replace in the saucepan with cold water and repeat the process 4 more times, to tenderise the fruit and draw out any excess bitterness. Allow the fruit to drain thoroughly.

Place the drained strips in a small saucepan and cover with the cold sugar syrup. Bring to a bare simmer and cook uncovered for about 20 minutes, or until the fruit appears translucent. Don't allow the syrup to cook too fast otherwise it will reduce, thicken and toughen the fruit. Drain off the syrup and save it for making lemonade. Place the strips on a wire rack to cool and to allow all of the excess syrup to drain off.

Toss in caster sugar and store in an airtight box in a cool place until needed.

Almond praline

Praline powder, ground fine or coarse, has a delicious nutty and caramel flavour and is an essential item in the pastry kitchen. It is used in ice creams, mousses, soufflés, cakes, icings, sweet sauces, biscuits and creams. It can be sprinkled over seasonal berries or scattered over peaches or nectarines before or after roasting. I sometimes just fold it into softly whipped cream to serve with a chocolate cake or pudding. Its uses are too varied to list them all. The praline keeps for several weeks in a sealed container.

Keys to success
Use a **heavy saucepan** to make the praline.

Allow the sugar to become a dark caramel and **do stir** with a wooden spoon if it cooks unevenly.

Pour the praline on to a prepared tray immediately it is cooked.

Do not touch or grind the praline until it is completely cold.

The ingredients
Unskinned almonds have more flavour than the pre-skinned variety.

Makes 220g   110g granulated sugar
110g unskinned almonds

Line a baking sheet or tray with baking parchment or a heatproof non-stick baking mat. Alternatively, use a light brushing of a bland oil such as sunflower.

Place the sugar and almonds in a heavy low-sided saucepan and put on a medium heat. Slowly the sugar will heat, melt and start to caramelise. This will not happen evenly, and using a wooden spoon you will have to gently push the almonds around the pan as the sugar caramelises. The almonds will start to make a cracking sound as they get roasted in the sugar. When all the sugar is a rich chestnut colour,

quickly coat the nuts in the caramel, using the wooden spoon, and immediately turn them out on to the prepared tray. The cooking time will have been about 10 minutes. Do not touch the mixture with your bare hands under any circumstances, as the caramel will be molten and lava-like. If you wish to draw a few individual almonds aside from the bulk of it to be used as a decoration, do it now with the aid of a fork before the mixture sets. Allow to cool completely – it will set into a solid slab.

Break the slab of praline into small coarse pieces and grind a few pieces at a time to the powder texture of choice, using a food processor. I use the pulse button so that I can control the size of the grind more accurately. It is worth saying that the sound of the praline being ground is very loud and you may think you will damage your machine, but I have ground a lot of praline in my time and have never found this to be the case.

Store the praline in a sealed container in a dry place.

Hazelnut praline

Preheat the oven to 180°C/350°F/gas 4.

Place 110g hazelnuts on a roasting tray and roast for about 15 minutes, until the skins are starting to lift and flake and the nuts are golden brown. Remove the tray from the oven and allow the nuts to cool. Place the cold nuts in a clean kitchen towel, gather up the edges of the towel, and rub the base of the towel on the palm of your hand to loosen the skins as much as possible. You will not get every last piece of skin off, and that is fine. Proceed to cook the skinned hazelnuts with sugar as for the almond praline recipe, above.

The trick is to be able to recognise what fruit, local or otherwise, is at its best at any particular time of the year and to use it then.

Fruit fools, compotes and salads

When I was learning how to cook, making a perfect fruit salad was regarded as one of the most difficult tasks in the pastry kitchen. In theory the task was a simple one: fresh fruit chopped or sliced and sweetened. What could be the problem? The problem was the same one that applies to many 'simple' dishes: it is all in the detail. The biggest issue was what combination of fruit to use and to ensure that the various fruit were in perfect condition. This called for a bit of organisation and careful ordering to get the slower-ripening and more quickly-ripening fruit ready on the same day. After that, the detail was in how evenly and to what thickness the fruit was sliced, how much sugar to use so as to enhance but not over-sweeten the fresh taste of the fruit, and how to mix the fruit without breaking and spoiling it. None of the problems were enormous ones, but they all needed careful consideration.

Compotes – fruit again, this time cooked in a thin syrup – can also be correctly described as 'simple', and are easier by comparison to a fresh fruit salad, but they too have their subtleties. For example, there is a considerable difference between a compote of rhubarb and stewed rhubarb.

Fools, a comforting mix of fruit either fresh or cooked, smashed or puréed and enriched with whipped cream, will also require the cook to concentrate, in an effort to achieve a balance of fruit and cream that favours both the fat and the fruit equally and allows neither element to dominate.

The time of year will determine where your fruit comes from and what recipe you choose to cook. From spring through summer and autumn you can rely on a good supply of home-grown fruit, and also, during those warmer months, of treats that rarely grow well here, such as peaches, nectarines, apricots and so on. During the dark winter months you will need more help from fruit that has been grown in a climate more sunny than ours, apart from what you may have frozen during the productive months here. The trick is to be able to recognise what fruit, local or otherwise, is at its best at any particular time of the year and to use it then.

I tend to gorge on fruits that grow successfully in our climate when they are in season, at their very best and delightfully at their cheapest. I then mostly forget about them until they appear the following year. I feel the same way about the best imported fruit – peaches and nectarines, for example. When the French and Italians are eating their home-grown and sun-ripened stone fruit, I want them then as well. I freeze a few prime locally produced fruits, but only the ones that I know will preserve well. I freeze for quality, not for sentiment, and only freeze fruit that I am confident will produce a delicious result later in the year.

I also indulge in the fruits with a unique flavour and a unique place in the calendar and that have thankfully escaped from being mass-produced due to their reluctance to conform, or travel, or that are not a worthwhile option for industrial-style production. These fruits can only be enjoyed in a certain place at a certain time.

The first dessert apple of the season, the Beauty of Bath, is a good example. Its season is short and it is a bad traveller. As children, our mother would quietly observe us eyeing up the tree bearing the forbidden fruit from about the middle of July. But we knew that the first day of August was the appointed moment for us to feast on the fruit, and generally we behaved accordingly. When finally the day arrived and we were allowed to climb the tree and claim the sweet bounty, our joy was noisy. The best of these apples were the ones eaten in the early morning or late evening, when the fruit was cold as well as sweet. Warnings about eating too many sometimes went unheeded, and we usually got the predicted hives. Cool pink calamine lotion was tenderly administered to our raised blotches. I remember how we would hold the apples up to our mother's face and say that her cheeks looked just like the skin of the apples. We thought we were paying her the highest possible compliment, because we thought few things could be as lovely as these apples or as lovely as her. She, elegantly as always, graciously accepted our childish plaudits and it was not until years later that I realised that the broken-veined and slightly blushed appearance of the apple may not have seemed quite the compliment we had meant it to be. Beauty is indeed in the eye of the beholder. To this day, I always rub the first of these apples against my cheek in a quiet act of remembrance.

In a couple of weeks these fragile apples were gone for another year and we moved on to the next tree that became ripe and ready. More itchy hives and more soothing lotion followed.

Fruit fools

Keys to success

Always choose **perfectly ripe and seasonal fruit**, regardless of whether it is to be cooked or not. Berries such as raspberries, loganberries, tayberries, blackberries and blackcurrants can be **frozen at the height of their season** and make excellent fools at a later stage of the year when seasonal fruit is just not a great option.

Fruit that is being cooked for a fool should be **quite tender** to ensure the creamy consistency of the finished dish.

Raw fruit can be puréed or coarsely mashed.

Generally, cream that is being added to fruit to make a fool should be **thickly whipped**, so that the finished consistency of the dish will be similar to **softly whipped** cream.

The mixing of the sweetened fruit and cream should be a **gentle business**, using a flexible rubber spatula. How thoroughly you wish to mix the two is up to you. The less you mix, the streakier and more dramatic the effect will be.

Serve a thin crisp biscuit, such as Vanilla Shortbread, with the fool.

Rhubarb fool with Sacristains

The first tender pink stalks of rhubarb are always a great treat. Expensive and scarce, their appearance heralds the arrival of spring and they never taste better than in the first few weeks of the season. Buy exactly the quantity you need and try not to let any go to waste.

The trick is trying to get the balance of fruit and cream right. Too much cream dilutes the flavour of the fruit and is too rich, and too little cream can leave the fool tasting a bit underwhelming. The consistency of the whipped cream is another crucial element. If the cream is too soft, the fool will be runny and more like a soup. If the cream is too stiffly whipped, the fool can become grainy. So look at your poached fruit and gauge the necessary consistency of the cream accordingly.

Serve crisp, buttery vanilla shortbread biscuits with the fool or, as I am suggesting in this case, an almondy, sugary, caramelised Sacristain.

The ingredients
The first of the new season rhubarb, forced and grown under glass or plastic, with its pinkish red stalks can be eaten raw or cooked. It combines in its raw state with blood oranges to make a delicious and refreshing salad. When buying it, the leaves should be firm and glossy and the stalks firm, well coloured and neither too thick nor too thin (about the thickness of your thumb). Avoid green stalks of rhubarb completely, unless you are making a chutney, in which case a few green stalks will do no harm.

Serves 6–8   450g rhubarb, cut into 2cm pieces
175–225g caster or granulated sugar
2 tablespoons water
300ml regular, double or whipping cream, whipped until quite stiff
Sacristains (see page 441), 1 or 2 per person

Place the rhubarb, sugar and water in a small stainless steel saucepan and stir to mix. This seems like a very small amount of water, but the rhubarb will release its own juice as it cooks and the less water you use the better the flavour of the fruit will be. Cover with a greaseproof paper lid and a very tight-fitting saucepan lid and bring to a simmer on a low heat. Cook gently until the rhubarb is collapsed and tender, about 20 minutes.

Sit a sieve over a bowl and drop the cooked rhubarb in, allowing the excess syrup to drain into the bowl. Do not press the rhubarb. Allow the fruit and the syrup to cool completely. Place the cooled rhubarb in a bowl and mix gently with some of the strained syrup to break it up. Do not turn it into a purée, as it is nice to come across distinguishable little pieces of the fruit as you eat the fool. Fold in the whipped cream and add a little more of the strained syrup if the consistency is not soft enough. Handle gently and do not over-mix.

Serve chilled. Drizzle some of the leftover syrup over the top, or serve it with a Compote of Rhubarb with Clementine Juice and Vanilla (see page 421). Serve the Sacristains or shortbread biscuits separately.

Raspberry fool with vanilla shortbreads

This is one of those recipes that somehow is greater than the sum of its parts. Raspberries, sugar and cream, three easy-to-source ingredients, produce a rich and luscious result. When available and in season, I use fresh raspberries. However, this is excellent made with frozen berries and I have not quite decided whether it may not actually be better made with the frozen fruit. Soft fruit becomes tarter when frozen and this seems to accentuate the flavour when the fool is made with the frozen berries. Serve Vanilla Shortbread Biscuits with the fool.

The ingredients
Raspberries, best-quality fresh or frozen, work equally well here. The berries can also be replaced very successfully with tart loganberries or tayberries, or even a mixture of all three.

Serves 8–10   450g raspberries, fresh or frozen
150–225g caster sugar
600ml regular, double or whipping cream, whipped
    until quite stiff
Vanilla Shortbread Biscuits (see page 437)

Lay the raspberries out flat on a dish. Sprinkle on the caster sugar and allow to macerate for 1 hour. If you are using frozen berries this should be long enough for them to defrost.

Purée the fruit and sugar in a liquidiser or blender. Pass the purée through a sieve to remove the seeds. Discard the seeds. Gently fold in the whipped cream. If you wish to create a 'swirly' effect, just be a little light-handed with the folding in of the cream. The fool is now ready to be served with the shortbread biscuits, or can be chilled for serving later.

Raspberry ice cream

If you have some of the fool left over, freeze it until set and frozen.

Fruit compotes

Keys to success
Ripe and seasonal fruit will yield the best compotes.

However, fruit suitable for compotes such as raspberries, loganberries, tayberries and currants, red, white and black, will when **frozen in prime condition** at the height of their local growing season, yield an excellent compote.

The cooked fruit in a compote should be **perfectly tender** and still holding its shape.

When serving a compote, it is crucial to serve plenty of the sweetened **poaching syrup** with the fruit.

Compote of plums with red wine and star anise

Plums that are hard and boring when raw can be transformed into something delicious when poached in a simple syrup. Here the syrup is half water and half red wine, the wine adding a lovely warming depth to the flavour. The star anise, a lovely spice, is perfect with the plums. The cooked plums should be holding their shape perfectly, but still tender enough to fall away from the stone with a gentle push of a fork or spoon. Serve these plums warm or chilled – they are delicious with whipped cream, yoghurt or crème fraîche, or with Yoghurt and Star Anise Cream (see page 515). Any of the wine and plum syrup left over after eating the plums can be made into a lovely jelly. The syrup also makes an excellent cocktail when diluted with sparkling water and stiffened with a splash of vodka.

The ingredients

Dark red or blood plums are ideal here. Unusually, I don't mind if they are hard, as they are transformed in the cooking to a state of tender deliciousness.

Star anise is a lovely spice, and its distinctive and quite beautiful star-shaped appearance is as lovely as its heady aroma. A word of caution, though: if you are heavy-handed with it, its forthright flavour and heady scent can move from being sweet and exotic to being more reminiscent of cheap pot-pourri – not good.

Serves 8

900g plums
550g caster or granulated sugar
2–3 star anise
300ml cold water
300ml red wine

Put the plums, sugar, star anise, water and wine into a saucepan and bring slowly to a simmer. Cover the pan and poach the plums at a simmer on a gentle heat until they are just starting to tenderise. This will take about 20 minutes, but keep a good eye on them – different varieties of plum, and plums in different stages of ripeness, will vary in cooking times. The plums should be holding their shape and feeling a little underdone in the middle when you remove them from the heat. They will continue to soften as the syrup cools. Serve warm, at room temperature or chilled.

Compote of raspberries with sweet geranium

This is a great recipe that can be used all year round. I use fresh berries in summer and autumn, and frozen ones in winter.

The geranium leaves come from the lemon-scented geranium, and they add a highly scented and delicious flavour to the syrup and the fruit. You will find this geranium in a good garden centre and it

is well worth having. It can sit outside in a sunny spot in summer and needs to come back to a sunny windowsill, conservatory or glasshouse for the winter months. It is immensely useful and I also use it to flavour mousses and soufflés, sorbets, granitas and ice creams. It also pairs beautifully with blackberries and apples, or better still a combination of both of those fruits. I have on occasions replaced the geranium with mint, lemon balm or lemon verbena with excellent results.

Serve these berries with Raspberry Fool or Raspberry Ice Cream (see pages 414 and 416) or with Chocolate and Caramel Mousse or Soft Vanilla Meringues (see pages 521 and 476).

The ingredients
Ripe fresh or best-quality frozen berries are equally successful here. If using frozen berries, there is no need to defrost them before use.

The water in the ingredients should be cold so that it draws the flavour out of the leaves and into the syrup as it comes up to the boil.

Serves 6   600g raspberries, fresh or frozen
400ml cold water
350g caster or granulated sugar
6–8 sweet geranium leaves

Put the berries into a large heatproof bowl. Put the cold water, sugar and geranium leaves into a saucepan and slowly bring to the boil, stirring occasionally to make sure the sugar dissolves. Allow to simmer for 2 minutes.

If using frozen berries, pour the boiling syrup straight over them, straining out the leaves as you go. If using fresh berries, allow the syrup to cool for 5 minutes before straining and pouring over the fruit. The fruit can be eaten immediately while still warm, which is lovely during the winter months, or you can leave it for a couple of hours and serve chilled. It keeps for several days in the fridge.

Compote of rhubarb
with clementine juice and vanilla

This may seem like an unusual combination, but believe me, it works really well. The cooked rhubarb should be perfectly tender and still holding its shape, in a syrup perfumed with vanilla and citrus juice.

The rhubarb is delicious served with Rhubarb Fool (see page 412), in which case it should definitely be chilled, or with Vanilla or Brown Bread Ice Cream (see page 467).

The ingredients
Bright red and firm rhubarb stalks are required here. Watch out for a
lovely variety of rhubarb called Timperley Red.

Clementines have the most delicious juice and are best here, though
any of the sweet oranges from the mandarin orange family such as
satsumas or tangerines will do.

Serves 4 450g red rhubarb stalks, cut at an angle into 5cm pieces
175g caster sugar
1 vanilla pod
125ml clementine or tangerine juice

Preheat the oven to 200°C/400°F/gas 6.

Place all the ingredients in a baking dish they fit into snugly. Cover tightly with tinfoil and seal well. Put into the preheated oven and cook for about 1 hour. I usually have a look at them after 45 minutes, testing the pieces with a skewer to see how tender they are, but generally I find it takes the full hour to cook. Serve warm or chilled.

Fruit salads

Keys to success

If your fruit is not **perfectly ripe** and in perfect condition, you will not produce a beautiful salad. The fruit is being served uncooked, so there is nowhere for hard, flavourless fruit to hide.

Take great **care when cutting, peeling and slicing** the fruit, so as to ensure a neat and even result that will not only look better but eat better as well.

When sweetening fruit for a salad, **don't overdo it**. The sugar is there to enhance the flavour of the fruit, not to overpower it. On the other hand, it is not clever to have the fruit too sharp – remember that eating the fruit is supposed to be a pleasurable experience, not a cheek-caving, lip-puckering ordeal.

When combining several types of fruit in a salad, take care with the proportions so as to have a good, even balance.

When mixing the fruit, use a flexible rubber spatula wielded with **care and delicacy** so as not to break the fruit and end up with a mush.

Most fruit salads will benefit from an hour of maceration before serving to draw the juices out of the fruit and for the various flavours to mingle. After the hour, the fruit starts to lose its texture and freshness of taste.

Sugared peaches with blueberries

When peaches are ripe and delicious at the height of summer, there are few things I prefer more than this simple dish. You can take it a step further by adding a sprinkling of raspberries or, when available, alpine strawberries. I eat this on its own or with peach sorbet, and for a real celebration with a splash of fizzy wine such as Prosecco or Blanc de Blanc, just before it goes to the table. A few really tender spearmint leaves could be gently torn over the salad at the last minute and that too would be lovely.

Wait until you see great peaches before you decide to make this dish, or else plan ahead and have your peaches in stock to guarantee that they will be perfectly ripe. Fully ripe nectarines are great here as well.

The ingredients

Peaches will be at their best in late July, August and early September. Watch out for unblemished fruit. Pick one up and smell it and if it doesn't transport you to a peach orchard, don't bother with it. White-fleshed peaches are particularly good, and keep an eye out for the variety of flat peach called Saturna, which is delicious. These flat peaches look as if someone sat on them, but when properly ripe they taste terrific. When perfectly ripe, yellow-fleshed peaches are just about an equal to the lauded white fruit. It is also worth keeping an eye out in good food shops or farmers' markets, as very occasionally a mild spring followed by a hot summer will yield home-grown peaches, and varieties such as Perrigrin, or the nectarine called Lord Napier, can be outstanding. However, regardless of climactic conditions, your geographical location, or the flesh colour of peach, only the ripe peach will do.

Blueberries have achieved legendary status in the last few years for their health benefits. High in vitamin C, and a beneficial antioxidant, they are now classed as a superfood. If you were to believe all the health benefits associated with them, you might eat nothing else. They certainly taste wonderful, and are being grown in larger quantities in this country with each passing year. As long as they

look and smell fresh, they are generally fine. They are well worth freezing, especially for people who like to include them as a regular part of their diet. Buy them at the height of the season in August and freeze them as they are.

Serves 4   4–6 ripe peaches
2 tablespoons caster sugar
1 lemon
150g blueberries

To peel the peaches, cut a small shallow cross in the stem end of the fruit. Place them in a heatproof bowl and pour over boiling water to cover the fruit – the water must be absolutely boiling. Count out 10 seconds and immediately remove the fruit with a slotted spoon and gently submerge them in iced water. After a few seconds, remove them from the chilled water and the skins should slip off easily.

Slice the peach flesh off the stone in 5mm slices into a bowl. Sprinkle them with a little sugar and a few drops of lemon juice as you go. Depending on how sweet the fruit is, you may not need all the sugar, and be mean with the lemon juice, as you don't want its flavour and sharpness to dominate. The lemon juice is in this dish to prevent the peaches from discolouring and to enhance the flavour of the fruit with its acidity. When all the peaches are sliced, add the blueberries and mix gently with a flexible rubber spatula. Already the sugar will be dissolving to a delicious syrup. Taste, being sure to get a piece of peach and a blueberry on the spoon, and decide if you need to add any remaining sugar. Serve the peaches as soon as all the sugar has dissolved to a rich syrup, or cover and chill for serving later.

If you are adding a few raspberries or alpine strawberries, stir them in very gently, using the rubber spatula so as not to break up the fruit.

Strawberries with honey, lemon and mint

Once upon a time, you could eat strawberries straight from the plant and expect a delicious experience. That is not the case now, except for a few exceptional varieties that are grown for the quality of their taste and not, as most commercial strawberries are, for appearance, longevity and hardiness.

This salad is really quick and easy to make and is both refreshing and delicious. Try to find honey produced close to where you live, and unwaxed lemons. Do not chop the mint until you are ready to add it to the fruit, as it will oxidise and lose its fresh sweet flavour if chopped in advance. Serve this salad on its own or with vanilla ice cream, or with a sugar biscuit and softly whipped cream.

The ingredients

Choose the ripest and freshest strawberries you can find. The freshness of the calyx or green stalk of the fruit is the best indicator as to the freshness of the fruit – it should be bright green and looking as fresh as a daisy. Watch out for a variety of strawberry called Gariguette and when you see it, buy it, as it has a flavour and sweetness that has long been bred out of most of the commercial varieties. If you find it you can cut down on the suggested quantity of honey in the recipe.

Spearmint, the smooth and tender-leaved variety, with its aroma of French markets and Moroccan tea, is best here.

Serves 4 450g strawberries
1–2 tablespoons honey
1–2 tablespoons lemon juice
2 tablespoons mint leaves

Hull the strawberries and slice thickly into a bowl. Mix the honey and lemon juice together. Chop the mint and immediately add to the honey. Taste to check that the balance of honey and lemon is correct. It should be neither too sweet nor too tart.

Add the honey mixture to the fruit and toss gently. Taste again, remembering that it is the sweetness of the strawberries that will really determine if more honey or lemon is needed. Serve immediately, or chill and serve within the hour.

Salad of oranges, dates and mint

This is a lovely refreshing salad which I like to serve when the new season oranges from Italy and dates from Morocco arrive in the shops in December. I scramble around in the garden trying to find a few surviving mint leaves to freshen it up. If the mint has all been scorched by the frost, I just use a sprinkling of pomegranate seeds. This dish can be served on its own with perhaps a little yoghurt.

The ingredients
In the shops here, oranges start to get good in early December, as the Italian ones arrive on the market. These oranges are usually around for a couple of months and are sweet and full of juice, light years away from the hard little scuds we have to put up with for most of the rest of the year. Colour in oranges is not an indication of quality, and avoid rock-hard light ones in favour of firm and heavy-feeling fruit.

Medjool dates, fat, meaty and shiny, arrive in the shops in December, usually the same time as the good oranges, a fortuitous bit of timing. Watch out for another wonderful variety of date called Barhi, which Alice Waters introduced me to at the Berkeley farmers' market in California.

Orange flower or orange blossom water is a perfumed distillation from the fresh blossoms of Seville oranges and can be found in good food shops and chemists.

Serves 4–6   5 oranges

1 tablespoon caster sugar or 1 dessertspoon honey

12 dates

2 tablespoons orange flower water

1 tablespoon mint leaves

2 tablespoons pomegranate seeds (optional)

Remove the zest from one of the oranges with a fine grater or a Microplane. Juice the zested orange and put into a bowl with the zest. With a sharp knife, remove the skin and pith from the remaining oranges. Slice or segment the oranges and add to the juice and zest with the caster sugar or honey.

Halve the dates lengthways, remove the stones and add to the oranges. Sprinkle on the orange flower water. Chop the mint leaves and gently mix all the ingredients together, being careful not to break up the orange pieces. If using the pomegranate seeds, add now. Cover and chill before serving.

Exotic fruit salad in lime syrup

This salad can be made all year round, varying the fruit according to availability and the season. Take particular care when choosing the fruit. If underripe fruit is chosen the results will be disappointing, so don't hesitate to leave one of the suggested fruit out if it is not up to scratch.

The lime syrup will keep in the fridge for several days and also makes an excellent base for lemonade. You can omit the lime syrup if you like, and just sprinkle the prepared fruit as you go with the sugar, lime zest and juice. You will have less juice in the finished salad, but the flavour will be delicious and intense.

The ingredients

Limes will vary a bit in colour, ranging from dark green to pale green depending on where they come from, but they should all have a lustrous quality and feel heavy in proportion to their size.

Pineapples can play games with you when you are trying to choose one that is ripe and ready. The colour of the skin is not an accurate guide to ripeness, as green pineapples can be just lovely, but the green leaves give a much more correct suggestion as to what is going on underneath the heavy skin. If the leaves look tired and discoloured, you can be pretty sure that the flesh inside will have similar defects. Avoid fruit that looks in any way bruised or damaged and particularly avoid any fruit with mould on the skin or leaves, as the flesh will also taste mouldy. Once you are happy with the visuals of the fruit, smell it and trust your nose. The fruit should be sweet-smelling and of course it should smell of pineapple.

Melon is another fruit that should look unblemished before you even pick it up, and will also give you a lot of information by its aroma. If it smells of melon and yields slightly when pressed at the end where the flower was, then all should be well providing you can give it a couple of days to arrive at peak condition in your kitchen. Watch out for green-fleshed Ogen melons – these mostly come from Israel and we see them during the autumn. Orange-fleshed Charentais and Cavaillon, confusingly the same variety and from France, and lovely Cantaloupe from Italy, are all summer melons.

Mangoes, like many imported fruits, are picked under-ripe to make them easier to transport. Generally, you need to allow a few days for them to ripen at room temperature. To test if they are ripe, press with the heel of your thumb, it should yield slightly. Watch out for the yellow skinned Alphonso mangoes, arriving in the shops towards the end of April, they are some of the best of the year.

Passion fruit with their ugly, dimpled and wrinkly skins, give no indication on the outside as to the deliciousness that lies within. When buying, avoid the smooth skinned ones, as they will not be properly ripe, but do make sure there is no mould on the skin, as in that case the flavour of the flesh may be tainted.

Kiwi fruit, a fruit that has somewhat gone out of fashion, can be excellent. Its lack of popularity may be due to the Nouvelle Cuisine movement in Europe in the late 70s and 80s when it ended up in all sorts of inappropriate places at the hands of some misguided chefs. If you have forgotten about them, perhaps this might be the time to reacquaint yourself with this hairy little fellow. Stunningly beautiful when out of their skin and closely observed, they are sweet and flavoursome when perfectly ripe. A ripe kiwi will yield slightly to pressure when pressed and should have an unblemished and unbroken skin. Overripe and soft kiwis will ruin a dish. Watch out for the golden kiwi, a relatively recent arrival here.

Serves 10

LIME SYRUP
225g sugar
225ml water
2 limes

FRUIT
1 pineapple, peeled, cored and cut into neat 3cm chunks
1 melon, halved, seeds removed, cut into 3cm chunks or into balls with the aid of a melon baller
2–4 kiwi fruit, peeled and sliced
1 mango, peeled and sliced
2–4 passion fruit, halved and sieved if you don't like the seeds
Seeds of ½–1 pomegranate
2 bananas, peeled and sliced

Put the sugar and water into a saucepan and bring to the boil, stirring occasionally. Simmer for 1 minute, then take off the heat and allow to cool completely. Remove the zest from the limes with a fine grater or Microplane, and add with the juice to the cooled syrup. Prepare your fruit as suggested in the ingredient list and add to the syrup. Do not add the bananas until just before serving. Serve chilled.

I wonder how many people make biscuits any more. Have they been lost and forgotten under the tsunami of cupcakes? They are a lovely and genteel offering and can be exactly what is required at 11 a.m., or 3 p.m., or after dinner.

Biscuits

A bowl of perfectly ripe autumn pears, a plate of biscuits, say Caramel and Almond Thins, and a glass of sweet wine... lovely.

Sometimes perfection is achievable, and with a carefully chosen and cooked biscuit, the scenario mentioned above is easily within your grasp. Biscuits are funny, though, and pretty as they may be, they rarely arrive at the table making a big song and dance. They are more a case of good tailoring rather than fancy accessorising, but they do arouse a funny set of emotions. There is none of the indulgent naughtiness associated with creamier or more lavish preparations. There will be no finger-pointing from fellow diners here when with a hovering digit you get to choose your own biscuit, which is exactly the shade that you like and not for sharing. It is quite acceptable to have a second one, and due to their generally slim and precise presentation, you might even sneak in a third. This multiple self-serving is a scenario that is unthinkable in the case of a cake or a tart. Biscuits just don't carry that sort of baggage. They require none of the last-minute fru-fruing that some sweet things do and are unusual in that they can be exactly what is required at 11 a.m., or 3 p.m. or after dinner, and all of that without guilt. Generally, the most stressful decision you have to make when serving them is in respect of what serving plate will show them at their best. It is also worth mentioning that anyone who aspires to god-like status due to their superior domestic standards will, on nonchalant presentation of the freshly stocked biscuit tin to the unexpected visitor, be catapulted into a sphere previously unimagined by budding kitchen deities.

So do I like biscuits, do I think they are worthwhile, do I think that with the previously mentioned pears or other similarly ripe fruit, with a fruit compote or fool, with a simple ice, they can be as smart as anything you might offer? Yes, without doubt. Piled high, laid flat, spread out for dramatic effect or straight from the tin, a well-made homemade biscuit is a treat.

I wonder, though, how many people make biscuits any more. Have they been lost and forgotten under the tsunami of cupcakes that has swept all in its path? That previously lovely and genteel offering that only appeared at teatime seems to get bigger, more psychedelic, more vulgar and more forgettable by the day.

So let us keep our biscuits small, thin, crisp and buttery; with a multitude of flavourings, shapes and sizes, biscuits are a simple skill that is worth mastering. Most of the recipes are easy, and good quality ingredients as always will be reflected in the finished taste and texture. Some of the biscuit recipes here are best eaten on the day they are made; others will keep in a tightly sealed tin for several days. Some of the biscuit doughs are frozen in an uncooked state and can then be sliced directly from frozen on to a baking tray lined with baking parchment, with no rolling required, and cooked as you need them, so they're really quick and perfect for those who like to plan ahead and are also a safety valve in the event of unexpected visitors. The remaining frozen dough goes straight back into the freezer for use another day.

Keys to success

The pastry kitchen is unforgiving – if you don't **weigh your ingredients accurately**, you cannot be guaranteed a good result.

When butter is called for in a recipe, **there is no substitute** that will yield as delicious a result. **The butter can be salted or unsalted**. I generally state my preference in each recipe.

Where the use of baking parchment is suggested, it is there for a good reason, generally to ensure that your biscuits will **definitely not stick to the tray** they are being cooked on.

Though some of the biscuits keep well in a sealed tin or box, there is no doubt that they **all taste better when freshly baked.**

Vanilla shortbread biscuits

I have many different biscuit recipes that I like, but I think this one is immensely useful and it has many possible variations. This is a classic example of a few simple ingredients, accurately measured and carefully cooked, producing a consistently good result. The value of such a recipe cannot be overstated, as you can rely on its good humour and reliability. The biscuit is crisp, sweet and buttery and the addition of some vanilla seed, scraped from a vanilla pod, adds a lovely flavour.

In their simplest form, cooked as flat biscuits, these can be served with tea or coffee. They can be sandwiched together with soft fruit such as strawberries and raspberries to make an elegant little afternoon tea treat or dessert. Gently pressed into tartlet tins and cooked, they make delicious receptacles for jams, jellies and preserves. I sometimes put a teaspoon of jam and a few berries on to the raw rolled tartlets and bake them to make very delicate jam and fruit tarts. Like most buttery pastries, these are without doubt best eaten on the day they are made, though they do keep well in a biscuit tin for a couple of days.

You will know that I am a big fan of an accurate weighing scale, measuring jug and spoons. I like to give myself every chance of success, and when I know that I have the correct amount of ingredients in my bowl, that is already a good start. Biscuits and pastries are much less forgiving than, say, a slow-cooked stew, so cooking times are also crucial. Here the rules and guidelines really matter, and because I think this is such a marvellous recipe, I would really like it to work properly for you so that it may become a regular and most useful part of your repertoire. So quite plain, and without bells and whistles, this biscuit punches above its weight in terms of texture and flavour. It is a classic example of the value of using butter and where possible the value of eating a buttery biscuit or pastry on the day it is made. If you make this biscuit with salted butter it will taste like an Irish or English delight; if you use unsalted butter, immediately it tastes more of France or Italy. There may be better biscuit recipes than this but there are few that are so straightforward, and that reward so generously for such a small amount of effort.

The ingredients

A vanilla pod or bean with its pungent and aromatic aroma is an essential ingredient in the sweet kitchen and indeed sometimes finds its way into the savoury kitchen as well. If possible buy pods that are flecked with a white crystal coating which contains vanillin; known as frosted vanilla, these are generally the most highly flavoured beans. Avoid pods that feel dry to the touch to the point of being brittle. Store the pods in an airtight container or in a jar of caster sugar to make your own homemade vanilla-flavoured sugar.

Makes 20
- 170g plain white flour
- 3cm piece of vanilla pod
- 110g butter, diced
- 55g caster sugar

Preheat the oven to 180°C/350°F/gas 4.

Put the flour into a bowl. Split open the vanilla pod with a knife and then, with the back of the knife, scrape the tiny little seeds into the flour. Mix thoroughly to disperse the dry vanilla through the flour. Add the butter and sugar and rub them into the flour until the mixture resembles coarse breadcrumbs. Keep rubbing and it will come together into a mass. Knead lightly to form a smooth dough. Do not be tempted to add any liquid. If you have measured the ingredients accurately it will work. If it feels a little soft, chill for 15 minutes.

Roll out on a floured surface to a thickness of 3mm. Cut out the shapes of choice with pastry cutters (you will get about 20 biscuits if you use an 8cm cutter) and transfer to a baking tray. Gather up the trimmings, lightly shake off the excess flour and roll and shape again. Bake in the preheated oven until golden. Immediately remove from the baking sheet and place on a wire rack to cool. If you leave them on the oven tray they will stick and burn.

The biscuits can be simply served with a light dusting of caster or icing sugar. Best eaten on the day they're made, but they will keep for 2–3 days in an airtight box or biscuit tin.

Sugar biscuits

Crisp, golden, caramelised, thin and elegant, these long slipper-shaped biscuits can be served with ices, sorbets, mousses and soufflés, or just with coffee. Scraps of puff or flaky pastry will work perfectly here. The pastry is rolled in icing sugar and cooks to a crisp caramel. I like to make my own puff pastry (see page 44). If you are going to use shop-bought pastry, use the very best all-butter variety that you can find.

The ingredients
The puff or flaky pastry you use must be made with butter, as any-thing less will produce an ordinary biscuit. That would be a pity, as these biscuits can be fantastic. Use the pastry chilled from the fridge and don't allow it to warm up, otherwise it will become dif-ficult to handle.

Makes 14   100g icing sugar, sieved
             200g puff pastry

Preheat the oven to 220°C/450°F/gas 7.

Dust your work surface and the pastry with some of the icing sugar. Roll the pastry into a 25cm square and dust with more icing sugar. Fold the left-hand and right-hand side of the square of pastry half-way towards the middle. Fold again so that the two sides meet in the middle of the pastry. Now fold one side on top of the other and firm it gently in place with the heel of your hand. Cut the pastry into 2.5cm pieces. Turn these pieces on their side with the cut side up. Dust again with icing sugar, flatten with the heel of your hand and roll into long tongue-shaped biscuits as thin as a sheet of pasta. They should be about 15–20cm long and 4–5cm wide. If the pastry starts to come apart at the folds when you are rolling it, just pinch it together and keep going. Use more icing sugar if the pastry is stick-ing to the work surface or the rolling pin.

Place on a baking sheet, then bake until golden brown. They may need to be flipped over during the cooking. Be brave and allow them to become well caramelised. Remove from the oven, then with a slice or palette knife place them on a wire rack to cool. They will become crisp and brittle.

Best eaten on the day they're made, but they will keep for a day or two in an airtight box or biscuit tin.

Sacristains: almond and sugar pastry twists

I hope most people have had one of those moments when you taste something so delicious that it suddenly explains why a particular cuisine or dish has achieved an exalted and revered position. I think these biscuits can produce such an effect.

If you want to produce a pastry or biscuit that makes your eyes roll with pleasure, there are two words you will need to remember – butter and freshness. The pastry being used, puff pastry in this case, needs to be made with butter and it needs to be really fresh. The pastry and biscuits should be made, cooked and eaten on the same day. Anything less than butter and freshness will only produce a mediocre result.

These biscuits are one of the reasons why we used to, and sometimes still think, that French pâtisseries are a little outpost of heaven on earth. Sugar-coated, almond-studded and slightly caramelised twists of crisp, fluffy and buttery pastry. Divine.

The ingredients
Butter puff or flaky pastry, as fresh as possible, is needed here.

The almonds, with their skins left on, will retain much more flavour than previously skinned ones.

Makes 15   Flour, for dusting
             200g puff or flaky pastry (see page 44)
             1 egg, beaten
             115g unskinned whole almonds, coarsely chopped
             75g granulated sugar

Preheat the oven to 200°C/400°F/gas 6.

Lightly dust the work surface and the pastry with flour. Roll the pastry into a rectangle, 30cm wide and 20cm long. Brush off any excess flour. Brush the pastry with beaten egg. Sprinkle on half the almonds and half the sugar and press them into the pastry by giving it one firm roll with your rolling pin. Carefully flip the pastry over, again brushing off excess flour, and repeat with the egg, almonds and sugar. Again press in the nuts and sugar with the rolling pin. Cut the dough into 15 strips about 2cm wide and 20cm long.

Line an oven tray with baking parchment. Catch the pastry strips at each end one at a time, and twist them several times to give the pastry four or five obvious twists. Lay them as you go on the paper, leaving 3cm of space between them. Bake in the oven for 15 minutes, until risen and richly caramelised. Remove from the tray and allow to cool and crisp on a wire rack.

Best eaten on the day they're made, but they will keep for a day or two in an airtight box or biscuit tin.

Chocolate biscuits

These biscuits are particularly festive-looking at Christmas when you can shower them with all manner of shiny edible decorations – hundreds and thousands, coloured sugars and so on. They cut beautifully into different shapes, so this may be the moment to use your fanciest biscuit cutters. Like the Currant and Candied Fruit Biscuits on page 450, though, they can be enjoyed at any time of the year. During the summer months these biscuits are delicious sandwiched together with lightly sweetened berries such as raspberries, loganberries or tayberries, and vanilla ice cream or whipped cream.

The ingredients
Cocoa powder, another important ingredient in the sweet kitchen, should be dark and completely unsweetened.

The pure vanilla extract used here should not be confused with vanilla essence. The extract is pure, dark, perfumed and low in sugar, indeed sometimes with no sugar at all. Generally, the pure extracts contain at least 35% alcohol. The essences tend to be low in vanilla and alcohol and high in sugar, a pale imitation of the real thing. It is quite easy to make your own extract by macerating slashed vanilla beans in water and brandy, bearing in mind the 35% of alcohol as a general rule.

Makes 36
140g salted butter, at room temperature, but not hot and oily
1 tablespoon vegetable oil
125g caster sugar
1 egg, beaten
1 teaspoon vanilla extract
225g plain flour
35g cocoa powder
1 teaspoon baking powder

Place the butter, oil and caster sugar in a bowl. By hand with a wooden spoon, or with the aid of a machine, cream together until light and fluffy in consistency and pale in colour. Add the egg and vanilla and continue to beat until well blended and smooth. Sieve the flour, cocoa and baking powder on to the mixture and blend in until it comes together and no longer looks streaky. Do not over-mix. Chill the mixture for at least 30 minutes.

Preheat the oven to 180°C/350°F/gas 4.

Roll out half the mixture at a time to about 5mm thick, using a little flour to prevent it from sticking. Alternatively, roll it between sheets of baking parchment. Cut out the biscuits with your cutter of choice (you should get about 36 if you use a 5cm cutter), then, using a palette knife, place on a baking sheet lined with baking parchment. Leave a little space between the biscuits, as they swell slightly when cooking. Bake in the preheated oven for about 8 minutes. The biscuits will rise slightly and feel gently set to the touch. They crisp up as they cool. Place the baking sheet on a wire rack and allow them to cool, still on the baking parchment.

Serve dusted with a little icing sugar or caster sugar, or ice with one of the icings suggested below. If you are using the icing and wish to sprinkle the biscuits with edible decorations, make sure to do that as soon as the biscuits are iced so that the decorations will stick on to the still slightly moist icing.

Best eaten on the day they're made, but they will keep for 2–3 days in an airtight box or biscuit tin.

Lemon glacé icing

For 30 biscuits   110g icing sugar
Zest of 1 lemon
About 1 tablespoon lemon juice

Sieve the icing sugar into a bowl. With a wooden spoon, carefully mix in the lemon zest and enough juice to make a spreadable icing. Beat until smooth and glossy. The consistency will be that of thick cream.

Coffee glacé icing

For 30 biscuits   110g icing sugar
1 dessertspoon coffee essence, such as Irel or Camp
1 tablespoon boiling water (approx.)

Sieve the icing sugar into a bowl and add the coffee essence. With a wooden spoon, add enough boiling water to achieve a smooth and glossy icing. The consistency will be that of thick cream.

Dark chocolate icing

For 30 biscuits   75g icing sugar
25g cocoa powder
40g butter
40ml water
50g caster sugar

Sieve the icing sugar and cocoa powder into a bowl. Put the butter, water and caster sugar into a small saucepan and stir on a low heat until the sugar has dissolved. Bring to the boil and immediately beat into the dry ingredients. Continue to beat with a wooden spoon until smooth and glossy. The icing will thicken as it cools.

Caramel and almond thins

These thin, crisp and delicious biscuits have many different uses. The original recipe comes from Chez Panisse, in Berkeley, California, where for forty years the inspirational Alice Waters and her team have been celebrating all that is good and local in food. I was lucky enough to spend a month in the kitchens of Chez Panisse a few years ago. I tasted these biscuits there and have adjusted the recipe slightly to suit our measurements and ingredients. They can be served with tea and coffee. They are good with ice cream and sorbets. They are fine enough to be served as a petit four. I also serve them with a blackberry and apple fool in the autumn and mango fool in winter. They are very handy, as the slab of uncooked biscuit keeps in the freezer and you can slice off thin sheets and cook them as needed.

The ingredients
If possible, grind the cinnamon freshly for this recipe. This is easily done in a spice grinder or clean coffee grinder. Otherwise, use the freshest ground cinnamon that you can find.

Flaked almonds with their skins still attached have a more interesting flavour than skinned ones, but if that is all you can find, these biscuits will still be delicious.

Makes 60
250g plain flour
¼ teaspoon bicarbonate of soda
100g salted butter
½ teaspoon ground cinnamon
5 tablespoons water
300g soft light brown sugar
110g flaked almonds, unskinned if possible

Sieve the flour and bicarbonate of soda into a bowl. Put the butter, cinnamon and water into a saucepan on a low heat until just melted. Do not allow to boil. Remove from the heat and add the sugar. Stir into the flour mixture with the almonds.

Place the dough on a piece of strong plastic (not cling film) or baking parchment and form it into a neat rectangular slab, about 23cm wide, 2.5cm thick, and 9cm long. I use the sides of a shallow baking tray to help me to achieve neat and straight edges. Put into the freezer until firm.

Preheat the oven to 180°C/350°F/gas 4. Slice the dough into 3mm thick slices and place them on a baking sheet lined with baking parchment, allowing a little room between the raw biscuits for expansion during cooking. Bake for 10 minutes, until golden brown. Slide the biscuits, still on the paper, on to a wire rack to cool.

Best eaten on the day they're made, but they will keep for 2–3 days in an airtight box or biscuit tin.

Currant and candied fruit biscuits

This is another Chez Panisse-inspired biscuit. I particularly like them at Christmas time, when I make them and give them as gifts, but in fact they are great at any time of the year. Apart from serving them with tea or coffee, I sometimes accompany them with Praline Ice Cream (see page 460).

This biscuit dough is prepared ahead, formed into a roll, wrapped in cling film and frozen. When you need a few biscuits, simply slice them off the roll and bake. The cooked biscuits keep well for several days in an airtight container.

The ingredients

Currants are tiny raisins made from drying a variety of small black grape. Like raisins and sultanas, they vary enormously in quality, so seek out ones that, when you taste them, remind you that this little dried fruit was once actually a grape. Store them in a sealed container.

Candied peel can be made from many different members of the citrus family, such as oranges, lemons, limes, grapefruits, tangerines, pomelos and so on. Like the dried fruit mentioned above, it varies in quality, and perhaps the safest way, apart of course from making your own (see page 399), is to buy it in large pieces so that the fruit it was made from is still somewhat recognisable. The pre-chopped versions tend to taste of nothing but sugar. The difference between good candied peel and the run-of-the-mill commercial brands is enormous.

Makes 70

275g salted butter, at room temperature but not warm and oily

225g caster sugar

1 egg, beaten

1 teaspoon vanilla extract

275g plain flour

75g currants

75g candied orange and lemon peel, finely chopped

By hand or in a food mixer, cream the butter and sugar until light and fluffy. Add the egg and vanilla and mix in thoroughly. Stir in the flour, currants and candied peel and mix gently but thoroughly to just combine the ingredients.

Form the dough into two logs, about 4cm in diameter. Place each log on a sheet of heavy plastic (I use a heavy duty plastic freezer bag which I cut open to make bigger), and form into a neat roll while squeezing the plastic to attain a neat finish. Twist the ends of the plastic to seal the roll and place in the freezer until frozen.

When ready to cook the biscuits, preheat the oven to 180°C/350°F/ gas 4 and line a baking sheet with baking parchment.

Slice the dough into 3mm rounds and place on the paper, leaving 1cm of space between the biscuits. Bake for about 12 minutes, until the biscuits are golden. Cool on the baking parchment and enjoy.

Best eaten on the day they're made, but they will keep for 2–3 days in an airtight box or biscuit tin.

Regardless of the recipe you are using, there is no doubt in my mind that the flavour, texture and colour of homemade ices are significantly better than the shop bought alternative, so it really is worth the effort involved.

Ice creams, sorbets and granitas

Most people like ice cream or iced desserts, and whether it is to cool you down on a summer's day or to serve proudly after dinner at any time of the year, without doubt it is worth trying to make your own. There are various different techniques for making ices, and hundreds, possibly thousands of different flavourings that may be added. Some recipes are entirely simple, just a matter of mixing softly whipped cream through a sweetened fruit purée and freezing it, or flavouring syrup and freezing that; others are more complicated and will involve making custard or an egg mousse. Some ices will involve an ice cream machine for freezing, others can simply be frozen in a domestic freezer. An ice cream machine is indeed a luxury, and whereas I would not be without mine, I can honestly say you could have a life-time of great ice cream if you don't have one. Regardless of the recipe you are using, there is no doubt in my mind that the flavour, texture and colour of homemade ices are significantly better than the shop-bought alternative, so it really is worth the effort involved.

Ice creams

Ice creams can be made using several different techniques. A custard-based ice cream is just that, a chilled custard with the addition of cream and sometimes milk, and the flavouring of choice. These ice creams have to be frozen or churned in an ice cream machine. The word 'churned' refers to the way the ice cream machine constantly keeps the mixture moving or churning as it freezes. This constant movement, with the aid of the rotating paddle in the machine, breaks down large ice crystals in the mixture and freezes it to an evenly smooth and frozen consistency. This technique makes what is generally regarded as the smoothest and most tender of all ice creams, and the technique offers the cook myriad choices when it comes to flavour additions. A classic.

An egg mousse ice cream is based on a mousse made with syrup and egg yolks. The flavouring and softly whipped cream are carefully folded into this mousse and then the mixture is frozen in a conventional freezer with no further mixing required. These ice creams must not be frozen in an ice cream machine, because due to the high proportion of cream in the mixture, the churning of the machine will give the resulting frozen mixture an unpleasantly heavy and buttery consistency. This ice cream is generally richer than a custard-based one, as it is made with pure cream only and no milk. The texture of this ice cream is firmer than the custard-based ice cream and its consistency has been described as being like 'crushed velvet'. Slightly old-fashioned but with a timeless texture and flavour, this is a great technique that produces superb ice creams.

Other ice creams can be made by sweetening and flavouring softly whipped cream and freezing it in a conventional freezer. Sometimes the recipes are entirely simple and the results extremely good.

Sorbets

Easy to make, sorbets are light ices made with dairy-free mixtures which are frozen in an ice cream machine to achieve their distinctive and perfectly smooth consistency. Due to their lightness, and willingness to accept and preserve refreshing flavours such as herbs and fruit, they are sometimes served as a refreshing starter or palate-cleansing course as well as being served at the end of a meal. With the aid of the ice cream machine, sorbets can be very quickly frozen and there are few better methods to trap and ice a flavour than a sorbet. Any sorbet recipe can be made into the coarser but still lovely granita.

Granitas

Granitas, like sorbets, are dairy-free and are also easy. However, they are frozen in a conventional freezer, so an ice cream machine is not required. When the mixture first freezes and sets, it is removed from the freezer, broken up with a fork or a whisk and refrozen. This process is repeated several more times and the resulting texture is considerably coarser than a sorbet, ending up with small shard-like pieces of flavoured ice that, like a sorbet, can be served as a delicious and refreshing course at the beginning, during or at the end of a meal.

Parfaits
A parfait is sweet, smooth, iced and refined, but with a lighter texture than ice cream. Generally, the parfait is set into a mould, either individual serving size or larger ones, before being frozen in a conventional freezer.

Keys to success
Measure all ingredients accurately.

The cream should be rich **regular or double cream**.

Fruit, if used, should be **perfectly ripe**.

Sorbets and granitas should be eaten **within a day or two** of being made. They will keep safely in a freezer for longer, but will start to lose flavour and texture.

All ices should be tightly covered when in the freezer.

Vanilla ice cream

This method makes ice cream with an old-fashioned taste and texture. I love it. Based on a egg mousse, it produces a rich and lovely result with a firmer texture than a custard-based ice cream. This type of ice cream was often used to create extravagant multi-layered iced confections known as 'bombes', which are out of fashion now, but still fantastic to eat. A thick syrup, poured on to beaten egg yolks, creates a rich mousse. The vanilla and whipped cream are simply folded into the mousse and the ice cream is placed in a freezer to set. No ice cream machine is required here, as pure cream is used and, because of the richness of that cream, the mixture requires no churning.

The ingredients
Use the best eggs you can get, and that quality will be reflected in the flavour, texture and colour of the ice cream. Save your egg whites for meringues, soufflés or for adding to mashed potatoes to make them light and fluffy.

I like to use both vanilla extract and the seeds extracted from a vanilla pod for this recipe. You can use one or the other if that is what you have.

Serves 8   110g caster or granulated sugar
120ml water
4 large egg yolks
1 teaspoon vanilla extract plus the addition of the seeds
from a 4cm piece of vanilla pod
1.2 litres regular, double or whipping cream, softly whipped

Place the sugar and water in a heavy-based saucepan and bring to the boil. Stir the sugar gently a few times with a wooden spoon to encourage it to dissolve before the water comes to the boil. Once the syrup comes to the boil do not stir it again, as it can cause the syrup to crystallise.

Boiling syrup to a thick thread

While the syrup is cooking at a gentle boil, whisk up the egg yolks to a light, pale and fluffy mousse. When the syrup reaches the 'thread' stage it will look thick and have large bubbles breaking on the surface, and when a metal spoon is dipped into the syrup, it will fall off in a slowish, thick, viscous stream, leaving an obvious thread at the end. If you are using a sugar thermometer the temperature of the syrup will be 106–113°C/223–236°F. Remove the syrup from the heat and immediately pour on to the egg yolks in a quick steady stream, with the whisk running at full speed all of the time. Make sure you do not pour the syrup down on top of the rotating whisk, but allow it to hit the side of the bowl and run down on to the egg yolks. If the syrup hits the whisk first, it tends to fly off and stick to the sides of the bowl and never come in contact with the egg yolks. Continue to whisk to a thick mousse. This can take 15 minutes to happen. You will know it is thick enough when the whisk will almost stand up on its own in the mousse.

Allow the mousse to cool. I put the bowl in the fridge for 20 minutes or so, and then with a rubber spatula fold in the vanilla and cream thoroughly. Place in a covered freezer container and freeze. It will be frozen and ready to eat after 6 hours. Remove from the freezer 10 minutes before serving. Use the ice cream as soon as possible, though it will keep for several months.

Praline ice cream

4–6 tablespoons coarse almond praline powder
(see page 403)

Make as above, adding the praline to the vanilla ice cream when half set and then returning it to the freezer.

Peach sorbet

This recipe sounds too good to be true, but if you have really ripe peaches, the resulting sorbet is delicious. The sorbet is best frozen in an ice cream machine or sorbetière, but excellent results can be achieved in a normal deep freeze and I include instructions for turning this mixture into a granita or an ice. Serve it just as it is or with Sugared Peaches with Blueberries (see page 423). I also sometimes like to combine it with a raspberry cream and a crisp, buttery biscuit such as a Sugar Biscuit or a Sacristain (see pages 440 and 441). The peaches in this recipe can be successfully replaced with nectarines.

The ingredients

Really ripe peaches are crucial here, so think ahead with your shopping and if necessary have the peaches ripening in your kitchen for a few days before making the sorbet.

Serves 6
- 700g ripe peaches
- 175g caster sugar
- 3 tablespoons lemon juice

Place a small Pyrex bowl or freezer container in your freezer to chill.

Begin by peeling the peaches. With a small sharp knife, make a small cross in the top and bottom of the peaches and place them in a deep bowl. Pour over boiling water and keep them immersed for 10 seconds. Drain immediately and cool in cold water for a minute or two. Drain again, then peel off the skins. Slice the flesh off the stones, and place the flesh in a blender with the sugar and lemon juice. Purée until the fruit is smooth and silky and the sugar has dissolved.

Freeze in an ice cream machine or sorbetière until quite frozen. Place in the chilled container, smooth the top, cover and keep in the freezer until ready to serve.

Serve in neat scoops, with sugared peach and blueberry salad and a few small and tender mint leaves if available.

Peach granita

If you don't have a machine for freezing the mixture you can proceed as follows and make what is called a granita. This will be coarser in texture than the sorbet, but will still be delicious and refreshing to eat.

Put the puréed mixture from the peach sorbet recipe into a shallow bowl. Cover and freeze. When partially frozen, remove and break up with a fork or a whisk to attain a slushy consistency. Replace in the freezer and repeat the process twice more. Serve as above.

Peach ice

Here is another option for freezing the mixture, failing an ice cream machine or sorbetière.

Freeze the mixture until completely frozen. Remove from the freezer and break up thoroughly with a whisk or in a food processor. Beat 2 egg whites to soft peaks. Add 1 tablespoon of caster sugar and continue beating to stiff peaks, just like stiff meringue. Fold into the mixture and refreeze. The resulting texture will be midway between a sorbet and a granita. Serve as above.

Raspberry cream

Serves 6-8   225g raspberries
75–120g caster sugar
300ml regular, double or whipping cream, whipped
   until quite stiff

Sprinkle the raspberries with the caster sugar and allow to sit for 30 minutes. Crush the berries and sugar coarsely, not rendering them into a purée. Fold in the whipped cream to create a streaked effect.

Serve with the peach sorbet.

Lemon verbena granita

This is a master recipe in that the leaf of choice, lemon verbena in this case, can be successfully replaced by others. The first time I made this recipe, I used blackcurrant leaves, as in the leaves from a blackcurrant bush. For a few weeks in May, the leaves are highly scented and you end up with an ice that is pure white in colour, but tastes intensely of blackcurrants. Fabulous.

Interestingly, the leaves of redcurrant or white currant bushes are not scented at all and not suitable for this recipe. If you have currant bushes in your garden they will not be in fruit when you are making this recipe, in which case you may not be able to remember which bush is which – just pick a leaf off each bush, rub it between your fingers to release its aroma, and if it smells intensely of currant, then that's it. Many other leaves work brilliantly too, such as spearmint, lemon balm and rose or lemon-scented geranium. Elderflowers, though not a leaf but with a heady Muscat-flavoured scent, also work really well. As this is a granita we are expecting a slightly coarse, flaky and icy texture, so forget about your ice cream scoop here and just spoon it into pretty serving dishes. You will not need an ice cream machine, though if you have one and freeze the mixture in the machine, it will then be a sorbet.

The recipe is simple, but watch out for the subtleties involved, such as using cold water with the sugar when cooking the leaves to draw out their flavour, and allowing the syrup to cool completely before adding the lemon juice. The granita will keep for several weeks in the freezer, but is considerably better when eaten as soon as possible after it has been frozen.

This granita of lemon verbena is good on its own but is even better when served with a splash of dry sparkling wine. Serve as a light and refreshing dessert or as an equally light and refreshing starter on a scorching summer's day.

The ingredients

Lemon verbena, a wonderful citrus-scented herb, is used to flavour many sweet dishes such as mousses, creams and ices. The sharp pointy leaves are intensely lemony, making an utterly refreshing ice.

Serves 6–8   3 handfuls of lemon verbena leaves
225g caster or granulated sugar
600ml cold water
3 lemons

Put the leaves, sugar and water into a saucepan and place over a moderate heat. Stir occasionally to encourage the sugar to dissolve, and bring it to a simmer. Continue to simmer gently for 2 minutes, then remove from the heat and allow to cool until it is completely cold. You will end up with a pale green syrup. Juice the lemons and add to the syrup, and right before your eyes you will see the green tinge leaving your syrup. Strain out the leaves through a sieve – I usually press on the leaves to extract as much flavour as I can. Place the strained syrup in a wide container and freeze until set.

Remove from the freezer and break up the ice with a fork. It will look like a slushy mess. Refreeze and repeat the process twice more, three times if you can bear it, and eventually you will end up with the distinctive shard-like consistency of a granita. Refreeze, covered, until you are ready to serve it.

I serve this in coloured glasses or glass bowls, with a single relevant leaf to decorate and a splash of chilled sparkling wine.

Brown bread ice cream

I think this is a brilliant recipe – it's really simple and tastes great. I use it year round. In autumn and winter I serve it with poached pears or citrus fruit, and in spring and summer I serve it with all of the different fruits as they arrive in season. It works really well with the first rhubarb, then with gooseberries and so on, and it's heavenly when paired with roast peaches or nectarines in high summer.

The ingredients
Wholemeal bread, lightly processed into coarse crumbs about the size of peas, is ideal here.

Serves 6–8   175g coarse wholemeal breadcrumbs (brown soda breadcrumbs are ideal)
600ml regular, double or whipping cream
125g soft light brown sugar (or icing sugar)
2 egg yolks
1 tablespoon dark rum, or whiskey or brandy
2 egg whites

Preheat the oven to 190°C/375°F/gas mark 5. Spread the bread-crumbs out on a baking tray and toast in the oven for about 20 minutes. They should become crisp and slightly browned.

Meanwhile, beat the cream with the sugar until softly whipped. Mix the egg yolks with the rum, if using, and add to the cream mixture, beating it in well.

When the breadcrumbs are cool, fold them into the cream mixture gently and thoroughly, so that they are evenly distributed. Lastly, whip the whites of the eggs stiffly and fold into the mixture. Freeze in the usual way, in a covered container. There is no need to stir up this ice cream.

Kiwi fruit granita with passion fruit and orange sauce

This is a really simple and lovely ice. The sauce is delicious with it and makes the whole combination into a thoroughly refreshing dessert.

Freshly squeezed orange juice comes from an orange and not a man-made container of any description. Passion fruit juice I can only consider if freshly released from nature's packaging.

I serve this with Sugar Biscuits (see page 440).

Serves 6–8 110g caster sugar
Zest and juice of 1 lime
700g kiwi fruit (about 9 fruit)

THE SAUCE
225ml freshly squeezed orange juice
3 passion fruit, halved and contents sieved to extract the juice
40–50g caster sugar, or to taste

Put the sugar into a bowl and add the zest and juice of the lime. Peel the kiwi fruit, using a swivel-top peeler, and make sure you remove the woody piece from the stalk end of the fruit. Chop the peeled kiwis coarsely and add to the sugar and lime. Blend briefly until almost smooth in a liquidiser or using a hand-held blender. If you over-blend them the little black seeds may be crushed, in which case the granita may become a bit peppery and the colour will be spoiled.

Place the bowl in the freezer to freeze and set. When the mixture is semi-frozen and slushy-looking, remove and whisk it vigorously to break up the large crystals of kiwi ice. Replace the mixture in the freezer and repeat the process three more times. By then the ice should be a granita and ready to serve when it suits you.

For the sauce, mix the orange juice and passion fruit juice in a bowl and add the sugar. Whisk vigorously to dissolve the sugar completely. Taste and correct the sweetness if necessary. Serve the granita in coarse shards, with some of the sauce poured over.

The mixture needs to be whisked to very stiff peaks – think shaving foam – so stiff that you can confidently turn the whisking bowl upside down with no fear of the mixture falling out.

Meringues

Most people like meringues and some people love them. Plain with softly whipped cream, fruit-swirled, chocolate-layered, nut-encrusted, citrus-filled, vanilla-flecked, there is almost no end to it, but meringues can plague the life of some cooks. Sometimes they are spot on, as in crisp, light and perfect, and the next time they will be soggy, chewy and just not right. Why is that so? We will endeavour in this chapter to remove as many of the pitfalls as possible, and for that reason I will concentrate on what I consider to be straight-forward meringue recipes. There are other techniques for making meringues apart from the ones I mention here, but they will have to wait for another day. If we succeed with the recipes listed here, I suspect it really will satisfy most people's meringue requirements.

Once you grasp, understand and follow the rules involved, there is no reason why you cannot make dozens of variations on the theme. In all these recipes the sugar is added in one go, which avoids having to fold sugar into the beaten egg whites and lessens the chance of deflating your meringue. Some of the meringues are cooked until crisp, others are soft. It is sometimes at times like this, when I reach for my food mixer, that I spare a little thought for all the cooks downstairs, in the kitchens of grand houses, hotels and restaurants, who, before the advent of the machines that we rely so happily on nowadays, whisked up, by the sweat of their brow, marvellous confections for the delectation of those upstairs. Bless their memory and their upper arms.

Meringue whisked to a soft peak

Keys to success

Measure all the ingredients accurately. Remembering that 1 egg white weighs 25g.

All equipment should be **spotlessly clean**.

Egg whites that are **a few days old** are better than really fresh ones.

The whites should be **free of any spots of egg yolk or shell**.

Whisking of egg whites and sugar for meringues **rarely takes less than 10 minutes** and sometimes, depending on your particular whisking machine, can take as long as 20 minutes.

The mixture needs to be whisked to **very stiff peaks** – think shaving foam – so stiff that you can confidently turn the whisking bowl upside down with no fear of the whisked mixture falling out.

Prepare your parchment-lined trays while the meringue is beating.

The meringue mixture needs to be shaped on to the parchment paper and go into the preheated oven **immediately** it is whisked.

The meringues are cooked when they **lift off** the parchment paper with no resistance.

The ideal way to cool meringues is to turn off the oven and allow them to cool completely in there.

If you are in a rush to cool the meringues, you can of course remove them from the oven and allow them to cool, still on the baking parchment, at room temperature. **They may craze a little – not the end of the world.**

If storing meringues for a few days, place them in an airtight tin generously lined with kitchen paper. The paper acts as a shock absorber and will also absorb moisture – the enemy of all meringues.

Soft vanilla meringues
with strawberries, honey, lemon and mint

These meringues are cooked quite quickly and have a thin crisp exterior and a marshmallow-like centre. The meringues, due to their softness, need to be eaten within 4 hours of being made. If you want to keep them for longer, reduce the oven temperature by 50° or to gas mark 2 and cook for a further hour, in which case they will lose some of their softness and become drier. The strawberry salad is simple, and when made with fruit that is bang in season is quite delicious. It can be enjoyed on its own, but will also be perfect with a vanilla ice cream or just cream and a sugar biscuit. A really ripe peach or nectarine sliced into the strawberries is also lovely.

The ingredients
Strawberries have suffered enormously from being bred for high yields and durability rather than flavour, and from being regarded as a year-round item on the shop shelf. Most commercially farmed strawberries are only interesting if they are smothered in lots of sugar, and we seem to have forgotten that strawberries used to be sweet enough to eat straight from the plant without a shuddering reaction due to their bitterness. In an ideal world a strawberry would never see the inside of a fridge, as it really dulls the flavour, and you really have to ask yourself whether it is OK that some strawberries will keep for weeks in a fridge. So for the few short weeks during the summer when locally grown strawberries are at their peak, try to find a farmers' market or shop where hopefully the only entrapment the berries will have endured is the road trip from the farm to the stall. Better still, grow a few of your own in a bag or a box and pluck them and eat them still warm from the plant, having only endured a journey of seconds.

Serves 4   2 egg whites
110g caster sugar
½ a vanilla pod
Strawberries with lemon, honey and mint. Use half the
quantity of the recipe on page 426.

476

Preheat the oven to 150°C/300°F/gas 2 and line a baking sheet or tray with baking parchment.

Place the egg whites and sugar in a spotlessly clean bowl. Whisk, preferably using an electric mixer, until the mixture becomes meringue-like and holds stiff peaks that look like shaving foam or stiffly whipped cream. Split the vanilla pod lengthways and scrape out the seeds. With a flexible spatula, fold the seeds thoroughly and quickly into the stiff meringue.

Drop blobs of the meringue on to the paper on the baking sheet. The blobs can be as big or as small as you like. Place the tray in the pre-heated oven and cook for about 45 minutes. As soon as the meringues will lift off the paper with no resistance, they are ready. Turn off the oven and leave to cool, or remove and cool at room temperature. As this is a soft and quick-cooking meringue, they will not keep as well as slow-cooked, dry meringues, so ideally they need to be eaten on the day they are made.

Oeufs à la neige

Oeufs à la neige, snow eggs, floating islands, îles flottante... whatever you choose to call these, they are one of my favourite sweets. These extremely light meringues are poached in slightly sweetened milk until just set, and glazed with a thin, crisp caramel coating. Crème anglaise is the most essential sauce to serve with the meringue – hence the name floating islands, as the meringue floats lightly in the golden pool of sauce.

Fresh or poached fruit is also an excellent accompaniment. Summer berries, green gooseberries poached with elderflowers, rhubarb poached with angelica, mangoes with lime, poached plums, a salad of winter citrus are just a few of the options. The oeufs are sometimes garnished with crystallised violets or pralines.

The meringue is best served on the day it is made, ideally within

Springy oeufs poaching in barely simmering milk

4 hours, but will still be good the next day, if somewhat deflated. Great care needs to be taken when poaching the meringue. The milk in the saucepan should barely simmer, and a wide saucepan with low sides makes the process much easier. I have used a spotlessly clean, low-sided, heavy roasting tin on occasions and it worked perfectly.

The ingredients
Egg whites that are a couple of days old, or even frozen ones that have been defrosted, work perfectly here.

The milk that will be left over after poaching the meringue can be used in the crème anglaise, or can be saved for heating again and serving with coffee if sweetened milk is to your taste.

Serves 10
6 egg whites
110g caster sugar
Crème anglaise to serve (see page 397)

POACHING LIQUID
1 litre full-fat milk
55g caster sugar

CARAMEL
200g caster sugar

Put the milk and the sugar for the poaching liquid into a wide shallow pan and heat to a bare simmer. Make sure your chosen pan is big enough to accommodate all the meringue eggs in one go, as this meringue mixture is particularly light and will not hang around while you cook one batch. You just want to see a few bubbles bursting around the edge of the pan.

In a spotlessly clean bowl, whisk the egg whites until they reach the soft peak stage. The egg white will still be frothy and light and barely hold a peak on the whisk. Still whisking, add the caster sugar in a steady stream and continue whisking for about 5 minutes, until the meringue is firm and glossy and can easily be shaped with a spoon.

With a tablespoon, shape the meringue into 10 quenelle or egg shapes. Don't worry if the shapes are a bit abstract. Gently slide each egg into the hot milk as you go. After about 4 minutes the top of the quenelles will start to feel a bit firmer, so carefully turn them over to cook on the other side. I use a palette knife or rubber spatula for this. After a further 3 minutes, check to see that the meringue is firm and bouncy to the touch, and if pressed gently will not stick to your finger. Remove with a slotted spoon on to a tray lined with a clean tea towel to drain. The cooked meringue can now be refrigerated for several hours.

To glaze the meringues, gently lift them on to a wire rack, leaving at least 2cm between them. Sit the wire rack on a tray lined with kitchen foil. Put the sugar for the caramel coating into a heavy saucepan on a low heat. There is no water required for this caramel, so it will look quite odd as it cooks. The lack of water gives a crisper and thinner caramel coating to the oeufs. Stir at intervals, until the sugar starts to caramelise. It will look quite lumpy and uneven and you may think it is a disaster, but persevere with the stirring, and as if by magic, it smoothens out at the last minute to reveal the smooth chestnut-coloured caramel that you require.

As soon as all the sugar is dissolved and the colour is correct, immediately, gently and generously spoon the caramel over the eggs. The eggs must not be touching, otherwise the caramel will stick them together. Do not touch them until the caramel is cold and completely set, as it may stick to your finger and give you a nasty burn.

To serve the meringues, lift them off the wire rack. This may require a bit of jiggling to loosen them. Sit them in a pool of crème anglaise and float them off to the table, where you deserve to be greeted by thunderous applause.

Raspberry Alaska with sparkling sauce

There is something gloriously old-fashioned about baked Alaska. The very name shrieks of grand hotel dining rooms, with highly polished copper, brass and silver, starched uniforms and expressions, and the pudding silently gliding to the table with a hush and a silent cacophony of bells and whistles.

Warm meringue, chilly creamy raspberry ice cream and a chocolate biscuit base are the elements of my interpretation of this classic dish. The sauce gets its sparkle from the sparkling wine that is added to it at the last moment so that it arrives to the table fizzing. The remaining wine can be drunk while eating the pudding.

The ice cream, biscuit base and sauce can be made ahead, several days if you wish, so the last-minute assembly is pretty straightforward. The entire dish can be assembled, coated with the meringue and frozen for 2 hours before being put into the oven. The Alaskas must be served immediately they come out of the oven.

The ingredients

The ice cream is the same recipe as the Raspberry Fool on page 414, divided between 8 individual portion containers lined with cling film and frozen. This part of the recipe can be done several days ahead.

The chocolate biscuits are the Chocolate Biscuits on page 443, cut 1cm wider than the width of the ice cream containers and cooked. The biscuits will keep in an airtight tin for several days.

Serves 8

MERINGUE
50g egg white or 2 egg whites
110g caster sugar

RASPBERRY SAUCE
120g fresh or frozen raspberries
50g caster sugar
Lemon juice, to taste
50ml dry sparkling wine, such as Cava or Prosecco

RASPBERRY ICE CREAM
see page 416

CHOCOLATE BISCUIT
see page 443

To make the raspberry sauce, purée the raspberries and caster sugar in a blender or with a hand-held device, to a smooth and shiny purée. Sieve out the seeds, then taste and adjust the sweetness with lemon juice if necessary. Decant into a pretty jug and chill. Do not add the sparkling wine until you are about to serve.

To assemble the Alaska, preheat the oven to 230°C/450°F/gas 8. Remove the raspberry ice creams from the freezer and remove from their containers. Sit each one on a biscuit and pop them into the fridge.

Whisk the egg whites in a spotlessly clean bowl until frothy. Add the sugar in a quick steady stream and continue whisking until the meringue is firm, glossy and holding stiff peaks. Immediately spread the meringue over the raspberry ices, completely concealing them with meringue. You can do this with a palette knife or, if you prefer, with a piping bag fitted with a medium-sized star or plain piping nozzle. Place the meringue-covered Alaskas on the tray or dish that you are going to bake them on. The dish must be robust enough to stand 4 minutes in the very hot oven.

The Alaskas can be prepared to this point and put back into the freezer for 2 hours, or you can bake them now if you are ready to serve them. Either way, just before you put them in the oven dust them lightly with icing sugar. Bake for 3–4 minutes, or until they are a rich golden colour. Add the sparkling wine to the sauce. Serve immediately on your favourite dish and pass the sauce separately.

Meringue Christmas tree with white chocolate, pomegranate and rosewater

Yes, I know this sounds a bit cheesy, but it really is delicious. Anyway, it's for Christmas and when I make this I go all out and throw a few (unlisted) hundreds and thousands at it and maybe some (unlisted) gold and silver dragées. Fabulous, but just once a year, mind.

The confection sounds much more difficult to make and assemble than it is, and even if it's not the most perfectly shaped tree in the world, don't worry – this tree just screams of love, and those to whom you present it will know you love them and forgive you for any constructional inadequacies. Get all the elements prepared and have fun assembling the tree. The white chocolate can be replaced with dark if that is more to your taste.

The ingredients
White chocolate is not really chocolate at all, but a mixture of cocoa butter, sugar and flavouring. It can be temperamental, and it really pays to buy the best quality because some of the cheaper versions are difficult to melt. Melt it as you would conventional chocolate, but with a little extra vigilance.

Rosewater, a fragrant liquid extracted from rose petals, is, when used with discretion, a wonderful flavouring. Widely used in the cooking of the Middle East and the Indian subcontinent, it is now easily available in this part of the world. It is another ingredient that does not benefit from being kept for years, as the flavour dulls.

Serves 10–12 MERINGUES
175g egg white or 6 egg whites
350g icing sugar

300ml regular, double or whipping cream
2–4 tablespoons rosewater, or to taste
55–110g white chocolate, melted
1 pomegranate, seeds removed

Place the egg whites and sugar in a spotlessly clean mixing bowl. Start beating slowly, just until the sugar is incorporated with the egg whites, and continue to beat to very stiff peaks.

While the egg whites are beating, line two oven trays with parchment paper and preheat the oven to 150°C/300°F/gas 2. Using a dessertspoon, drop the meringue on to the paper in little blobs, or use a piping bag fitted with a medium-sized nozzle and pipe it into sticks. Bake the meringues until they lift off the paper with no resistance. This will take approximately 60 minutes. Allow to cool completely.

Whip the cream to stiff peaks and add the rosewater to taste. Melt the chocolate gently in a low oven or over a bowl of barely simmering water.

To assemble the tree, choose a large, flat serving plate on which you plan to present it, as once the tree is assembled it is too difficult to move it. Sandwich all the meringues together in pairs with the rosewater cream before you start the assembly. Drizzle a little of the melted chocolate in a circle on the base of the plate, then arrange a circular layer of the meringues on it as a base, pressing them into the chocolate. Allow this to set if you wish, but you can continue if it feels sturdy. Keep building up the meringues in a classic Christmas tree shape, dipping a corner or side of each meringue in the melted chocolate as you go to help them stick together.

When the tree-shaped meringue has been achieved, drizzle some of the remaining chocolate down the sides of the tree. Now place some pomegranate seeds on the chocolate drizzles, as if you were decorating a Christmas tree with baubles. Put aside in a cool place to set. The fridge is ideal, but if the tree is too big for your fridge, put it in front of a slightly open window to chill and set.

To serve, decorate with holly leaves, a dusting of icing sugar and very good-quality chocolate or cocoa powder. Serve with any leftover rosewater cream and a raspberry sauce if you wish.

There is always a place for warm puddings, and while some, such as the Roast Peaches, are definitely seasonal, others, such as the Buttermilk and Lemon Puddings, can be a year-round treat.

Warm puddings

Here are a few puddings that I like best when served warm or at least at room temperature. The selection will see you through the year, and while some, such as the Roast Peaches, are definitely seasonal, others, such as the Buttermilk and Lemon Puddings, can be a year-round treat, served on their own or better still accompanied by the fresh fruit of the moment or a fruit compote.

The Chocolate and Cherry Bread and Butter Pudding and the Chocolate, Prune and Armagnac Puddings are without doubt made for chocolate-lovers. They are rich and sumptuous and a real treat. The Lemon Verbena Cream Pots are light and delicate.

Roast peaches or nectarines with almond praline cream

This is a very simple recipe that will reward you greatly as long as the fruit you choose is ripe. It may seem strange to make a warm dish to serve during the warmer months of July and August when these fruits are in season, but this is a dreamy dish and when served with the chilled praline cream it is perfect. I don't serve the fruit straight from the oven, but allow it to cool slightly – if you serve the fruit roasting hot, you don't get the full flavour that it has to offer.

The ingredients

Peaches and nectarines should be perfectly ripe for this dish. Look out for unblemished fruit with a strong aroma. A ripe peach will smell of peach and will hold the print of the heel of your thumb if gently pressed. This is a practice that should only be performed if you are in doubt about the ripeness of the fruit.

Serves 8   8 peaches or nectarines
25g butter
2 tablespoons runny honey
2 tablespoons lemon juice

ALMOND PRALINE CREAM
2 tablespoons coarse almond praline (see page 403)
300ml regular, double or whipping cream, softly whipped

Preheat the oven to 220°C/435°F/gas 7.

Halve the fruit and remove the stones. Place the fruit, cut side up, in a tightly-fitting ovenproof dish. Melt the butter and stir in the honey and lemon juice. Spoon over the fruit and place in the preheated oven for about 20 minutes, or until the fruit is tender. A thin metal skewer should pierce the fruit with no resistance.

Fold the praline into the cream, making sure not to mix it too much otherwise the cream may over-whip and become grainy. Chill until needed.

Once the fruit is cooked, allow it to cool for 10 minutes or so before serving. Pass the praline cream separately, and be sure to serve some of the cooking juices with the fruit.

Vanilla or Brown Bread Ice-Cream (see page 467) or Peach Sorbet (see page 461) are also delicious with these peaches.

Chocolate, prune and Armagnac puddings with chocolate sauce

These puddings are delicious and without doubt made for chocolate lovers. Although not molten in the centre, they are soft and yielding. The combination of ingredients is a classic one but has timeless appeal. The cooked puddings will sit happily in a warm oven for at least an hour before serving, and indeed could be made ahead of time, allowed to cool and reheated in a bain-marie in a warm oven. The prunes in the recipe can be replaced with cherries, a delicious variation, in which case I would soak them in kirsch. Cognac can replace the slightly dryer Armagnac with the prunes.

The pudding can be cooked in a large dish, or in individual ramekins or even teacups.

The ingredients
Best-quality chocolate, 62% cocoa solids, is best for this pudding. I use Valrhona.

Prunes vary in quality, so look out for juicy-looking ones with their stones still in. I get the ones known as Agen prunes, grown in the Aquitaine region in the south-west of France. The same variety is grown successfully in California as well.

Armagnac, a brandy from the Armagnac region, which is close to Aquitaine, is dryer than the brandy from Cognac and seems to have an affinity with the flavour of the prunes, though either will do.

Cream of tartar, or tartaric acid, adds stability to the beaten egg whites, resulting in a more luscious texture in the cooked pudding.

Serves 10   THE PRUNES
225g prunes, weighed after removing the stones
4 tablespoons Armagnac or brandy

THE PUDDING
150g best-quality chocolate, 62% cocoa solids
150g unsalted butter
150ml warm water
110g caster sugar
1 teaspoon vanilla extract
4 eggs
110g plain white flour
Pinch of cream of tartar

TO SERVE
A dusting of icing sugar
Softly whipped cream

Put the prunes into a bowl with the brandy and leave to soak overnight.

Preheat the oven to 200°C/400°F/gas 6 and get ready either a 2 litre ovenproof pie or gratin dish, or ten 200ml ramekins or teacups of a similar volume. If you plan to serve the individual puddings unmoulded from their containers, you will need to paint them with melted butter before adding the mixture. You will also need a roasting tin about 4cm deep, large enough to accommodate the ramekins or dish.

Cut the chocolate into small pieces and put it into a Pyrex bowl with the butter. Place over a saucepan of cold water, making sure the bottom of the bowl does not touch the water. Place on a low heat – don't let the water do more than simmer. While the chocolate is melting, tear or chop the Armagnac-soaked prunes into smaller pieces, about 1cm, and either divide them between the ramekins or spread them over the base of the large dish. If there is some Armagnac that has not soaked into the prunes, save it for adding to the cream later.

When the chocolate is nearly melted, remove the bowl from the saucepan and stir with a flexible rubber spatula to blend the chocolate with the butter. Add the water, sugar and vanilla and mix with a whisk until smooth. Separate the eggs, placing the whites in a spotlessly clean bowl for whisking later. Whisk the yolks into the chocolate mixture, followed by the sieved flour.

Whisk the egg whites with a pinch of cream of tartar until holding soft but definite peaks. Do not allow them to over-whip and take on a grainy appearance. Stir a quarter of the egg white into the chocolate mixture and fold in the remainder with a heavy flexible spatula, making sure no lumps of egg white remain unblended.

Divide the mixture between the ramekins, or put it all into the one dish, and immediately place in the roasting tin. Pour boiling water into the tin, to come halfway up the sides of the ramekins or dish. Cook in the oven for 10 minutes, then lower the temperature to 160°C/325°F/gas 3 for a further 10 minutes if using individual dishes or a further 20 minutes for a large dish. The puddings will appear cooked on top but will feel a little soft and molten in the centre.

Remove the roasting tin carefully from the oven and allow the puddings to sit for at least 10 minutes before serving.

The individual puddings can be turned out on to warmed plates for serving. The large dish can be brought to the table as it is. Regardless, I dust the puddings with a little sieved icing sugar just before serving.

Pass softly whipped cream separately. I sometimes serve chocolate sauce with these as well.

Lemon verbena cream pots

Lemon verbena, with its slim, sharp and pointy leaves, is intensely flavoured and is lovely in these little creams. I usually serve them warm, but have also enjoyed them served cold.

The verbena, which for this recipe needs to be fresh and not dried, grows very easily in a sunny position and the leaves are also used in sorbets and ices, to flavour whipped cream and to make a simple and refreshing tea. They can be very successfully replaced with lemon balm or lemon-scented geranium leaves, or even mint.

Serves 8
2 stalks or 20 leaves of lemon verbena
350ml full-fat milk
100ml regular or double cream
6 large egg yolks
160g caster sugar

Preheat the oven to 180°C/350°F/gas 4 and get ready 8 ramekins or espresso cups. You will also need a roasting tin about 4cm deep, large enough to accommodate the ramekins.

Chop the verbena leaves coarsely. Place them in a small saucepan and add the milk and cream. Bring slowly to the boil. Turn the heat down as low as it will go, cover the saucepan and leave on the heat for 10 minutes. Remove from the heat and allow to stand for a further 10 minutes.

Put the egg yolks and sugar into a bowl and beat with a whisk until thick and slightly pale.

With a hand-held blender, buzz the verbena leaves in the milk very briefly. A couple of pulses of the machine should do it. You just want to break up the leaves so they look the size of large tea leaves. Now strain the milk through a fine sieve. Some of the smaller bits of verbena leaf will go through the sieve and that's fine. The larger pieces will remain in the sieve. Press heavily on the leaves to extract as much of the liquid as possible.

Pour the sieved milk on to the egg and sugar mixture while continuously whisking, then divide between the ramekins or cups and place them gently in the roasting tin. Pour in boiling water to come halfway up the sides of the ramekins, then lay a sheet of dampened greaseproof paper over the top. Cook in the oven for 30 minutes, then have a look to see if they are lightly set. The centres of the creams should ripple lightly when shaken. If they are not sufficiently set, replace in the oven for a further 5 minutes and check again. When cooked, remove from the oven and allow to cool.

Serve the creams barely warm or chilled. I sometimes serve them with a small dribble of Rose Petal and Cherry Syrup (see page 395).

Buttermilk and lemon puddings with caramel and pineapple

These comforting upside-down puddings are best eaten warm, though they are still delicious at room temperature. Whereas that warmth may seem most appropriate during the cooler months in autumn and winter, I enjoy these at any time of the year. The combination of caramel and pineapple with the light pudding is delicious, but the fruit you choose to serve with these can be a seasonal decision. Strawberries, diced and lightly sugared, are very good with it. Blueberries, crushed just before eating and also lightly sugared, are excellent. In spring, compote of rhubarb works very well and, a little later, the hard bitter green gooseberries poached with elderflower and combined with the caramel sauce are just lovely. I have also served these in December, placing a teaspoon of mincemeat into each mould before adding the mixture, and ended up with lovely light Christmassy mini puddings. I served them with vanilla custard.

This can be cooked in one large dish or in ramekins or teacups. If you are taking the option of individual servings and planning to serve them turned out on to serving plates, bear in mind that the top will be soft and runny and that is the way it should be.

The ingredients

Buttermilk, with its slightly sour taste, adds depth to the flavour of these puddings.

Choose a pineapple with lovely fresh leaves and a decent sweet pineapple aroma.

Serves 8 40g butter, melted
120g plain flour
190g caster sugar
125ml freshly squeezed lemon juice
1 tablespoon finely grated lemon zest
350ml buttermilk
3 eggs

TO SERVE
1 pineapple
225ml Caramel Sauce (see page 391)
Softly whipped cream

Preheat the oven to 180°C/350°F/gas 4 and get ready either a 2 litre ovenproof pie or gratin dish, or ten 200ml ramekins or teacups of a similar volume. You will also need a roasting tin about 4cm deep, large enough to accommodate the ramekins or dish.

Brush the ramekins or teacups lightly but thoroughly with half the melted butter. If you are baking the pudding in a single large serving dish, there is no need to butter it – you will not be turning it out.

Sieve the flour into a large bowl and add 140g of caster sugar, the lemon juice and zest and buttermilk and whisk for a couple of minutes until smooth.

Separate the eggs, placing the whites in a spotlessly clean bowl for whisking later. Put the yolks into another bowl and mix with the rest of the melted butter, then stir into the buttermilk mixture.

Whisk the egg whites until they are lightly frothy, then add the remaining 50g of caster sugar and continue whisking until the mixture forms soft but definite peaks. Stir a quarter of the egg white into the buttermilk mixture, then lightly fold in the rest until thoroughly mixed together.

Either divide the mixture between the buttered ramekins or put it into a large dish, and place in the roasting tin. Pour in boiling water to come halfway up the sides of the ramekins or dish, and cook in the oven for 25 minutes, until the puddings are lightly browned and feeling gently set. The larger single dish may take 5 minutes longer. Carefully remove the roasting tin from the oven. The puddings will stay warm sitting in the water for about an hour.

Peel the pineapple and cut in half lengthways. Cut each of the halves, again lengthways, into three long wedges. Remove the hard core, and cut these wedges crossways into neat 5mm slices.

To serve the individual puddings, carefully invert on to warm plates. The tops will be a little soft and runny, and that is what you want. If you have made one large pudding, serve it straight from the dish at the table. Serve with the sliced pineapple, a drizzle of the caramel sauce and some chilled softly whipped cream.

Chocolate and cherry bread and butter pudding

This is a rich chocolate lover's pudding and a lovely combination of flavours and textures. Removing the stones from the cherries is not nearly as torturous as you might think. It is one of those jobs that if you think too much about it, you may be put off, so I just get cracking, always wearing an apron as the cherries tend to spray their very dark juice round and about. I place them one at a time on a chopping board, press them with the back of a knife and remove the stone. You can of course use a cherry-stoning device. Serve the pudding warm.

The ingredients

Find the best white bread for this pudding.

Fresh, fat, dark and ripe cherries such as the Bing variety are needed.

Best-quality chocolate, 62% cocoa solids, yields a result that is neither too sweet nor too bitter.

Serves 8–10   200g cherries, weighed after removing the stones
2 tablespoons brandy
55g butter, at room temperature
12 slices of good-quality sliced white bread, crusts removed
175g chocolate, 62% cocoa solids, chopped into 1cm pieces
175g caster sugar
4 large eggs, beaten
450ml regular or double cream
230ml full-fat milk
1 teaspoon vanilla extract

TO SERVE
A dusting of icing sugar
Softly whipped cream

A square or rectangular dish, ceramic or pottery, can be used for assembling and cooking the pudding. It should be about 6cm deep, with sides of 20–22cm.

First, put the stoned cherries into a bowl. Add the brandy and set aside to macerate while you prepare the bread. When ready to make the pudding, drain the cherries, reserving the brandy.

Butter the bread and arrange 4 slices, buttered side down, in one layer in your baking dish. Sprinkle half the chocolate and half the cherries in an even layer over the bread. Arrange another layer of bread, buttered side down, on top. Add the rest of the chocolate and cherries and place the final layer of bread on top, buttered side down.

Put the sugar, eggs, cream, milk and vanilla into a bowl and add the reserved brandy. Whisk together and pour over the dish. Allow to stand at room temperature for 1 hour or in the fridge overnight.

Preheat the oven to 180°C/350°F/gas 4. Place the pudding in a roasting tin and pour in boiling water to come halfway up the sides of the dish. Cook in the oven for 1 hour, or until set and the top is golden and crisp.

The cooked pudding will sit happily and stay warm for an hour or so in the oven, still in the roasting tin with the heat turned off, though do remember it is really much nicer when served warm. Dust the pudding with icing sugar and serve on warm plates with softly whipped cream.

For some cooks the sighting of the word gelatine in a recipe is enough to have them flicking over the page – it has an unjustified reputation for being difficult.

Cold puddings

If you have always yearned to create quivering jellies and delicate and gently set chilled mousses or soufflés, there is one technique you will have to master, and that is the use of gelatine.

Gelatine comes in two forms: powdered and sheet, also sometimes called leaf gelatine. One teaspoon of powdered gelatine has the same setting power as one of the sheets or leaves.

For some cooks the sighting of the word gelatine in a recipe is enough to have them flicking over the page. It strikes fear into some, as it has an unjustified reputation for being difficult. This is a pity, because when you know the rules involved, which are both few and simple, you will find that gelatine is really easy to use. Once mastered, it opens up a huge range of recipes that otherwise cannot even be considered.

Either form of gelatine can be used in a recipe where gelatine is called for. Some cooks prefer to use one or the other. I will explain how to use both and you can then choose which suits you best, but without it you will have to forgo those trembling sweet moments.

There is another setting agent called agar-agar, which is extracted from various seaweeds and is suitable for vegetarians. The use of this product is not as formulaic as the powdered and leaf gelatins, and the instructions accompanying different brands should be read and followed accordingly.

Keys to success for powdered gelatine

Measuring the gelatine: always **accurately measure the gelatine** and the mixture to be set. Remember you are using an exact amount of gelatine to set an exact amount of a mixture to a certain consistency, so you must be scientific in your approach. Too much gelatine will have a set that is too firm. Too little will result in a set that will not hold its shape and may collapse on presentation.

Sponging the gelatine: moisten the measured gelatine with the liquid as suggested in the recipe. I always use a Pyrex jug or heavy ceramic bowl for this task, as either is heavy enough not to allow the gelatine to overheat when being melted – it also gives a clearer picture of what is going on. I avoid plastic or stainless steel as I find them too light – the melting gelatine sticks to these materials, which means it is not in your mixture where you need it to be. Generally, **I use 1 tablespoon of liquid to 1 teaspoon of gelatine**. In a matter of minutes the moistened gelatine will take on the appearance of a sponge, hence the expression 'sponging the gelatine'.

Dissolving the gelatine: place the jug or bowl with the sponged gelatine **into a saucepan of barely simmering water**. Make sure the water in the saucepan comes up no higher than halfway on the sides of the jug or bowl, as you don't want any of it splashing into the gelatine. After a few minutes, and this will depend on the quantity of gelatine being dissolved, the sponge will dissolve into a clear liquid. Avoid the temptation to stir. It is unnecessary and can cause the gelatine to become cloudy, in which case it is difficult to be sure that it is completely dissolved. What you want to see is a completely clear liquid – then you know the granules of gelatine are dissolved and ready for the next stage

Mixing the gelatine: you never add the dissolved gelatine straight into the mixture to be set, as it can block due to the change of temperature and leave you with little balls of gelatine in the finished dish. So, remove the gelatine from the saucepan and allow to sit and cool slightly for 1 minute. Add 2–3 tablespoons of the mixture to the gelatine and stir to mix. Add another 2 tablespoons and

Powdered gelatine sponging

keep mixing. Then add the gelatine to the larger volume of mixture and immediately fold it through with a rubber spatula until completely and evenly mixed in. Put the mixture into the serving dish of choice, and place in the fridge for a minimum of 3 hours to chill and set. Once the mixture is set, it will remain in that condition while chilled for several days, though with most set puddings, the sooner they are eaten, the more delicious they will be.

Keys to success for sheet or leaf gelatine

Measuring the gelatine: measure the quantity of sheets necessary for the recipe you are cooking. If you have a half or quarter teaspoon measurement, use half or quarter of a sheet of gelatine. **I usually cut them with scissors to achieve a neat and accurate result.**

Dissolving the gelatine: place the gelatine sheets in a bowl and cover with water. In a few minutes they will collapse and look like wilting pieces of cellophane. Lift them out of the water, shaking off the excess, and place in a very small saucepan with 1 tablespoon of the liquid for each leaf of gelatine. Place on a very gentle heat and stir to dissolve. Remove from the heat. This step of the technique takes only a matter of 2–3 minutes.

Mixing the gelatine: never add the dissolved sheets of gelatine straight into the mixture to be set, as it can block due to the change of temperature and leave you with obvious pieces of gelatine in the finished dish. Add 2–3 tablespoons of the mixture to be set to the dissolved gelatine leaves and stir to mix. Add another 2 tablespoons and mix again. Now add the gelatine to the larger volume of mixture and fold it through with a rubber spatula until completely and evenly mixed in. Place the mixture in the serving dish of choice and place in the fridge for a minimum of 3 hours to chill and set. Once the mixture is set, it will remain in that condition while chilled for several days. The sooner you eat it though, the more fresh-tasting and delicious it will be.

The sponged gelatine gently dissolving

Raspberry jelly
with lemon and mint cream

I love jelly, and this recipe came about as a result of that greedy interest! Use firm, ripe berries – indeed, the recipe can be changed to include a mixture of berries such as loganberries, tayberries and a few currants. The jellies will keep perfectly in the fridge for a couple of days, as long as they are covered. I like to set the jelly in individual portions, either in glasses or oiled ramekins which can then be turned out and served as quivering little free-standing jewel-like offerings. Of course you can set all the jelly in a large bowl, something like an old-fashioned jelly mould which can be turned out to create an extravagant presentation. Otherwise, use a glass bowl so that you can see the lovely berries suspended in the lightly set jelly, and serve it straight from the bowl.

The ingredients
Ripe, firm raspberries are necessary here for superior flavour and
   texture.

The framboise or raspberry liqueur is optional, though crème de cas-
   sis would do very nicely instead.

I am suggesting powdered gelatine in the recipe, but it can be replaced
   with the corresponding amount of leaf gelatine.

Serves 8–10 Sunflower or grapeseed oil, for brushing
2½ teaspoons gelatine
3 tablespoons water
450g raspberries

SYRUP
225ml cold water
225g sugar
4 sprigs of spearmint
1 dessertspoon framboise raspberry liqueur (optional)
1 tablespoon lemon juice

MINT CREAM
15 spearmint leaves
1 tablespoon lemon juice
150ml regular or double cream

Prepare 8–10 individual jelly moulds, ramekins, espresso cups or small glasses. Alternatively, you can use your favourite serving bowl. Brush the moulds of choice with a little non-scented oil such as sunflower or grapeseed oil, and place them upside down on a sheet of kitchen paper to allow any excess oil to run off. If you are not planning to serve the jellies turned out you do not have to oil the receptacle.

To make the syrup, put the water, sugar and mint sprigs into a pan and bring to the boil. Simmer gently for 2 minutes, then take off the heat and allow to cool completely. Add the framboise, if using, and the lemon juice.

Measure the gelatine into a Pyrex jug or ceramic bowl. Add the water and allow to sponge. Place the sponged gelatine in a saucepan of gently simmering water to dissolve. The sponge will dissolve unaided into a clear liquid. There should be no undissolved grains of gelatine in the liquid.

Strain the cooled mint syrup through a sieve, pressing every drop of liquid through. Add 2 tablespoons of the syrup to the gelatine and stir, then add another 2 tablespoons and stir again. Pour this into the remaining syrup and mix well.

Put the raspberries into a bowl. Add the gelatine mixture and mix with a gentle touch so as not to crush the berries. Put the mixture into the prepared moulds and place in the fridge to set. This will take about 3 hours, sometimes quicker.

Meanwhile, make the mint cream. Place the mint leaves in a bowl and crush them with the back of a spoon to coarsely tear them. Add the lemon juice, then stir in the cream, which will thicken slightly. If it thickens too much, add a little water to thin it out. The consistency should be that of pouring cream.

To serve, turn out the jellies on to the plate of choice and drizzle with a little mint cream. Decorate with more mint leaves, and a few raspberries if you have them left over.

Yoghurt and star anise cream

This gently set cream or mousse is a lovely combination of flavours. You can set the cream or mousse in individual moulds or one large one, and turn it out if you wish. Use whatever dish suits your situation. The mousse will keep in the fridge for several days. Poached rhubarb or plums are heaven with it, or just some strawberries, sliced and lightly sweetened with caster sugar. I sometimes make a jelly from plum poaching syrup and pour that on top of the set cream, where it sets and makes a really festive presentation and a perfect taste and texture marriage.

The ingredients
Star anise is a highly scented spice and needs to be used with discretion so as not to end up with a dish that is overpowered by its heady aroma.

I use full-fat organic yoghurt for this cream.

Serves 8–10   3 star anise
230ml full-fat milk
175g caster sugar
200ml regular or double cream
3 rounded teaspoons powdered gelatine or 3 sheets
  of gelatine
425ml natural, unsweetened yoghurt

Use a pestle and mortar to grind the star anise coarsely into roughly 5mm pieces. Put the star anise, milk, sugar and cream into a saucepan over a low heat and stir until the sugar has dissolved and the mixture is tepid. This takes about 5 minutes. Do not let the milk boil or the flavour will be spoiled. The purpose of gently warming the milk is to draw the flavour out of the spice and to encourage the sugar to dissolve. Remove from the heat and allow to cool and infuse.

Put 3 tablespoons of water in a small bowl or jug and sprinkle in the gelatine. Stir gently to mix, then allow to 'sponge' and stiffen. Place the jug in a saucepan of simmering water until the gelatine has dissolved into a clear liquid, with no trace of gelatine granules visible. Do not stir the gelatine as it dissolves.

Strain the milk to remove the star anise and add 4 tablespoons to the gelatine. Mix gently, then combine with the rest of the milk and mix well. Add the yoghurt and whisk gently to a smooth consistency. Pour into the serving dish or dishes of your choice. Remember that if you wish to turn the pudding out, your chosen mould or moulds need to be brushed with a non-scented oil first.

Place in the fridge to set for at least 3 hours.

Rhubarb trifle
with almonds and pistachios

This trifle is based on the classic preparation with fruit, sponge, liqueur, custard and a final topping of whipped cream. I use the recipe as a master plan throughout the year. Rhubarb is the first fruit to be used. It will be followed by gooseberries, then strawberries, followed by currants and so on, so it is immensely useful. The great thing about a trifle is that it can be prepared ahead, ideally the day before, and the finishing touches of cream and an appropriate decoration are quickly and easily achieved.

The custard, also referred to as pastry cream, is lightened up by the addition of two of the whisked egg whites, thereby adding a volume of air and achieving a rather more foamy result.

When assembling a trifle, the balance of the assembly of the ingredients is important so as to end up with a consistency that is neither too wet nor too dry. I like to put it together while the custard is still slightly warm, as this creates a more sumptuous consistency.

I like to use a glass bowl for serving the trifle, but in fact the volume of the bowl is much more important than the style of it, as the volume will affect the proportions of the finished dish.

The ingredients
Use deep pinky red and firm stalks of rhubarb here to ensure a rich
  flavour of the fruit.

Try to ensure that the almonds and pistachios are as fresh as possible.
  Like all nuts they can be dull and even rancid when old.

Serves 8
450g pink or bright red rhubarb stalks
175g caster sugar
125ml water
1 sponge cake (see the Whisked-up Sponge cake, page 532)
6 tablespoons kirsch (optional)

PASTRY CREAM
300ml milk
½ a vanilla pod or 1 teaspoon vanilla extract
3 eggs
110g caster sugar
25g plain flour

FINISHING THE TRIFLE
425ml softly whipped cream
50g toasted flaked almonds
30g shelled unsalted pistachios

Put the chopped rhubarb, sugar and water into a small stainless steel saucepan. Cover, then place on a moderate heat and bring to a simmer. Cook covered until the rhubarb is completely tender and just beginning to collapse. I use a glass saucepan lid or a Pyrex plate for covering the saucepan so that I can more easily see what is happening. You don't really want the rhubarb to collapse to a stringy consistency, as the trifle is better to eat if the rhubarb still has some degree of its identity intact. However, it is crucial that all the rhubarb is tender. Allow it to cool somewhat while you proceed with the pastry cream.

Bring the milk to just below boiling point with the vanilla pod, if using. If using vanilla extract, add it later. Allow the heated milk to sit and infuse off the heat. Separate 2 of the eggs and place the whites in a spotlessly clean bowl for whisking later. Put the 2 egg yolks and the remaining whole egg into a bowl with the caster sugar and whisk until light and fluffy. Gently whisk in the flour until thoroughly mixed in. If you are using a vanilla pod, at this point, split it or cut a tiny piece off one end and squeeze the vanilla seeds into the sugar and egg mixture. If you are using vanilla extract, add it now.

Pour the still warm milk over the mixture and whisk in well. Return the mixture to a clean saucepan and stir it continuously with a combination of a flat-bottomed wooden spoon and a whisk. The flat-bottomed wooden spoon prevents the custard from sticking to the bottom of the pan and the whisk breaks down any lumps as they form. Allow the mixture to come to the boil and then simmer, still stirring, for 2 minutes. This simmering of the custard is vital to get it to thicken properly and to ensure that the raw taste of the flour is cooked out.

Remove the custard from the heat, transfer to a clean bowl and allow to cool for 5 minutes. Whisk the egg whites to stiffish peaks and fold into the custard. The result should be air-filled and slightly foamy.

To assemble the trifle, use a bowl not less than 1 litre but no bigger than 1.3 litres in volume. Cut the sponge cake in half horizontally to achieve two neat discs. Place one of the discs, cut side down, in the bottom of your chosen bowl. The shape of your bowl will determine how much you need to manipulate the sponge to make it fit. If it starts to come up the sides of the bowl, that is absolutely fine.

Add the kirsch, if using, to the poached rhubarb. Spoon about half the rhubarb and its juice over the sponge, making sure the cake is thoroughly moistened. Spoon over half the pastry cream and place the remaining cake, cut side up, on top. Again, you may have to bully the sponge into place. Don't be afraid to cut off little bits and do a bit of patching if necessary. Spoon over the rest of the rhubarb. Finish with the remaining pastry cream and smooth off the surface with the back of a spoon. I often get a skewer to the trifle at this stage and prod it a few times, making unnoticeable holes right down to the bottom of the bowl to encourage the juices to moisten the sponge.

Cover the bowl and chill for at least 8 hours or, better still, overnight. Before serving, spread the softly whipped cream over the trifle and sprinkle over the cooled toasted almonds and the pistachios.

Rhubarb and strawberry trifle
When the cooked rhubarb is nearly cooled, add 250g of sliced ripe fresh strawberries. Assemble the trifle as in the recipe above.

Apple, blackberry and geranium trifle
This is a lovely autumn version for you to try. If you don't have the geranium leaves, it is still worth making, though the perfumed geranium takes it on to another level. Replace the rhubarb in the master recipe with 450g of Bramley cooking apples, peeled, cored and roughly chopped, and 100g of blackberries, and cook with the sugar, water and 4 sweet geranium leaves until it collapses to a frothy fluff, stained pink by the berries. Remove the collapsed geranium leaves before assembling the trifle according to the master recipe. Sweet sherry could replace the kirsch here.

Blood orange jelly

I love when the blood oranges arrive, generally in late January. They have a wonderful flavour and the ruby-coloured flesh and juice is just a joy.

Serves 6–8
4 blood and 2 normal oranges
Juice of 1 lemon
225ml sugar syrup (see page 390)
1 dessertspoon finely chopped mint
1 teaspoon orange liqueur such as Grand Marnier
2 teaspoons gelatine
2 tablespoons water

SAUCE
225ml fresh orange juice
2 – 4 teaspoons caster sugar
1 tablespoons freshly chopped mint

Grate the zest from the two normal oranges using a microplane or the finest side of your grater. Over a bowl, to catch any juice, carefully peel and segment all of the oranges. Squeeze the juice from any flesh remaining on the skin over the segments. Add the lemon juice, syrup, chopped mint and liqueur, if using, and mix gently. Now strain all of the liquid off the oranges and measure out 300ml. Reserve any surplus liquid.

Measure the gelatine into a Pyrex jug or bowl and add the water. Allow to sponge, placing it in the fridge if you wish to speed up this process. Place the sponged gelatine in a saucepan of gently simmering water and allow to dissolve. As soon as the gelatine is completely liquid and clear, remove from the saucepan. Add the measured orange liquid to the gelatine, stirring as you pour. Add this to the orange segments and gently mix. Divide between the moulds and place in the fridge to set. Allow 4 hours to be certain, but it will sometimes set in 2 hours.

Sweeten the orange juice for the sauce to taste with the caster sugar and add the mint. Serve the jellies, turned out of their moulds if that is your preference, with a little of the sauce.

Chocolate and caramel mousse

This is a rich and concentrated mousse with a texture that I really like. The combination of the chocolate and the burnt sugar caramel works really well. I serve this with caramel sauce and thick pouring cream. Sometimes I can get Jersey cream, and that's just heavenly.

Serves 6   225g chocolate (62% or 70%), chopped into 1 cm pieces
50g butter, diced
4 eggs
225g caster or granulated sugar
225ml water
1 teaspoon vanilla extract

Place the chocolate and butter in a Pyrex bowl. Place the bowl over a saucepan of cold water, making sure the water is not touching the bottom of the bowl, and place the pan on the heat. Bring the water to a simmer and immediately turn off the heat, allowing the butter and-chocolate to melt gently in the bowl.

Separate the eggs, putting the whites into a spotlessly clean bowl for whisking later. Whisk the yolks to a pale mousse.

To make the caramel, put the sugar and 125ml of water into a heavy-based saucepan and place on a low heat. Stir occasionally to encourage the sugar to dissolve before the liquid comes to a boil. Once it boils and has become a syrup, remove the spoon and do not stir again. Allow the syrup to become a dark chestnut-coloured caramel. If it is colouring unevenly in the saucepan, tilt the pan gently to and fro to get it to even out by running the dark caramel into the paler syrup.

Do not be tempted to stir, as if you put a cold spoon into the caramel, it will 'block' and go solid – a disaster. Keep going until the caramel is a deep chestnut colour and almost burnt. Then immediately and quickly add the remaining 100ml of water, hot if possible to prevent less spluttering.

Now the caramel will look a bit odd, but once you put the saucepan back on the heat it will cook to a single consistency again. Cook it until it thickens again – when you dip a spoon into the caramel and allow it to drop off, it will fall in a thickish thread. Pour this gradually on to the whisked egg yolks, whisking all the time. A food mixer with a whisk attachment or a hand-held electric whisk will do this job perfectly. The mixture will whisk to a mousse in a matter of minutes. Stir the melted chocolate and the vanilla extract into the mousse. You may need to be a little vigorous with the stirring.

Whisk the egg whites to stiff peaks. Do not allow them to over-whip and become grainy. Stir a quarter of the egg white into the mousse to soften it, then fold in the remaining three-quarters lightly yet thoroughly. Pour the mixture into a shallow serving dish. There will not be a lot of mousse, but it is rich, so the servings should be small. Place the mousse in the fridge to chill for 4 hours.

Serve with a dark caramel sauce and thick pouring cream. Perfectly ripe raspberries, particularly the autumn varieties, are delicious served with this mousse.

For the cook, there is great satisfaction the moment you open the oven door to reveal a perfectly risen and coloured cake.

A few cakes

I like my cake fresh. I am talking same day fresh, and then I love cake. It is a pity that so much cake is forgettable. Inferior ingredients, within and without, yielding a brute of a thing that is often forced to sit on a chilly counter waiting for yet another poor expectant sweet tooth to be treated to mediocrity. Perhaps I am overstating it, but when you witness the reaction provoked by a freshly baked cake, made using good ingredients – well, it just seems such a shame that there is not more fresh cake about.

Nothing compares to the texture, flavour and smell of a cake baked on the same day it is going to be eaten. Other than that, but with the notable exception of a couple of fruit cakes, I can leave them. If I am having cake, which I generally don't really need, it has to be fabulously good, a treat. Its excellence must override that feeling that this item of food is superfluous to my needs, that it is so good – and that doesn't mean grand and complicated, which of course it can be, but so honestly good – that it will make my day better, and if I have to wait a week or a month or longer for another piece which will induce similar feelings, well so be it. I can wait. What's the point in diluting something so pleasure-filling with masquerading upstarts?

For the cook, there is great satisfaction the moment you open the oven door to reveal a perfectly risen and coloured cake. It certainly makes me sigh with pleasure. The pleasure is compounded on presentation of the finished treat to family and friends.

The exceptions to the freshly baked cake are the fruit-filled heavyweights such as Christmas and Easter cakes. These cakes are traditionally cooked months ahead of the planned time of eating and allowed to 'mature'. The theory is that they improve as they age. I now feel that they actually lose their charm the longer they sit, as the fruit seems to lose its fresh flavour and the texture of the cake becomes ever more dense as moisture slowly evaporates. Of course, part of the reason for making them so far ahead was the cook being organised, a situation I applaud, but considering the cost of these cakes that are often made to mark important life events, they really need to taste delicious when you get to eat them. As a result I now try to start eating them within a week of making them and have no hesitation about putting on the finishing layers of almond and white icing within that time span as well. Even a fruit-filled tea brack, which I include here and which is regarded as a keeper and indeed does keep well, is significantly better when eaten on the day or the day after it is made, when the tea-soaked fruit is still sweet and succulent.

Keys to success

To be assured of a good result, it is very important to have an organised and almost scientific approach to baking. It is all about the rules, and if you **follow the rules and use good ingredients**, you will be successful.

Correct measurements, tin sizes, temperatures and cooking times will work, incorrect ones won't. If I don't have the correct tin size, I don't make the cake. I don't mean to sound brutal, and I could generalise about cutting down or increasing the ingredient quantities to suit different sized tins, but really this is not a good approach.

Choose a cake recipe that is suitable for the occasion such as a Whisked-up Sponge for afternoon tea or Roast Hazelnut and Chocolate Cake for after dinner.

Read the recipe from start to finish once or twice so you know the steps involved.

Weigh out **all the ingredients** before you start to mix anything.

Have eggs and butter **at room temperature**.

Check if the recipe calls for salted or unsalted butter. Salted butter generally seems to suit the flavour of cakes from Ireland and Britain. But when we move across to France and Italy for a recipe, more often than not, the butter will be unsalted.

Preheat the oven.

In a whisking cake, such as the Whisked-up Sponge, the purpose of whisking is to introduce air to the ingredients. These tiny little bubbles of trapped air add to the volume and lightness of the mixture and are reflected in the light texture of the cooked cake. Once this airiness is achieved by the whisking, the ensuing folding in of further ingredients, with a strong flexible spatula, must be done with a **light but determined hand**. There is no advantage to spending 2 minutes folding in flour or beaten egg whites when it can be done in 30 seconds.

Folding whisked-up egg whites into a heavier mixture, such as the Roast Hazelnut and Chocolate Cake, will require a **bit more determination** and take a little bit longer than for the sponge or tea cake.

When mixing a cake such as the Almond and Lemon Cake or the Tea Brack, it is just that, mixing, to bring all of the ingredients together. So no fancy stuff here, but remember once the ingredients come together to a single mixed consistency, that's that. **Further mixing may even be detrimental** and cause the cake to toughen slightly.

Cook the cake for the suggested time at the suggested temperature in the centre of the oven.

If you have a glass-fronted oven door you can check its progress without opening the oven door. If however your oven door is solid, you will just have to **be patient and brave** and wait until the time suggested in the recipe before having a look. It is generally disastrous

Folding sieved flour into the whisked-up eggs and sugar

to open the oven door too early, as it allows heat to escape, causing many cakes to collapse.

Check to see it is cooked by inserting a skewer into the centre of the cake, then withdrawing it to ascertain that the skewer is clean, indicating a cooked cake.

Remove from the oven just as soon as it is cooked and place on a wire rack to start cooling.

Don't turn the cake out of the tin until you are confident that it is **cooled enough to hold its shape** when it is unmoulded from the tin. You should be able to handle the cake without any heat discomfort.

Allow the cake to **cool completely** before filling and icing.

Serve the cake with the appropriate accompaniment such as whipped cream or a cup of tea or coffee.

Store any of the cakes that will keep well in airtight containers as directed in the recipe.

A whisked-up sponge cake

There are few cakes that I like better than this old-fashioned sponge. The cake should be light and filled with masses of tiny and invisible air bubbles, and it is then a most lovely vehicle for all sorts of fillings. Filled with cream and jam such as strawberry, raspberry, blackcurrant or apricot, it is a joy. Summer fruits such as sweet strawberries can be sliced or crushed and added to the filling. Raspberries, loganberries or tayberries, lightly sugared and left whole, peaches or nectarines, sliced and again lightly sugared, are all contenders for the filling.

My favourite filling is a combination of a soft fruit such as those mentioned above and a jam made from the same fruit, with some whipped cream. You can be creative here, and out of the home-grown fruit season, pineapple or lightly poached apricots make a perfect change. This is the cake I like to use when making trifle, and I sometimes freeze one of these to have it ready for that task.

Strictly speaking, this is a cake to serve with tea, but I think it is every bit good and special enough to serve after dinner. The sight of this coming to the table on your favourite cake plate will gladden all.

The ingredients
Good-quality free-range eggs make a big difference to any cake, and are especially noticeable in the colour and texture of this one.

Serves 8

Melted butter, for brushing
4 free-range eggs, at room temperature
110g caster sugar
1 teaspoon vanilla extract
110g plain flour

FILLING
225ml regular, double or whipping cream
2 generous tablespoons jam, such as raspberry,
    strawberry, blackcurrant
250g fresh fruit, such as raspberries or strawberries

Preheat the oven to 180°C/350°F/gas 4. Prepare two 23cm cake tins with sides about 5cm high – brush with melted butter, dust with flour, then tap and turn upside down to shake out any excess. Line the base with a snug-fitting disc of greaseproof paper or baking parchment.

Put the eggs, sugar and vanilla into the bowl of an electric mixer and whisk until the mixture increases in volume to become a light, pale and air-filled fluffy mousse. This will take at least 10 minutes and sometimes as long as 20 and is crucially important, as this is the part of the recipe where all the important air is incorporated into the mixture. If you are using a hand-held electric mixer, it may take even longer. When you lift the whisk out of the bowl and make a figure of eight with some of the mixture, it should hold that shape for several seconds to indicate a firm and air-filled mousse.

Sieve the flour, one-third at a time, on to the mousse and fold in gently with a long-handled rigid rubber spatula. When all of the flour is added, divide the mixture between the prepared tins, being careful not to knock air out by being rough or banging the tins.

Place the tins gently in the oven and cook for 20 minutes, or until the cakes are lightly browned and cooked. They will feel gently firm on top and will be barely shrinking from the sides of the tins. Remove from the oven and place them, still in their tins, on a wire rack to start cooling. After 10 minutes, gently remove the cakes from the tins and again place on the wire rack to cool.

When the cakes are completely cool, whip the cream to soft peaks. Remove the parchment paper and spread the jam on the base of the cake, followed by the cream and then the fruit.

Place the top on the cake and, if you wish, sprinkle with a light dusting of caster sugar for a traditional but delicious lightly sparkling finish.

Tea brack

This is a rich fruit-filled brack flavoured with Earl Grey or Lapsang tea. It is a taste of the past, but quite delicious. The brack, best on the day it is made, keeps well in a tin for several weeks and I like to serve it with a cup of tea. I cut it into thin slices and serve it lightly buttered.

Try to search out the best dried fruit, which should look plump and juicy when you are buying it. Organic dried fruit tends to be much better than the alternative, but of course is more expensive. The same goes for glacé cherries and candied peel.

The recipe is quite straightforward, so as long as you measure your ingredients accurately, use the correct size of tin and cook the brack for the correct amount of time at the correct temperature, you should get a lovely result.

The ingredients

Raisins and sultanas are varieties of grapes that have been dried slowly to preserve them for baking and other recipes. The quality varies a lot, so search out good-quality fruit – it should look plump and juicy and taste fruity when you buy it.

Glacé cherries are best when undyed and an unglamorous natural dark colour. They are less sweet and are more flavoursome than their more colourful cousins.

Candied peel, like raisins, sultanas and glacé cherries, also varies a lot in quality and some of the commercially produced peels taste of nothing except sugar. Good-quality candied peel will still taste of the fruit it was before candying, such as orange, lemon or grapefruit.

Serves 10–12   200g raisins

200g sultanas

450ml tea, made with best-quality Indian Breakfast tea
    leaves and a large pinch of Earl Grey or Lapsang
    tea leaves (don't forget to strain out the leaves
    before adding them to the fruit)

55g whole unskinned almonds

55g organic undyed glacé cherries, quartered

55g candied peel, cut into 5mm pieces

110g soft dark brown sugar

110g caster sugar

1 egg

400g plain flour

1 level teaspoon baking powder

The day before you are going to bake the brack, put the raisins and sultanas into a bowl and pour over the strained measured tea. Cover and leave overnight for the fruit to soak up the tea.

Next day the fruit should be plump and lovely and infused with the flavour of the tea. If there is still some tea that has not been soaked up by the fruit, leave it in the bowl – it all goes into the brack mixture.

Preheat the oven to 180°C/350°F/gas 4. Line a rectangular loaf tin, 30cm long x 11cm wide x 7cm deep, with baking parchment.

To remove the skins from the almonds, place the nuts in a small saucepan of boiling water and simmer for 1 minute. Remove and strain, then cool under a cold running tap. Pinch off the skins, then give the nuts a quick dry in a clean cloth and chop them coarsely by hand or in a food processor.

Add the chopped nuts to the soaked fruit along with the glacé cherries, candied peel, sugars and egg and stir with a wooden spoon until well blended. Sieve the flour and baking powder over the mixture and stir again until all is thoroughly mixed. The mixture may look a little soft but that is quite all right.

Pour into the lined tin and gently smooth the top, then bake in the oven for about 90 minutes. To test that the cake is cooked, insert a skewer into the brack and withdraw it. If the skewer is clean it is cooked; if it is in any way moist, it is not cooked and should be returned to the oven and tested again after another 5–10 minutes.

Place the cooked brack, still in its tin, on a wire rack for 15–20 minutes. Then remove, still in its wrapping of baking parchment, to cool completely. I like to leave the brack in the baking parchment until I am ready to eat it. Wrap it in cling film or place in an airtight container to keep it fresh.

Serve thinly or thickly sliced and lightly buttered.

Roast hazelnut and chocolate cake

This is a rich moist cake with a shiny glossy icing and makes a wonderful dessert cake. The cake can be made and iced a day ahead, which makes it perfect for a party.

The ingredients
Unsalted butter is less aggressively flavoured than the salted variety and its more delicate flavour suits the chocolate and hazelnuts very well.

Best-quality chocolate is needed here to give a truly full-flavoured cake.

Serves 10
Melted butter, for brushing
185g hazelnuts
185g unsalted butter
185g chocolate, 62% cocoa solids
6 eggs, separated
185g caster sugar

ICING
175g chocolate, 62% cocoa solids
2 tablespoons very strong coffee
175g unsalted butter

Preheat the oven to 190°C/375°F/gas 5. Line a 25.5cm springform tin with a disc of baking parchment and brush the sides with a light but thorough coating of melted butter.

Place the hazelnuts on a baking sheet and put into the preheated oven for about 10 minutes, until the nuts are roasted to a golden colour and the skins are starting to lift. Remove from the oven and allow to cool. When the nuts are cooled, place them in a clean tea towel and rub the bottom of the towel around on the palm of your hand. The skins will start to lift off the nuts. Remove as much of the skin as you can, but there may be little flecks of skin that will not budge and that's OK. Grind the peeled hazelnuts to a coarse powder in a food processor.

Place the butter and chocolate in a heavy Pyrex bowl and put over a saucepan of cold water on a very low heat. Make sure the bottom of the bowl does not touch the water. Allow to melt gently.

While the chocolate is melting, put the egg yolks and sugar into the bowl of an electric mixer and beat until light and pale. When the chocolate and butter have melted, remove the bowl from the saucepan and stir with a rubber spatula to achieve a smooth and silky consistency. Allow to cool for 3 minutes, then mix gently but thoroughly into the egg yolk and sugar mixture. Stir in the hazelnuts.

Place the egg whites in a spotlessly clean bowl and beat to stiff peaks. Stir a fifth of the egg whites into the chocolate to lighten it slightly, then fold in the rest with a rubber spatula. Make sure all the egg white is properly folded into the chocolate mixture.

Pour the mixture into the tin and gently smooth the top. Do not bang the tin.

Bake in the oven for 20 minutes, then reduce the oven temperature to 160°C/325°F/gas 3 and cook for a further 30 minutes. Do not be alarmed if there is a crack in the top of the cake, as this will seal up as the cake cools. Also, what is now the top ends up as the bottom, well out of view and all in all very forgiving.

Remove the tin from the oven and place on a wire cooling rack. Place a slightly damp cloth over the top of the tin and allow to cool completely. The cake will collapse slightly, indicating a soft and luscious texture.

While the cake is cooling, make the icing. Place the chocolate and coffee in a Pyrex bowl and melt as before, starting it off over a saucepan of cold water. Remove from the heat when nearly melted, stir with a rubber spatula and allow to cool for 8 minutes. Now whisk in the diced butter, 3 or 4 pieces at a time. A hand-held electric mixer is best for this, but failing that, a balloon whisk will do very well. Do not add the next lot of butter until the previous addition has been completely incorporated. Gradually the icing should start to thicken slightly. The finished consistency should be spreadable, like soft but not melted butter.

If the icing becomes runny, it means you have added the butter too quickly. If this happens, place the runny icing in the fridge to chill. Stir it regularly and gradually and it will thicken to a spreadable consistency.

To remove the cake from the tin – the cake should still be slightly warm – run a blunt kitchen knife around the inside of the tin to loosen the edges. Unclip the tin to remove the sides. Invert the cake on to a large flat plate. The bottom of the cake has now become the top. Remove the disc of baking parchment and allow the cake to cool completely before spreading the glossy icing over the sides and top of the cake with a palette knife.

The cake is now ready to be served, or will keep quite happily until the next day, in fact it will still be tasting good in a couple of days' time. I prefer not to refrigerate it, but to keep it in the coolest part of the kitchen. Clearly, if it is high summer, and you can't find a cool spot in the kitchen, you will have to chill it.

Serve the cake in small slices, with softly whipped cream. In the case of this cake I find that it can also stand up to the aggressive nature of crème fraîche.

A plain cake in a tin

This is a terrific cake and in its simplest form, as given here, it is perfect with a cup of tea. I don't see any reason, though, why you couldn't serve it as a dessert cake, still very slightly warm from the oven, with a bowl of sweet strawberries and softly whipped cream. I find many ways to vary it all the way through the year and I've listed those variations below.

As with any cake you make where you begin by whisking eggs and sugar to create an air-filled base, a light hand is required when folding in the remaining ingredients.

The cake is best on the day it is made, ideally before it gets completely cold, which is possible with this cake, as it is neither iced nor filled, just sliced and eaten. It is still excellent the next day, and will happily keep for a few days after that if stored in an airtight container.

The ingredients

As with all cakes, free-range eggs make a big difference to the flavour, texture and colour of the finished cake.

Serves 8

100g butter
3 free-range eggs
200g caster sugar
Finely grated zest of 1 lemon or 1 orange
300g plain flour
3 teaspoons baking powder
150ml full-fat milk
100ml regular or double cream
1 teaspoon vanilla extract

Preheat the oven to 200°C/400°F/gas 6. Line a loaf-shaped cake tin, 30cm long x 10cm wide x 7cm deep, with baking parchment. Melt the butter over a low heat until liquid and leave to cool.

Place the eggs and sugar in the bowl of an electric mixer, or use a hand-held electric mixer, and whisk until the mixture is pale, light and air-filled. This takes about 10 minutes. To check that the mixture is ready, lift a little out of the bowl, using the whisk, and allow it to drop back in gently in a figure of eight. It should visibly hold that shape for a few seconds.

Gently pour the melted butter over the mixture, followed immediately by the grated citrus zest, sieved flour and baking powder. Using a heavy rubber spatula, fold the ingredients together with a light hand, making sure the dry ingredients are properly mixed into the wet.

Gradually incorporate the milk, cream and vanilla, again with a light hand to attain a smooth thick, batter-like consistency. Don't be alarmed if the mixture looks strange when you add the milk and cream. Just keep mixing and it will come together perfectly.

Pour the mixture into the prepared tin, smooth the top lightly and bake in the oven for 40 minutes. To check whether the cake is cooked, insert a thin metal skewer into the cake and withdraw it. If the skewer emerges clean, the cake is cooked; if it is sticky or moist, the cake is not and should be cooked for a further 5 minutes. Place the cooked cake, still in its tin, on a cooling rack and allow to settle and cool for 15 minutes. Lift the cooling cake out of the tin still in the baking parchment and replace on the rack to cool further.

This cake tastes great while still slightly warm. Serve it just as it is, cut into neat slices, about 2cm thick. If you are not using the cake immediately, leave it in the baking parchment, allow it to cool completely, then wrap, with the parchment still on, in cling film and place in an airtight container.

Anise seed cake

Add 1 teaspoon of anise seeds to the cake with the flour and baking powder.

Cherry cake

Add 100g of washed and quartered organic glacé cherries to the sieved flour before adding to the cake mixture.

Lexia raisin cake

Add 100g of Lexia or other good-quality raisins to the sieved flour before adding to the cake mixture.

Yoghurt and lemon cake
with sherried raisins

This is a Middle Eastern recipe that I like very much. I serve it as a dessert cake, and sometimes, during the winter months, with a seasonal Salad of Dates and Oranges rather than the sherried raisins. This cake rises in the cooking and then falls a little, to present itself looking like a cross between a cake and a tart.

Serves 6–8   Melted butter for brushing
4 large eggs
100g caster sugar
1 teaspoon vanilla extract
60g plain flour
400g Greek-style yoghurt
Grated zest and juice of 1 lemon

SHERRIED RAISINS
75g raisins
75ml oloroso or Pedro Ximénez sherry

To make the sherried raisins, place the raisins and sherry in a small saucepan. Bring to a gentle simmer and immediately remove from the heat. Set aside to macerate for at least 1 hour.

Preheat the oven to 180°C/350°F/gas 4. Prepare a 23cm springform tin by brushing the sides with melted butter. Line the base of the tin with a disc of baking parchment.

Separate the eggs and place the whites in a clean bowl for whisking later. With an electric mixer or a hand-held device, whisk the egg yolks, sugar and vanilla to a thick pale cream. Sieve the flour and fold it into the egg and sugar mixture with the yoghurt, lemon zest and juice and mix to a smooth consistency.

Whisk the egg whites to stiff but not dry peaks and fold lightly but thoroughly into the mixture. Pour into the prepared tin and bake for

50–60 minutes, until the top is browned and the cake looks set and firm. The cake will have risen and then fallen during the cooking. Remove the tin from the oven and place on a wire rack. After 5 minutes, run a blunt table knife around the inside of the tin to loosen the edges. Now remove the sides of the tin and allow the cake to cool for a further 20 minutes.

Place a flat plate, serving side down, over the top of the cake. Invert the cake on to the plate so that the base of the tin is now uppermost. Remove the base of the tin and the baking parchment. Get another plate, the one you want to serve the cake on, and again invert the cake so you now have restored the cake to its correct serving position.

Serve slightly warm or at room temperature, with the sherried raisins spooned over the cake. Pass yoghurt or softly whipped cream separately.

Almond and lemon cake

This small, thin and rich almond cake has its roots in Pithiviers, the town in France that also gave us the classic and distinctively scored almond-filled puff pastry gâteau of the same name. This is a very simple cake that I first started making according to Jane Grigson's recipe from her wonderful *Good Things*, a book I love. I have changed the recipe slightly with the addition of lemon zest to the cake and the icing, and I peel and grind the almonds myself, so the texture is somewhat grittier than in the original recipe.

I mostly make it using hen's eggs, but on the occasions that I can find duck eggs, I find the cake to be considerably better, with the minimal ingredient list benefiting from the richer duck eggs. Don't be put off if you can't get duck eggs, as the cake is still excellent with the more readily available hen's eggs.

The lemon-flavoured fondant or glacé icing finishes the cake really nicely, and a final decoration of candied lemon or clementine

zest is pretty and delicious. I also sometimes use organic glacé cherries to decorate the cake and they combine really well with the almonds.

Serve the cake in small slices as a tea cake or with softly whipped cream and a small cup of strong and aromatic coffee after dinner.

Serves 6–8   110g unsalted butter, melted and cooled ,
plus extra for brushing
130g unskinned almonds
115g icing sugar, sieved
75g plain flour, sieved
Pinch of fine salt
3 free-range egg yolks, duck's or hen's
Finely grated zest of ½ a lemon

ICING
175g icing sugar
Finely grated zest of ½ a lemon
1½–2½ tablespoons warm water

DECORATION
Candied orange, lemon or clementine zest, either in
julienne form or diced, or organic glacé cherries
(see page 399)

Preheat the oven to 180°C/350°F/gas 4. Grease an 18cm round cake tin by lightly brushing it with a little melted butter, and line the base with a circle of baking parchment.

To peel the almonds, place them in a small saucepan of boiling water and simmer for 1 minute. Drain, then rinse in cold water. Drain again and squeeze the skins off the almonds. Pop them on to a clean dry cloth and dry them off. Place the almonds in a food processor and grind to a coarse and gritty powder.

Put the almonds into a bowl with the icing sugar, flour and a pinch of salt and mix well. Add the egg yolks, lemon zest and the cooled but still liquid melted butter and mix well with a wooden spoon – 30 seconds should do it. Place the somewhat firm mixture in the prepared tin and gently flatten the top with your outstretched fingers. Tap the tin gently on your work surface to ensure that the mixture is evenly spread through the tin and there are no trapped air bubbles.

Bake the cake in the oven for 40 minutes. The surface will be golden-coloured and should feel gently firm, but not hard, to indicate that it is cooked. Place the tin on a wire cooling rack and allow to cool for 5 minutes, then run a blunt knife around the inside of the tin to loosen the sides and turn the cake out on to the rack to cool completely.

While the cake is cooling, make the icing. Sieve the icing sugar into a bowl. Make a well in the centre and add the lemon zest and half the warm water. Using a wooden spoon, start drawing in the icing sugar and slowly an icing will start to form. Add more warm water as necessary and with caution to create an icing that when lifted from the bowl will fall back in, in a slowly disappearing trail. If the icing is too thin due to too much water being added, add a little more icing sugar to correct it.

Place the cake on an upturned plate and spread the icing over the top and sides of the cake. I use a palette knife dipped in boiling water and then dried to help spread it.

Sprinkle the candied zest or place the cherries on top of the cake while the icing is still molten. Allow the iced cake to sit and settle for a few minutes before transferring it to a pretty serving plate.

Store the cake at room temperature until you are ready to serve it, and pass a bowl of softly whipped cream separately.

Acknowledgements

Many people have had a hand in this book, but none more so than my editor Louise Haines. My good fortune in meeting Louise was facilitated by very kind words from Wendy Fogarty and dear friends Daisy Garnett and Nicholas Pearson. From there, Louise gently and kindly prised the book out of me and surrounded me with a team of lovely people to make my lengthy and rambling scribblings into a book. Georgia Mason edited with charm, as did Annie Lee. Laura Hynd came to Cork and we spent two lovely weeks with me cooking and Laura snapping to produce her gorgeous photographs. Alistair Hall, also a visitor to Cork, wrapped all the bits together in a really lovely design.

Throughout the process, I have no doubt bored people to tears and some must have thought the entire 'book thing' was just my imaginary friend. So, thank you to all my enduring friends who sustain me with their love and fine tables. Especially to Canice Sharkey, Diarmaid Falvey and Mary Jones, and Isaac and Rachel Allen in Cork. In London, Chloe Ponsonby and Blo Deady. In Paris, Risteard Keating and Charles Antoine Van Campenhout. In Tangier, Gordon Watson.

For my extraordinary and inspiring sister Darina Allen, her husband Tim and all at the Ballymaloe Cookery School, thank you.

For another extraordinary and inspiring woman, Myrtle Allen and all at Ballymaloe House, thank you.

At certain points encouraging words came from so many sources that I am sure I can't remember them all – forgive me, but all of your words mattered. I do remember advice and kindness from Sharon Hogan, Mike Hanrahan, Camilla Stoddart, Pamela Black, Susan McKeown, Josh Heller, Gillian Hegarty, Skye Gyngell, Jeremy Lee, Robyn Allen and Betty Lewis.

Thank you to all the cooks I have worked and laughed with; the students I have taught; the food writers whose words I have devoured; the farmers, gardeners, fishermen and all the producers of food who provide me with the ingredients that keep me very happy in the kitchen.

Meat cooking times

These are guidelines and will be a helpful aid to work out accurate cooking times, but you will also need to feel the texture of the cooked meat and check the internal temperature with the aid of a thin metal skewer or a meat thermometer. When testing the internal temperature of cooking meat, make sure the skewer or probe is not touching the bone.

It is important to bear in mind that the internal temperature of cooking meats will continue to rise when the meat has been removed from the oven or placed in an oven with the temperature reduced to rest.

Roasting beef
Preheat the oven to 230°C /450°F/gas 8 and cook the beef for 10 minutes before reducing the temperature to 180°C /350°F/gas 4 for the remaining cooking time.

For **beef on the bone**, such as **rib** or **sirloin:**

Cooking time	Internal temperature when cooked
10 minutes per 450g for rare	45–50°C/120–125°F
12 minutes per 450g for medium	60–65°C/140–145°F
18 minutes per 450g for well done	70 °C/160°F

For **beef off the bone** such as **fillet:**

Cooking time	Internal temperature when cooked
8 minutes per 450g for rare	45–50°C/120–125°F
10 minutes per 450g for medium	60–65°C/140–145°F
15 minutes per 450g for well done	70°C/160°F

Roasting Lamb

Preheat the oven to 180°C/350°F/gas 4.

For **lamb on the bone** such as **leg** or **rack**:

Cooking time	Internal temperature when cooked
15 minutes per 450g for medium/pink	60–65°C/140–150°F
20 minutes per 450g for well done.	75°C/165°F

For shoulder of lamb on the bone cooked to a melting tenderness, preheat the oven to 150°C/300°F/gas 2 and allow 40 minutes per 450g.

Roasting Pork

I like pork cooked through until no trace of pink remains and am suggesting a cooking time to reflect this preference. Preheat the oven to 190°C/375°F/gas 5.

For **pork on the bone** such as **leg** or **loin**:

Cooking time	Internal temperature when cooked
25 minutes per 450g	70°C/160–170°F

For shoulder of pork on the bone cooked to a melting tenderness, preheat the oven to 150°C/300°F/gas 2 and allow 60 minutes per 450g.

Roasting Chicken

Chicken must always be cooked until no trace of pink remains. Preheat the oven to 180°C/350°F/gas 4.

Cooking time	Internal temperature when cooked
20 minutes per 450g, plus an extra 20 minutes.	75–80°C/165–175°F

Index

Figures in italics indicate illustrations